King'

BATH
HISTORY

BATH
HISTORY

VOLUME VII

edited by Brenda J. Buchanan

Millstream Books
1998

Bath History gratefully acknowledges the support of the following organisations:

Bath & North East Somerset Heritage Services
Bath Archaeological Trust

The Editor wishes to thank the expert readers who have helped so greatly in the preparation of this volume.

It is regretted that due to production problems in the printing of this volume, certain illustrations fall below our customary high standard.

First published in 1998 by Millstream Books, 18 The Tyning, Bath BA2 6AL

Set in Palatino and printed in Great Britain by Antony Rowe Ltd, Chippenham

ISBN 0 948975 51 2

British Library Cataloguing-in-Publication Data:
a catalogue record for this book is available from The British Library

CONTENTS

In the Notes at the end of each article in this volume, the place of
publication of books is London unless otherwise stated.

NOTES ON CONTRIBUTORS

Christopher Woodward is Assistant Curator at the Sir John Soane's Museum, London. Until 1995 he was Curator-Director of The Building of Bath Museum, for whom he wrote the educational guide, *The Building of Bath*.

Jean Manco combines lecturing at Plymouth University with an independent consultancy on historic sites and buildings. Articles on Bath buildings have been published in *Bath History, Somerset Archaeology and Natural History* and *Architectural History*. Her book on St. John's Hospital, Bath will be published this year.

Trevor Fawcett, a former university librarian and FLA, was long active in art librarianship. His M.Phil. thesis on English provincial art, published in 1974, was followed by work on the bibliography and reproduction of the visual arts. He has written widely on urban history, especially on Georgian Norwich and Bath.

Hilary Arnold is a geography graduate who researched the Simcoe family's genealogy on behalf of several Canadian historical bodies, and lectured on her findings in Toronto and Montreal. The present article is based on a talk given in Bath in 1996. She has published in *Country Life* and in Yorkshire journals.

Deirdre Le Faye, of the Department of Medieval and Later Antiquities in the British Museum, has written widely on the life and times of Jane Austen and her family. She published the definitive biography, *Jane Austen: A Family Record*, in 1989; and *The Jane Austen Cookbook* (with Maggie Black) and a new edition of *Jane Austen's Letters*, in 1995.

Michael Forsyth is a practising architect who specialises in the conservation of historic buildings, and is Director of Studies of the post-graduate course on this subject at the University of Bath. He holds a Ph.D. of the University of Bristol. His publications include *Buildings for Music* (1985) and *Auditoria: Designing for the Performing Arts* (1987).

Owen Ward is a Visiting Fellow in the Centre for the History of Technology at the University of Bath. Recent publications in *International Molinology* and elsewhere have been concerned with the history of the millstone industry, and with more local water-powered sites. He is Chairman of the Bristol Industrial Archaeological Society.

Sally Festing has two Penguin biographies in print, *Gertrude Jekyll* and *Barbara Hepworth*. Her *Story of Lavender* has reached a second edition, and *Fishermen* (1979), a study of inshore fishing communities on the north Norfolk coast is currently being reprinted.

R. Angus Buchanan is Emeritus Professor of the History of Technology at the University of Bath, a Vice-President of the Society of Antiquaries, and a member of Bath Archaeological Trust. Publications include *Industrial Archaeology in Britain* and *The Power of the Machine*. He is working on 'The Life and Times of I. K. Brunel'.

'O LORD! BATH IS UNDONE; 'TIS UNDONE; 'TIS UNDONE!'[1]

Bath and the Pre-history of Architectural Conservation*

Christopher Woodward

'Old Bath' as depicted by Joseph Gilmore in 1694 is a lost city. The great Abbey, one of five city gates and a few yards of its fortified wall survived the Georgian building. The fine houses depicted in the margin of his map were all demolished. To the partisan of Georgian architecture the principal value of 'Old Bath' is as a foil to the more elegant city built on its ruins. However, Gilmore drew his map to celebrate the buildings of contemporary Bath, which a proud member of the local Chapman clan, tradesmen and Common Councilmen, described in 1664 as 'this antient, little, pretty City'.[2] As Jean Manco has shown, in the late sixteenth and seventeenth centuries Bath had been substantially rebuilt in a grander and more prosperous fashion as a result of the revival in popularity of the spa.[3]

Modern Bath has 5,000 listed buildings and all but a handful of these – more than 95% – date from between 1700 and 1830. Bath as rebuilt by the Georgians is the only city in Britain to be listed as a World Heritage Site *in toto*. Is there an irony in our impeccable preservation of a city built at the expense of another? No, in my view, but it is important to appreciate how the past saw its past. Georgian Bath was a blueprint of urban modernity but it also had an exceptional pride in its own antiquity. John Wood (1704-54), a native, attempted to demolish and rebuild the entire town as depicted by Gilmore but aspired to the title 'Restorer of Bath'.[4] How do we reconcile these apparent paradoxes?

We should first consider two important differences in perception. To begin with, 'architectural conservation' is a recent phenomenon: its influence on the course of architectural development was neglible until the Victorian age. Hitherto, the demolition of the old and its replacement by the new seemed as natural a process as the passing of the seasons. New was bigger and better; brick replaced wood, and stone replaced brick; windows grew

*A version of this article discussing the broader 'pre-history of conservation' appeared in the *Transactions of the Association for Studies in the Conservation of Historic Buildings* (1993)

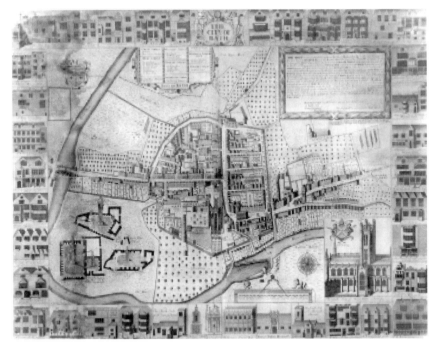

1. The City of Bath, drawn by Joseph Gilmore, 1694. (*Reproduced by courtesy of The Building of Bath Museum*)

larger, and panes of glass clearer. If any writer described a building as 'old' it was intended as a criticism.[5] The earliest local evidence for an adjustment in the meaning of the word of which I am aware is a letter to the *Bath Chronicle* in November 1850: 'As year by year, the memorials of Old Bath become more and more rare, and as they will ere long be obliterated I would call the attention of those interested in our local topography to an extensive portion of the wall of the Old City, which is now laid bare by the removal of the houses on the southern extremity of Orchard Street'.[6]

When John Wesley came to Bath in 1790 he saw the city during its greatest building boom: 'I took a view of the new buildings. There are at present none like them in England ...' He praised Lansdown Crescent and Bathwick New Town but concluded: 'And must all these fine buildings be burned up? Yea – Earth and heaven destroyed, Nor left even one in the mighty void!'[7] Architecture might be the most enduring of the arts but according to Christian doctrine every structure – whether marble temples or mud huts, Bath Abbey or Lansdown Crescent – would crumble into dust when the Last Trump sounded at some unspecified time in the future. The universal acceptance of this doctrine in earlier centuries defined a limit to our predecessors' expectations of posterity: ultimately, preservation was futile. In his 1838 survey of Bath's modern history, *The Annals of Bath*, Captain Mainwaring commented 'the fabrics of Mr Wood, with all other earthly tenements, must, at some point, be alike mingled in the same common dust'.[8]

There was also the example of Rome, whose ruins suggested that the decline and fall of every great civilization was inevitable. The architect John Soane (1753-1837) commissioned imaginary views of his Bank of England at some unspecified moment in the future. The neo–classical Bank was Soane's masterpiece and a symbol of modern Britain's power: will today's achievements be tomorrow's ruins, the paintings ask?

As T S Eliot began *East Coker*, a poem of 1940:

> In my beginning is my end. In succcession
> Houses rise and fall, crumble, are extended,
> Are removed, destroyed, restored, or in their place
> Is an open field, or a factory, or a by-pass.
> Old stone to new building, old timber to new fires,
> Old fires to ashes, and ashes to the earth,
> Which is already flesh, fur and faeces ...[9]

The past's acceptance of progress on the one hand and of the inevitability of decay on the other perhaps helps to explain why it was standard practice to recycle the materials of demolished structures for use in new buildings. More importantly, building materials represented a far higher proportion of the total cost of a building than they do today. Stone was expensive to transport while lime mortar – unlike modern cement mortar – is easily removed from old stones, allowing them to be re-laid in new walls on the same site. Modern archaeological research has demonstrated the Saxons' extensive use of *spolia* from Roman structures in the construction of the first Abbey at Bath and the city walls, confirming the observations made by the antiquary William Stukeley (1687-1765) in 1724: 'The walls round the city are for the most part intire, and perhaps [comprise] the old Roman work, except the upper part, which seems repaired with the ruins of Roman buildings; for the lewis holes are still left in many of the stones, and, to the shame of the repairers, many Roman inscriptions: some sawn across, to fit the size of the place, are still to be seen, some with the letters towards the city, others on the outside ...'[10]

John Wood's first project in Bath was the reconstruction of the lodgings at St. John's Hospital, Chapel Court, from 1727, and he was instructed by his client, the Duke of Chandos, that 'old wainscoting will serve very well to line the dark closets [the privies].'[11] Wood pulled down the Elizabethan structure recorded by Gilmore (fig.2) but incorporated its thick stone spine wall into his new building. When in 1716

2. St. John's Hospital, detail from Gilmore, fig.1.

William Killigrew built the Hospital's chapel, he was allowed to sieve rubbish from the adjacent length of city wall to use as an aggregate in his mortar.[12] Each year the Corporation paid a portion of its plumber's bill with old brass and lead,[13] and so on: in this way 'Old Bath' was partially digested into the new city.

At times, destruction could be more determined. The principal cause of this was religion. In the fourth century AD, the blocks of sculpted stone forming the image of Sulis-Minerva were removed from the pediment of the Roman Temple in the sacred precinct and re-used as paving slabs, laid face down. Bath Archaeological Trust has suggested that this action might have been a deliberate gesture by Christians determined to efface the Pagan Gods.[14] The outstanding episode was the Dissolution of the Monasteries in 1536 and 1539, and of the chantries, chapels and hospitals in 1545. It is thought that substantial remains survive of only one-third of the 650 monasteries once in existence.[15] The Priory at Bath was dissolved in 1539 and the Abbey Church was sold to a local landowner, Matthew Colthurst. Its most valuable materials – the lead roof and brass bells, its glass and iron – were sold to be recycled and the stone shell abandoned to the wind and rain. The cloister abutting its south wall was demolished but for the west range, which had been the Prior's Lodgings. As commonly happened, this prestigious accommodation was converted into a private dwelling, the Abbey House (fig.3). During the reign of Queen Elizabeth I,

The Abby House or Royal Lodgings

3. The Abbey House, detail from Gilmore, fig.1.

Colthurst's son Edmund donated the carcass of the Abbey to the citizens as their Parish Church, and it was restored through public donations. Common sense alone would have secured the Abbey's survival: begun as recently as 1499, it was a solid, modern structure and its renovation enabled the closure of three smaller and older parish churches.

The next episode of religiously-motivated destruction was the iconoclasm conducted under Parliamentary authority during the Civil War. The most notorious iconoclast was Dowsing in East Anglia who 'goes about the country like a bedlam breaking glasse windows'. One day in Ipswich he stripped eleven churches; on another in Clare, Suffolk, he boasted how his men 'broke down 1,000 pictures superstitious; I broke down 200'.[16] But the iconoclastic fury passed Bath by. Dr. John Wroughton's explanation is that the city was so whole-heartedly Puritan that there was no call for such demonstrative action.[17] A party of the city's Puritans did raid the Bishop's Palace at Wells, accusing Bishop Piers of Papist sympathies. The only evidence of vandalism in Bath is the defaced effigy of Sir William Waller, the Parliamentarian commander, in the Abbey. The damage has been attributed to Royalist troops billeted in the city but also to King James II himself; an anecdote suggested the King drew his sword and sliced off Waller's marble nose during his visit to the city in 1687.[18]

It was James II's visit that caused the little Cross Bath to become the focus of religious controversy. His Queen, Mary of Modena, came to bathe there in the hope the waters would help her conceive. She did, and jubilant Catholics celebrated the arrival of an heir – the 'Old Pretender' – by erecting a monument in the Cross Bath, in gratitude to its waters. Jean Manco has described how immediately after James II's overthrow the Corporation ordered the removal of its 'Papist' ornaments: a crown of thorns, inscriptions, and 'all other superstitious things belonging thereunto'.[19] The Cross was repeatedly vandalized because of its unpopular associations and was finally removed in 1783. A single cherub was rescued and placed in a niche at the north end of Old Bond Street where it survives as the city's only memento of Mary of Modena's momentous conception.

There are few recorded instances of such energetic religious vandalism in the eighteenth century but a suspicion of 'Popery' still overshadowed medieval structures. As late as 1794 Uvedale Price, in his influential *Essay on the Picturesque*, suggested that the ruins of monastic abbeys seen in the landscape had a value which was moral as well as pictorial: 'we may glory that the abodes of tyranny and superstition are in ruin'. In 1733 the citizens of Bristol removed the medieval market cross in their High Street, contending that it was a 'superstitious relic'; it was rescued and re-erected as a feature in the gardens at Stourhead.

The second argument for the removal of the High Cross – and possibly the real motivation – was that it obstructed traffic. The creation of wide, uncluttered thoroughfares was essential to urban improvement. During the eighteenth century the enthusiasm for 'Improvement' superseded religious fanaticism as the principal cause of the destruction of old architectural fabric. A town which had once boasted of the height of its church tower or the stoutness of its defensive walls now aspired to a new image of classical regularity: streets and open spaces should be rectilinear and broad, clean and lamp-lit, paved in stone and fronted with façades of uniform design. Our attraction to irregular, half-timbered house fronts jumbled in narrow, twisting streets is a legacy of a Victorian change in sentiment, in itself a reaction to Georgian regularity.

As rebuilt by the elder and younger Wood, Bath was the blueprint of the modern 'improved' city. John Gwynn prefaced his proposals for *London and Westminster Improved* of 1766 with the statement that 'there is not in the Kingdom one city, town or village wherein any regularity is observed, or atempt made towards magnificence or elegance, except the city of Bath'.[20] Few could fail to be impressed. In his *History and Antiquities of the County of Somerset* of 1791 Rev. John Collinson could set aside his antiquarian instincts to describe modern Bath 'as the pride of England and the admiration of foreigners. The old city walls are now built over, and in its pristine state [Bath is] almost wholly obliterated by modern improvements. The most superb edifices, raised by the most skilful architects, rise in every quarter, and compose one of the most beautiful cities in the world'.

In 1755 the Corporation demolished the north and south gates 'in order to render the streets and avenues in and to this city more extensive and commodious'.[21] The West Gate went in 1776 and only the East Gate survived, no doubt because it did not represent any obstruction to traffic. The fortified ramparts were demolished in a more piecemeal fashion, as developers of new terraces like Westgate Buildings obtained permission from the Corporation to demolish the necessary length of wall.

For much of the century, however, there was a dramatic contrast between the old, unreconstructed centre and the Upper Town created by the Woods on the farmland rising to the north of the city. John Wood was born in Bath in 1704, but by the age of 17 was in London building neat brick houses in the squares north of Oxford Street. At 21 he returned to Bath and two years later presented a proposal to the Corporation to rebuild the town in the modern style 'so far as it related to the Estates under their Guardianship'.[22] The Corporation 'thought proper to treat all my schemes as chimerical'[23] and Wood realised his vision of modern magnificence in the open fields which lay outside the walls, and beyond the Council's control. Wood's Queen Square (1729-39) was immediately recognised as the finest square in Britain while as a consequence of the Corporation's small-mindedness, Wood complained, in the old centre of Bath there was 'not a Street, lane, Alley or Throng whose sides are straight, or whose surface is upon a true depending line to give them the least beauty'.[24] A tourist's description of Bath as late as 1787 presents a tale of two cities: Royal Crescent was as impressive as the Temple of Solomon but the 'blind alleys ... which separate the old town from the new' were as bad as the notorious slums of St. Giles-in-the-Fields in London.[25]

In the old city sash windows gradually replaced iron casements, slate replaced tile, and many houses were refaced in stone. Chapman's Lodgings of 1652 still overlooked the King's Bath, however, and in 1790 a visitor commented on projecting timber jetties.[26] Progress was piecemeal until the decisive Bath Improvement Act of 1789 and, as Jane Root has described, Thomas Baldwin created Bath Street and Union Street and widened and refronted Stall Street and Cheap Street.[27] Half a decade earlier Wood had proposed the demolition of 'narrow, inconvenient'[28] Cheap Street in order to create a vast piazza fronted by the Abbey and the Pump Room. What survived of the old, crooked city at the close of the century?

Did Georgian Bath try to preserve its historic identity while transforming itself into a model of modernity?

The various reconstructions of the spa complex failed to unseat the seventeenth-century statue of King Bladud in the King's Bath: he was too strong a symbol of the collective local identity. The citizens cherished the legend of Bladud's discovery of the Hot Springs long into the second half of the eighteenth century, so Richard Warner tells us in his *Historical and Descriptive Account of Bath and its Environs* of 1802, although as early as 1724 William Stukeley had ridiculed the folklore, describing the painted statue with the legend inscribed on its plinth as 'a fanciful image of K. Bladud, with a silly account of his finding out these springs, more reasonably atttributed to the Romans'.[29] When the Stuart Guildhall was demolished in 1775 two of the statues on its façade were preserved: those of King Coel and King Edgar, each of whom played a role in the city's ancient folklore.

John Wood describes how he preserved an ornamental chimney-piece from one of the St. John's Hospital lodging houses he rebuilt: 'I have reserved the chief ornaments of the Chimney to this hour, because it is a testimony of that fame that ensured to our hot waters'. It had been donated by Lord Brooke in 1674 to express his gratitude to the spa waters which had cured his diabetes. In Wood's design for the west front of the new Hospital buildings he had proposed a pediment 'and in the Tympan[um] of it I proposed to place the Figure of the Head of Saint John the Baptist, together with several other Ornaments that embellished the old Frontispiece' in the centre of the east front of the old building, as drawn by Gilmore. However Wood's client, the Duke of Chandos, did not accept the design and St. John the Baptist disappeared from sight. Wood also describes a statue of Prince Bladud decorating the North Gate, poorly 'carv'd by some vile bungler's hands'; this figure was not rescued when the gate was demolished in 1755. The pieces of sculpture whose rescue from the Georgian bull-dozer has been described may have been exceptions to the rule.

In evaluating an old structure the eighteenth century distinguished between the building as a whole and individual features of symbolic signficance or ornamental beauty; a statue or a coat-of-arms might be preserved but the structure itself would be demolished and its materials recycled. This distinction was not only due to straightforward greed: It was also influenced by an understanding of a building's integrity which is fundamentally different to our own conceptions. The Venerable Bede described how the dying St. Aidan slumped against the wooden buttress of a church on Lindisfarne. The buttress was incorporated into a succession of churches built on the same site, in the belief that it would heal the sick and resist fire.[30] A fragmentary relic preserved the integrity of the whole, a view of posterity expressed by Francis Bacon as 'Time's shipwreck': 'antiquities are history defaced, or some remnants of history which have casually escaped the shipwreck of Time'.[31]

Since the eighteenth century, however, a more objective and less suggestive attitude has evolved: an historic building is evaluated as an entity and even a blank stone wall has an integrity which deserves to be respected. Dr. Chris Miele has suggested that this new approach may have begun in the 1830s with the first scholarly studies of Anglo-Saxon buildings, an architecture dominated by plain stone walls.[32] We are also influenced, no doubt, by John Ruskin's assertion that every stone dressed by the hand of a craftsman has a value in an age cheapened by mechanical mass-production.

The older way of understanding a fragmentary past is seen at its most complex and imaginative in the figure of the elder John Wood. As we have seen, he proposed to obliterate the town in which he was raised and to become the 'Restorer of Bath'. He saw beyond the visible reality of his environment to an imaginary, lost magnificence which he proposed to recreate. Three large rocks lying in a circle beside the road ascending Lansdown were, Wood assures us, the remains of 'a stupendous Altar; and the circular Foundation behind them seems to have borne other erect Stones, which, in all Probability, were set up by King Bladud for a Temple in honour of the Sun'.[33] As Tim Mowl has revealed, the Circus was imagined by Wood as a reconstruction of Bladud's circular temple on this site.[34] A second example is his attitude to the Abbey. He did not admire its Gothic ornamentation but contended that the dimensions of its ground plan and columns were abstracted from classical architecture: under its 'Gothick dress' the Abbey is 'really and truly an Egyptian hall of the Doric Order'.

As Tim Mowl and Eileen Harris[35] have each demonstrated, Wood was determined to reconcile the classical style of architecture of pagan Rome with the superior, and older, authority of God and Moses. He achieved this, in his own mind, by aggrandizing the legendary figure of Bladud who, he argued, was a Druid High Priest who had studied classical architecture with Pythagoras in the ancient East and introduced the classical style to Britain many centuries before the Romans arrived. Bladud had constructed his Druid capital at Bath and the modern city was only a fragment of a metropolis which had encompassed Stanton Drew, some miles to the south. In the postscript to the 1749 edition of his *Essay*, Wood wrote a diatribe against the farmers who continued to break up the ancient stones in the circle at Stanton Drew to use as building rubble: this destruction was 'rapacious ... base and ignoble'. This is the only occasion in his *Essay* when Wood criticises the destruction of old fabric.

In 1738 a Roman mosaic was discovered during the excavation of the foundations of Wood's new Mineral Water Hospital. The mosaic was preserved and recorded by Wood in a drawing which is exceptionally attentive and accurate for its time.[36] In no city in Britain was the ancient Roman heritage as strong a presence as in Bath. Its walls were studded with the inscriptions described by Stukeley and by John Leland, Librarian to Henry VIII: 'There be divers notable antiquitees engrav'd in stone that yet be sene yn the walles of Bath'. Every guidebook proclaimed the city's Roman antiquity and nearly every new development, it seems, discovered Roman traces underfoot. In 1791 Collinson described how 'The antiquities ... which have at different periods been cast up from among the ruinous foundations of the city are almost innumerable; vast masses of sculptured stone, columns, capitals, architraves and friezes of huge buildings; tessellated pavements, bricks of various shape and dimensions; paterae, urns, vases, lachrymatories, coins, silver and brass instruments of various kinds, having from time to time been discovered, and sold to strangers frequenting the city'.[37]

In 1727 workmen digging a sewer in Stall Street discovered the bronze bust of Minerva which today is the pride of the Roman Baths Museum. The bust was displayed in the Guidhall as a symbol of the city, and further discoveries were placed alongside in order 'to gratify the speculations of connoisseurs, and the reveries of the lovers of the vertu'.[38]

In the summer of 1755 the Roman Baths were discovered twenty feet below the Abbey House, which was being demolished for redevelopment. The ruins were drawn by the artist William Hoare and remained exposed to view until 1763 when the Duke of Kingston constructed a new suite of Baths on their site to capitalize on the hot springs which had bubbled up from the ruins.[39] The Baths disappeared until they were rediscovered in the 1880s; part of one Roman wall was demolished to provide a footing for a house in the new Abbey Square. Why were these ancient remains not preserved, when every year hundreds of Englishmen made pilgrimages to the ruins in Rome? The only explanation is the lack of appreciation for plain, unornamented masonry as expressed by one traveller in 1761: the Baths 'cannot be called good specimens of the famous and splendid Roman architecture, but it is obvious that they were built of bricks, without any great art or science, and probably by the Roman soldiers themselves, and it was not worth our while to go and see them'.[40]

4. The Museum of Antiquities, Hot Bath Street, Bath. The plan for this building, by John Palmer, then also working on alterations to the nearby Cross Bath, was approved by the Corporation in 1797. (*Photograph by Lesley Green-Armytage*)

By contrast, when labourers digging in Stall Street in 1790 discovered the portico of the Temple of Minerva and the sculpture of the Gorgon's head in its tympanum 'antiquarians poured in from all parts of the country to see the remarkable find', according to Barry Cunliffe,[41] and in 1800 the Corporation opened a small Museum of Antiquities in Hot Bath Street to display the fragments. The two battered figures mentioned earlier, King Coel and King Edgar, were placed in niches on the façade (fig.4).

This little building, which survives as a private house, was probably the earliest archaeological museum in Britain to be established by a municipal authority. The collection from the Guildhall was moved here, although the bust of Minerva remained as a symbol of the city. Can one suggest that Minerva had gradually supplanted Bladud in this civic role?

5. Illustration from the title-page of *Remains of two temples and other Roman antiquities discovered at Bath* by Samuel Lysons, 1802, showing an archaeological reconstruction of the temple of Minerva and the Sacred Precinct. This work was later incorporated in a three-volume edition of Lysons' *Reliquiae Britannico-Romanae*, published 1813-17. (*Reproduced by courtesy of Bath Central Library*)

John Carter's *Ancient Architecture of England* of 1795 presented the ruins of the Temple of Minerva as the most significant Roman remains to be discovered in Britain, and Samuel Lysons' collection of plates entitled *Remains of two temples and other Roman antiquities discovered at Bath*, of 1802, opened with a perspective view reconstructing the Temple and its magnificent precinct (fig.5). Carter owned a plaster cast made from a Roman bust found at Bath, then identified as Diana, and so did John Soane; Soane's is displayed in the Colonnade of his Museum at No.13 Lincoln's Inn Fields and was perhaps acquired at the auction held after Carter's death in 1817.[42] When the Corporation's Museum opened, the *Bath Herald* of 15 November 1800 reported 'we hear that Lord Powis has employed Mr. Lancashire, the statuary, to copy several of the most curious of these mutilated altars and mouldering ornaments to be placed among the choice antiquities of Powis Castle'. The idea of duplicating antiquities, whether in marble or in plaster, had originated in the Renaissance so that the collections of Rome could be admired and studied further afield. The application of these processes to the Temple of Minerva suggests that it was considered worthy of being bracketed with 'real' Roman architecture.

The antiquities accumulated up to 1800 had been accidental discoveries made by building labourers, but in the following decades active archaeology expanded the Corporation's collection. When Pierce Egan, author of *Walks Through Bath*, visited in the autumn of 1818 he referred to 'the numerous excavations now making in and about Bath'.[43] Six finds – a mosaic, a sepulchral urn, a sarcophagus, for example – had recently been added to the Museum. When workmen digging a new vault at the Abbey in 1835 discovered a mosaic and sold the pieces to the public, as earlier generations had always done, it prompted an indignant article in the *Bath Chronicle*.

The architectural conservation movement as we recognise it today was not a development of this increasing sensitivity to classical archaeology, however. Its roots lay in new soil: the Gothic Revival. To men educated in the classical taste the story of English architecture began with Inigo Jones. To the virtuoso John Evelyn (1620-1706), for example, only two structures in London as it existed before the Great Fire deserved to survive: the Banqueting House Jones built on Whitehall (1619-22) and the Corinthian portico he added to St Paul's (1634), but not the cathedral's medieval nave and tower.[44] Jones introduced the pure Renaissance style of Andrea Palladio to Britain; it was revived by Lord Burlington's circle in the early eighteenth century and imported to Bath by John Wood. Thus Richard Warner could write, in his 1802 history of the city, that the art of architecture 'began to dawn [at Bath] about the beginning of the last [eighteenth] century: for though, in the Roman times, Aquae Solis had exhibited many specimens of splendid architecture, yet in the trouble which succeeded their departure from Britain, these had been overshadowed and obliterated; and the art never shewed itself at Bath again till the time of Mr Wood, about the year 1728 ...'[45]

The idea that the history of architecture can be seen as a succession of styles, each with its own merits – that is, in essentially comparative terms – was not maturely developed until well into the nineteenth century. Originally, the word 'Gothic' was not so much a definition as a damnation: the term was invented in the Italian Renaissance to identify medieval architecture with the barbarian Goths who had destroyed Rome.[46] The structures depicted by Gilmore fell into the 'Gothic' category: although fashionable pediments, pilasters and strapwork patterns had been applied to many façades, their overall design was not controlled by classical proportion and measure and as a result they fell below the threshold acceptable to Palladian taste.

The Abbey House was one of the few notable domestic structures to be medieval in origin and, as discussed, its demolition began in the summer of 1755, supervised by the younger Wood on behalf of the Duke of Kingston. In his *Essay on the Waters* of 1756 the doctor Charles Lucas urged its disappearance: 'There can hardly be a greater affront than to find a rude irregular Gothic building upon the ruins of very magnificent and elegant Roman Baths and sudatories'. All the city's surviving medieval parish churches were demolished and rebuilt during the Georgian period. The Rev. John Penrose visited St. James's – where John Wood had been baptised – in 1766: 'It is an old church, has been often repaired and enlarged, and the Minister told me that ... it would soon be taken down and rebuilt, built larger, for that it is not half big enough to contain the People who would be glad to attend there'.[47] It was rebuilt in 1768-69.[48] As late as 1817 Bathwick's Parish Church was demolished and replaced by a much larger neo-Gothic structure; the ivy-clad tower of the old church survives on the riverside.

The first 'conservationists' were men for whom the neglected architecture of medieval England had richer associations than the classical style imported from Italy. When the antiquary William Stukeley visited York in 1740 he described the Minster as 'an astonishing beauty, [which] produces an effect superior (in my opinion) to any building upon earth ... I cannot persuade myself to except even St. Peter's in Rome ... I must needs prefer it to to the Pantheon itself'.[49] In the garden of his parsonage at Stamford he constructed a mock-medieval Hermitage which he decorated with stained glass rescued from the town's churches, where its replacement by clear glass was still in fashion.

Men such as Stukeley, however, were seen as somehow irrelevant to the graft of real life; antiquarians were an irresistible subject to satirists. Brown Willis (1682-1760) began an interest in the medieval as a boy at Westminster School and studied every cathedral in England and Wales except Carlisle.[50] In his obituary in the *Quarterly Review* he was described as 'having, with one of the honestest hearts in the world, one of the oddest heads that ever dropped from the moon. He wrote the worst hand of any man in England: it was more unintelligible than if he had learned to write by copying the inscriptions upon old tombstones ...' Willis had ruined his family's fortune by being 'far too deeply engaged with past ages to bestow any portions of his thoughts and cares upon the present'. The obituarist cited as conclusive evidence of his eccentricity that when visiting Bath Willis would insist on lodging, not in one of the new streets, but in the Abbey House.

The Society of Antiquaries had been formed in 1717 and one of its earliest actions was to pay ten shillings to erect two wooden posts to protect the medieval Waltham Cross from being damaged by passing traffic.[51] In 1792 it began its most important campaign: the programme to record all the nation's cathedrals. This initiative may have been prompted by William Chambers, Architect to King George III, who in 1791 had suggested 'a correct elegant publication of our own cathedrals and other buildings called Gothic, before they totally fall to ruin, it would be of real service to the arts of design; preserve the remembrance of an extraordinary stile of building now sinking into oblivion ...'[52] Chambers seems to accept the inevitability of our cathedrals crumbling to dust; the Antiquaries' programme was intended to record, not to preserve.

The Society appointed John Carter (1748-1817) as its draughtsman and he measured and drew first St. Stephen's Chapel at Westminster and next Exeter Cathedral. Then came Bath Abbey, 'being the last building of any magnitude erected in the country in a style purely Gothic, and almost the last one which remains exactly in the state in which it was originally designed'. The Antiquaries' publication of Carter's superb drawings in 1798 was the first scholarly analysis of the building.[53]

John Carter was the first man to campaign to prevent the destruction of medieval fabric. A quarrelsome and obsessive medievalist – described as 'John the Baptist to Pugin's Christ' by J. Mordaunt-Crook – he was convinced that Gothic was our true 'National Architecture' and superior to the classical, a foreign importation.[54] In 1795 he arrived at Durham to record the Cathedral and was outraged to discover that plans for destructive 'improvements' to designs by the architect James Wyatt were in progress. The Society of Antiquaries refused Carter's plea for intervention. When, in the summer of 1797, Wyatt applied for membership of the Antiquaries Carter organised a protest but was heavily out-voted. It was not the Society's role to intervene in modern controversies. Carter continued his campaign independently and by his death in 1817 had published over two hundred polemical articles in the *Gentleman's Magazine* opposing alterations to medieval buildings.

During these decades there was a significant change in attitude, not least due to the isolation enforced by the Napoleonic Wars: a new generation unable to make the Grand Tour to France and Italy was nurtured on its native heritage. In 1822 the Gothic Revivalist L.N. Cottingham could preface his publication of views of *The Chapel of Henry VII at Westminster Abbey* with a confident reference to 'the desire at present evinced for the preservation of this species of building'.

This new sympathy came too late to save 'old Bath' but had a dramatic impact on the appearance of the Abbey. Its tall, poised structure had always excited admiration but as late as 1755 the *Bath Guide* dismissed as 'the work of superstition' the sculpture on the west front which illustrated Bishop King's dream of angels and ladders. The description of these carvings as 'wretchedly executed' but the Abbey's interior as 'lofty and awful'[55] – 'awe-inspiring', that is – by the Cornish parson John Penrose, reflected the conventional taste of the mid-century, as did the refurbishment he described: 'The Church hath lately been cleansed and beautified; all the monuments, the Roofs, the Windows, the whole Church throughout is as neat as possible and during the Lent, all the cushions; the Pulpit, Desk, Mayor's, Communion-Table, and other cushions and cloths are covered with Black ... very decent'.[56] The Georgians liked their churches – so the Gothic Revivalists were later to say – to be as neatly and comfortably furnished and upholstered as their drawing rooms.

When the Society of Antiquaries published Carter's views of the Abbey in 1798 the only criticism made was of the 'miserable' modern houses built against the north elevation. The demolition of these began in 1823, thanks to a determined effort by the Rector and the Corporation. It was in the 1820s that the architecture of the Abbey began to enjoy a new measure of respect.

In 1825 *The History and Antiquities of Bath Abbey Church* was published by John Britton, a prolific and persuasive journalist who 'did more to promote the due appreciation of medieval art than any other contemporary writer'.[57] Britton devoted two pages to strong criticisms of the Abbey's condition and the intrusion of Georgian furnishings. It was a 'cause for regret, and even indignation' that Prior Byrde's Chantry Chapel was white-washed and dilapidated. The galleries fixed between the spandrels of the arches in the Choir should be removed. The altar and communion table should be in a more fitting style. The numerous marble monuments cluttered up the piers. The organ case was 'inappropriate and tasteless' (fig.6).[58] In 1833 all these faults were amended in a restoration which cost £27,000, although the raised galleries remained until G.G. Scott's restoration of the 1860s. A new stone organ screen in a style which corresponded with the architecture was commissioned from the architect Edward Blore who was, before Pugin, the most knowledgeable expert on Gothic detail. The City Architect George Manners oversaw the work and designed the new altar and communion table in a Gothic style.

6. Interior of Bath Abbey Church, from *The History and Antiquities of Bath Abbey Church* by John Britton, 1825. (*Reproduced by courtesy of The Building of Bath Museum*)

Prior Byrde's Chapel was restored to its original condition as a result of a successful fund-raising appeal and the architect for this work, Edward Davis (1802-1852), published *Gothic Ornaments Illustrative of Prior Birde's Oratory* in 1834. Davis's introduction to his book of lithographs underlines the change of attitude which had taken place. The Chapel 'was fated to experience the same neglect to which all Architecture of a Gothic character was so long exposed. For three centuries it was abandoned to the mercy of the parish officers; its fronts were defaced by monuments; the lower compartments of the windows were built up, and those parts permitted to remain exposed were washed and re–washed with coats of various hues, until all the sharpness of the carved work was lost, and much of the delicate tracery was altogether obliterated'.

On the exterior of the Abbey, George Manners added flying buttresses to the nave and octagonal pinnacles to the east front, replacing the square turrets which had been installed in the seventeenth century. To Manners, these alterations realised the original intentions of William and Robert Vertue, the architects of 1499, but to others they were an unnecessary interference in a structure sanctified by time. In March 1834 a correspondent wrote to the *Bath Chronicle*: 'The workmen employed upon the Abbey have this week removed the square faced towers which rose flush upon the eastern front. In their place octagonal towers are now building. Oh, that the mantle of Oliver King [the Bishop who built the Abbey] had fallen upon some of our citizens who could check the barbarism which dictates these changes!'[59]

The local historian Mainwaring dubbed the dispute 'pinnacle warfare'.[60] Manners' new pinnacles were rebuilt by G.G. Scott to a new design in the restoration of the 1860s; in 1905 T.G. Jackson in turn replaced Scott's. The 1830s argument indicates that Bath had reached a second and more mature stage in its attitude to conservation. The premise that certain buildings should be preserved for posterity was now widely accepted; the debate had moved on to ask not 'if' but 'how'. Did later alterations – such as the square turrets – which had weathered many years, deserve to survive, or should they be replaced by modern designs which were closer to the architects' original intentions? The 'pinnacle warfare' of the 1830s was essentially the 'restoration versus repair' debate which overshadowed the Victorian campaigns of architectural conservation and which still preoccupies us today.[61]

Notes

1   John Wood, *An Essay Towards a Description of Bath*, 2nd ed. (Bath, 1749),
        p. 225. Wood expressed vividly the anxieties felt by contemporaries at the
        changes taking place in his time: '... the Citizens, in general, were so uneasy
        at the Sight of every new House that was begun, that, in the utmost Despair
        they cry'd out, "O Lord! Bath is undone; 'tis undone; 'tis undone!"'.
2   Henry Chapman, *Thermae redivivae: The City of Bath described* (Bath, 1673).
3   Jean Manco, 'Bath and the Great Rebuilding' in *Bath History*, Vol. IV (Bath,
        1992), pp.25-51.
4   *Bath Journal*, 18 February 1754. Quoted in an account of the laying of the
        foundation stone of the Circus.
5   By contrast, 'venerable', 'antique' and 'ancient' were compliments.
6   Bath Central Library, Hunt Collection, cutting from the *Bath Chronicle*,
        November 1850.
7   *The Journal of the Rev. John Wesley, A.M.*, ed. N. Curnock, 8 vols. (1909-16),
        vol.8, p.46, entry for 3 March 1790, quoted in Trevor Fawcett, *Voices of
        Eighteenth-century Bath* (Bath, 1995), p.11.
8   R. Mainwaring, *The Annals of Bath* (Bath, 1838), p.451.
9   T.S. Eliot, *East Coker* (1940), II.1-7 from *Collected Poems 1909-62* (1974), p. 166.
10   William Stukeley, *Itinerarium Curiosum*, 2 vols. (2nd ed., 1776, based on
        1724 ed.), Vol.I, pp.146 and 148.
11   Huntington Library, California, Brydges MSS. Letter from the Duke of
        Chandos to John Wood, 8 June 1727.
12   St. John's Hospital Archive, Bath. Contract between William Killigrew and
        St. John's Hospital for the rebuilding of the chapel, 9 February 1716 .
13   Bath Record Office, Bath Chamberlain's Accounts. In 1755, for example, lead and
        brass to the value of £11 0s 5d was salvaged from the demolished North Gate.
14   Barry Cunliffe, *Roman Bath Rediscovered* (1971), p.17.
15   See M. Briggs, *Goths and Vandals* (1952), pp.20-24. This is the best general
        account of the history of architectural conservation although its account
        of the nineteenth and twentieth centuries has been superseded by
        publications such as *The Future of the Past*, ed. Jane Fawcett (1976).
16   Quotations from Briggs (1952), p.65.
17   Author's conversation with Dr. Wroughton, 1993.
18   This story is repeated, for example, in H. Storer's description of the Abbey
        in *Cathedral Churches ...* , Vol.VI (1819).
19   See Jean Manco, 'The Cross Bath' in *Bath History*, Vol.II (Gloucester, 1988), p.65.
20   John Gwynn, *London and Westminster Improved* (1766), p.13.
21   *The Bath Guide* (Bath, 1762).
22   Wood (1765 ed.), p.243.
23   *Ibid*.
24   Wood (1749 ed.), p.242.
25   Charles Dibdin, *A Musical Tour* (Sheffield, 1788), pp.33–34, letter ix, 21
        October 1787; quoted in T. Fawcett (1995), p.10.
26   *Gentleman's Magazine*, January 1790, quoted in Manco (1992).
27   Jane Root, 'Thomas Baldwin: His Public Career in Bath, 1775-1793', *Bath
        History*, Vol.V (Bath, 1994).

26

28   Wood (1749 ed.), p.340.
29   Stukeley, *Itinerarium Curiosum: Centuria I* (1724), p.128.
30   See N. Boulting, 'The Law's Delay' in *The Future of the Past*, ed. J. Fawcett (1976).
31   Francis Bacon, *Advancement of Learning*, ed. Joseph Dewey (1868), II, 2, section 1.
32   Author's conversation with Dr. Chris Miele of English Heritage, the authority on William Morris and the Society for the Protection of Ancient Buildings, 1998.
33   Wood (1765 ed.), p.119.
34   Tim Mowl and Brian Earnshaw, *John Wood: Architect of Obsession* (Bath, 1988), p.26 and pp.179–206.
35   Mowl, *ibid.*; Eileen Harris's analysis of Wood's theory is in her *English Architectural Books and Writers 1550-1785* (Cambridge, 1990), pp.480-491.
36   Cunliffe (1971), p. 75.
37   Rev. John Collinson, *The History and Antiquities of the County of Somerset* (Bath, 1791), p.102.
38   Collinson (1791), p.101.
39   Walter Ison, *The Georgian Buildings of Bath* (1948), p.54.
40   Friedrich Kielmansegge, *Diary of a Journey to England in the Years 1761-1762* (1902), pp.127–28, entry for October/November 1761; quoted in T. Fawcett (1995), p. 115.
41   Cunliffe (1971), p.9.
42   The plaster bust in Carter's collection was sold at Sotheby's, 24 February 1818 as Item 261. Soane's Library contains a copy of the catalogue.
43   Pierce Egan, *Walks Through Bath* (1819), pp.120-123.
44   Briggs (1952), p.89.
45   Rev. Richard Warner, *The History of Bath* (1801), p.95.
46   *Romanesque Architectural Criticism* by T. Bizarro (Cambridge, 1992) is an analysis of this changing stylistic terminology.
47   John Penrose, *Letters from Bath 1766-67*, ed. Brigitte Mitchell and Hubert Penrose (Bath, 1983); letter of 30 April 1766.
48   Ison (1948), pp.73-4.
49   Stuart Pigott, *William Stukeley* (2nd ed., 1987), p.122.
50   Information from the *Dictionary of National Biography*, pp.2286-87.
51   See Boulting (1976).
52   Chambers made his remarks in the third edition of his *Treatise On Civil Architecture* (1791) p.40. The Society of Antiquaries decided their programme on 30 March 1792: see J. Evans, *A History of the Society of Antiquaries* (1956), p.206.
53   John Carter, *Some Account of the Abbey Church at Bath* (1798).
54   See J. Mordaunt-Crook, *John Carter and the Mind of the Gothic Revival* (1995) for a study of Carter and the episode described below.
55   Penrose (1983), letter of 24 April 1766.
56   Penrose (1983), letter of 13 April 1767.
57   Charles Eastlake, *A History of the Gothic Revival* (1872), p.86.
58   John Britton, *The History and Antiquities of Bath Abbey Church* (1825), pp.92-93.
59   Bath Central Library, cutting in Hunt Collection.
60   Mainwaring (1838), p.424.
61   The fullest description is in J. Fawcett (1976), *passim*.

SAXON BATH: THE LEGACY OF ROME AND THE SAXON REBIRTH

Jean Manco

In 1984 Barry Cunliffe summarised what was known of Saxon Bath with his customary scholarship and insight.[1] However, the intervening years have brought a crop of fresh perspectives nationally and new discoveries locally. That must be my excuse for trampling the footsteps of a master. There has been a growing realisation that the Romano-British way of life did not vanish overnight. *Britannia* was part of the Roman Empire for 400 years, so it is scarcely surprising that elements of Roman culture were absorbed and became part of the British sense of identity. One such element was Christianity. By the time *Britannia* became independent in 410AD, Christianity had been the state religion for nearly twenty years. Evidence is mounting of its survival in the Bath region. The survival of Roman cantonal boundaries is even more significant for local history, for that made Bath a frontier town. In the long run the benefits of that precarious position outweighed the dangers. In war a refuge, in peace a market, Bath throve as a border crossing. Recognition of the Avon as an early frontier alters our view of Bath's hinterland. Instead of a Roman estate cocooning the city on both sides of the Avon, which survived into Saxon times,[2] picture a town thrust out under the eyes of the enemy, with its hinterland fanning out behind it. Only in the eighth century did Bath Abbey gain land south of the Avon.

Dobunni to Hwicce

The Romans had found Britain full of warring tribes, among them the Dobunni – the people of the Severn valley and the Cotswolds. The territory of the Dobunni can be estimated from the spread of their coins through North Somerset, Gloucestershire, Worcestershire, and part of Warwickshire. Differences in pottery may be a clue that those south of the Bristol Avon had formed a splinter group.[3] Under Roman administration, tribal areas became *civitates*. A schism between the northern and southern Dobunni would make the Bristol Avon the natural southern boundary of the Dobunnic *civitas*.[4] That territory looks remarkably similar to the old diocese of Worcester (fig.1), created for the Anglo-Saxon kingdom of the Hwicce – strong evidence of the continuity of a territorial unit from Roman to Anglo-Saxon. Probably after *Britannia* seceded from the empire in 409, it dissolved once more into local kingdoms, based on the Roman *civitates*.[5]

Within decades Saxons swept over the lowlands. The fifth-century *Gallic Chronicle* reports that the Saxons were in control of a large part of Britain in 441. Debate has raged over this source, while Gildas, our native source for the events of this period, is frustratingly imprecise. However, in a thorough re-interpretation of both, Nicholas Higham suggests that after a period in which victories were divided between Britons and Saxons, the Saxons achieved dominance and could impose treaty terms in 441. This left the highland zone as free British kingdoms and the east under Saxon control. The buffer zone between, including the Dobunni, seems to have remained British, but de-militarised, relying on Anglo-Saxon protection and paying tribute in return.[6] Such a divide could explain the creation of the Wansdyke. That massive earthwork would have made a sensible defence for the free British of the South-West.[7] While on their eastern flank the Wiltshire and Hampshire Avon was protected by the New Forest, on the north their best strategy would be a defensive line along the hills overlooking the Bristol Avon and the Kennet. The West Wansdyke was apparently built to a Roman pattern,[8] as one would expect of a people only decades out of the empire. Archaeological evidence also suggests an early post-Roman date for the East Wansdyke.[9]

Gildas describes the siege of Mount Badon as almost the last of the British victories.[10] Mount Badon was identified as Bath by that weaver of fables Geoffrey of Monmouth and this idea still has its adherents.[11] However, Gildas was a Briton writing when the Dobunnic polity was still British, so he would scarcely have described Bath by the Anglo-Saxon name *Baðon* (ð = 'th'). In any case a mount under siege would surely be a hillfort. Gildas seems to have been writing in the area now Dorset and Wiltshire.[12] The one battle he names would probably be that one strong in local memory, making the hillfort of Badbury Rings in Dorset the most likely Mount Badon.[13]

During the peace between Briton and Saxon, a Christian society continued in the British kingdoms with elements inherited from both the Roman and Celtic cultures. Latin continued in use. However, masonry building ceased, as part of a wider dislocation. Gildas bewails the

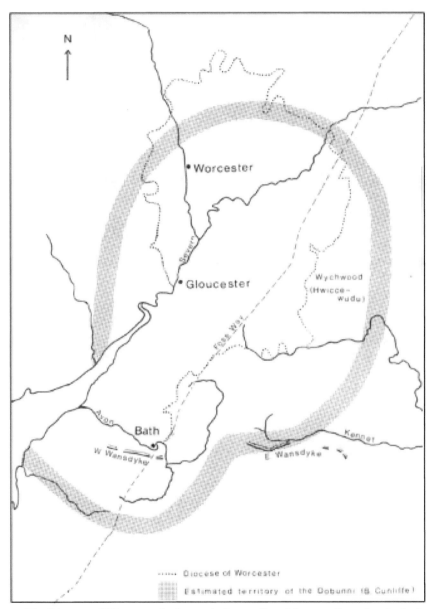

1. The Diocese of Worcester is shown in its medieval form, adjusted to include Bath. The territory of the Hwicce must have extended further east than this diocesan boundary originally, if it included Wychwood.

destruction of towns: 'The cities of our land are not populated even now as they once were; right to the present they are deserted, in ruins and unkempt.'[14] Although he attributed it to war, there were other forces at work. The Roman consumer-city, sustained by rents and taxes flowing in to town-dwellers, could not survive the end of the Western Empire. Towns decayed across Europe.[15] It is not a story of utter abandonment. While towns ceased to be major production centres, with large populations, some might remain as monasteries, episcopal seats or local markets. Around these foci life continued amid the ruins. Signs of sub-Roman occupation have been found in a cluster of Dobunnic towns and also Camerton, six miles south-west of Bath.[16] Bath itself is a special case. It was first and foremost a spa town. We shall consider later how well it fared in the new economic climate.

In the latter part of the sixth century the Anglo-Saxons began to expand their territory. *The Anglo-Saxon Chronicle*, compiled so long after these events, may not be reliable on the details. It describes a battle at Dyrham in 577 in which the West Saxons killed three British kings and captured three towns: Gloucester, Cirencester and Bath.[17] The repeated use of the number three, so popular in folktales, arouses suspicion. Some have doubted whether the entry is historical at all, but this seems excessively sceptical. If it were a later West Saxon invention to bolster their claim to the former Dobunnic territory,[18] why not add Worcester as well? The omission lends plausibility. We can picture the British leaders retreating beyond the Severn in 577.

A sixth to seventh-century Anglo-Saxon spearhead and knives tossed into a Roman ditch near Bath[19] suggests a small band of Anglo-Saxons captured and disarmed, but if they lost that skirmish, they certainly won the war. Even before 577, it would have been difficult for de-militarised British authorities to resist piecemeal Anglo-Saxon settlement. Angles appear to have drifted into Dobunnic territory from the north-east in the fifth and sixth centuries, leaving their mark in pagan burials and a sprinkling of pagan place-names.[20] Anglian settlers might well have resented the West Saxon advance just as much as the British. If the Angles were indeed mercenaries or exacting tribute, then the West Saxon victory would have usurped their position. It was some 60 years before the tide turned. In 628, says *The Anglo-Saxon Chronicle*, the West Saxons fought the (Anglian) Penda of Mercia at Cirencester and afterwards came to terms. It is clear from the subsequent history of the area that Penda won, but he had probably forged an alliance with local leaders, for the former Dobunnic polity was not amalgamated with Mercia. Instead it became the client kingdom of the Hwicce. The West Saxons, their expansion to the west and north blocked, overran the free British territory of the South-West from 658, so the Bristol Avon became a boundary between Wessex and the Hwicce.

Who were the Hwicce? The earliest surviving document to record the name is the Tribal Hidage, now thought to date from 626.[21] Bede tells us that the South Saxon queen Eafe 'had been baptised in her own country, the kingdom of the Hwicce. She was the daughter of Eanfrith, Eanhere's brother, both of whom were Christians, as were their people.'[22] The implication is that Eanfrith and Eanhere were of the royal family of the Hwicce; the context places them in the mid-seventh century. Their names and those of subsequent Hwiccian royalty were Anglo-Saxon. Place names show that Anglo-Saxon settlement was widespread in the Hwiccian area, Anglian in the north, Saxon in the south. However pagan burials seem to cluster to the north-east.[23] Bede, whose aim was to provide a detailed account of the conversion of the Anglo-Saxons, fails to tell us how the Hwicce became Christian. So the British Church was probably responsible, rather than Pope Gregory's mission to the Anglo-Saxons, the details of which Bede carefully researched. Incoming settlers could have been converted by Christian neighbours. Alternatively the royal family may have sprung from inter-marriage between a British ruling dynasty and an Anglo-Saxon military aristocracy. Bede shows that elsewhere such marriages could pave the way for the conversion of a whole people.

Two *eccles* place-names within the kingdom indicate the survival of Christian communities into the period of Anglo-Saxon incursion. There are also scattered clues to continuity of worship from sub-Roman to Anglo-Saxon. Probable British Christian burials have been found beneath Worcester Cathedral and St Mary de Lode, Gloucester.[24]

Aquæ Sulis to *Aquæmann*

In the late Roman period Christianity perhaps made little headway in *Aquæ Sulis* (Bath), where the worship of Sulis Minerva was an integral part of its function as a spa. A fourth-century curse tablet thrown into the Sacred Spring provides evidence of divided loyalties. The writer, Annianus, asks the Lady Goddess to retrieve six silver coins from whoever stole them, 'whether pagan or Christian'. Only a Christian would use such terminology. (Pagans did not refer to themselves as such.) Yet

Annianus did not shrink from invoking the power of Sulis.[25] If he attended a local church, it would probably have been outside the city walls. Sites for the churches of this new religion generally had to be found on the edges of towns, rather than the established centre. Those with cemeteries needed to be outside the city walls to comply with Roman law.[26] So the churches of St Michael in Broad Street and St Swithin in Walcot are possible sites.[27] Although St Swithin suggests a Saxon origin, in fact the medieval church at Walcot was dedicated to All Saints.[28]

Many pagan temples in Britain seem to have come to an abrupt end around 410.[29] Christian militancy was raging across the empire. Impatient with gradual conversion, militants destroyed temples and cult images. The failure of the pagan gods to wreak a terrible revenge undermined the whole pagan belief system. Who would worship a broken idol? At Uley in the Cotswolds the head of the cult image was hacked off and buried.[30] In Bath the head of Minerva seems to have been given much the same treatment. Also her temple façades were dismantled and parts turned face down as paving slabs, although the precise date of all this damage is unknown.[31] The Cross Bath could also have been a target. Two Roman carved stones were found tumbled into its spring. One was dedicated to Sulis Minerva, while the other bore scenes linked with Æsculapius.[32]

Uley is one of two pagan temples within a twenty-mile radius of Bath which were replaced by Christian religious sites.[33] So did a church spring up amid the ruins of the temple of Minerva? The medieval church of St Mary of Stalls was built on the site of the temple precinct and apparently on the same alignment, but the earliest burials in its cemetery are late Saxon.[34] So was a companion temple taken over by Christians? A Roman circular temple probably stood on or near the site of the present Abbey Church.[35] An early church beneath the present one is an attractive possibility. However there would be no compelling reason to convert a temple site if a more suitable building was available nearby. Unlike Roman temples, which were entered only by priests, churches needed to house a congregation. A *basilica* (assembly-hall) was ideal for the purpose.

The name *Aquæ Sulis* could have become an embarrassment in the Christian era. A religiously neutral name would be *Aquæmann*, simply adding the Old Welsh *mann* (place) to the familiar *aquæ*.[36] There is no contemporary evidence of a name-change, but the name occurs centuries later in a suggestive context. *Achamanni* and *Aquamania* for Bath suddenly appear in charters of Edgar from 965 to 972,[37] and are never used in later charters. Anglo-Saxon versions occur in *The Anglo-Saxon Chronicle* in one place only – the description of the coronation of Edgar in 973. He was crowned 'in the ancient borough of *Acemannes ceastre* – the men of this island call it by another name – *Bathan*'. Æthelweard, a kinsman and contemporary of Edgar, translated this as: 'in the city called *Akimannis castrum* by men of old, and by others *Bathum* for its boiling waters'.[38] So *Aquæmann* appears to be an antiquarian rediscovery favoured by Edgar. Since this had not regained general currency, the chroniclers felt obliged to explain which town was meant. Such a brief and literary revival is unlikely to explain the name *Akeman Street* for the road to Bath from St Albans.[39] Presumably this road name was adopted in the early Saxon period, while lowland Britain was Anglo-Saxon, but Bath remained British.

Christian ire was not directed against the baths themselves. After the destruction of the temple façades, the inner temple precinct was repaved and its gateway replaced by a new building, presumably to permit access to the Sacred Spring. It continued in use well into the fifth century and perhaps beyond.[40] The Sacred Spring fed a grand and sophisticated bathing complex. How much of this survived? In a Welsh compilation of the early ninth century, drawn from earlier British sources, 'The hot pool in the country of the Hwicce' was listed among the wonders of Britain:

> It is surrounded by a wall, made of brick and stone, and men may go there to bathe at any time, and every man may have the kind of bath he likes. If he wants, it will be a cold bath; if he wants a hot bath, it will be hot.[41]

It sounds as though the Roman baths were still in use when this was first written. The Romans liked to finish bathing with a cold plunge, so there were both hot and cold pools in the complex. The main spring was indeed surrounded by a wall of brick and stone; the masonry wall had tile bonding courses, characteristic of Roman construction.[42] But so grand a spa could only be sustained by a stream of paying visitors, the product of a wealthy society. The first decades of British independence seem to have brought an upturn in the economy. The imperial tax burden was a thing of the past.[43] But in the decline that followed, Bath would have suffered. Eventually the great baths would have to give way to a more modest spa, operating amid the ruins of once-great buildings. The bustle of shops, workshops and entertainment would cease. Bath would be pared down to its primary function.

Æt Baðum: At the Baths

For the Anglo-Saxons Bath was the town at the baths. The name first appears in a charter of 675 as *Hat Bathu*,[44] meaning hot baths (in the accusative plural). Thereafter it is always given in the dative plural *Baðum*, *Baðan* or *Baðon*, meaning 'at the baths'.[45] Bede wrote c.730 that Britain possessed 'warm springs and from them flow rivers which supply hot baths, suitable for all ages and both sexes in separate places and adapted to the needs of each.' This comes in his geographical introduction, drawn largely from earlier authors. However, this particular statement has no known antecedent and presumably reflects the use of the baths in Bede's own day.[46] By then the city had crumbled into ruin. In the same era as Bede, a Saxon poet described an unnamed city, clearly Bath, as 'Wondrous masonry, shattered by fate':

> There stood courts of stone;
> where a stream gushed in hot rippling floods,
> a wall enfolding all its bright bosom;
> baths that heated themselves: how convenient!
> Then over the grey stone hot streams poured
> to the round pool.[47]

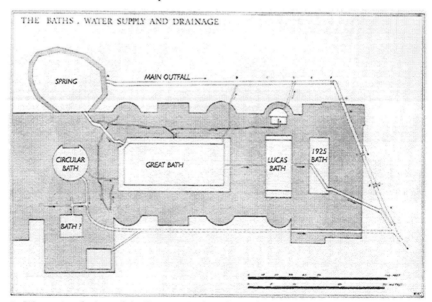

2. Water circulation of the Roman Baths. (*Reproduced by courtesy of Barry Cunliffe*)

That was not the Roman arrangement. In their time the hot spring fed the great bath and eventually ran down a drain east to the Avon, while the circular pool was a cold plunge (fig.2). The hot water seems to have been deliberately redirected into the circular bath,[48] probably to reduce the baths to manageable size. From there the water would have run south to the Avon (like the medieval drain).[49] That would have left the eastern baths dry and they were partly buried beneath a late Saxon cemetery.

The Anglo-Saxons called the reduced complex the *Alron* bath. It is only by lucky chance that the name is not lost to us. Deeds are our best source for place-names within the city and few survive from before 1235, when the name changed to the King's Bath. Geoffrey of Monmouth noted the old name around 1150. He confidently assumed *Alaron* to be a person. A modern editor also translated the *balneum Alrone* in two deeds as 'Alron's bath'.[50] But no such personal name is known. *Alron* seems to be a compound of *æl* (foreign) or *ald* (old) and *run* (writing). Perhaps Roman inscriptions could still be seen in the complex when the Anglo-Saxon language became the dominant one in Bath.

Abbess Berta's Convent

On 6 November 675 Osric, King of the Hwicce, granted the Abbess Berta 100 hides near Bath for the establishment of a convent.[51] This land would all have been within his territory, north of the Avon. His charter does not explicitly state that the convent was to be built in Bath. However, Bath would be the likely choice, the city wall providing a degree of protection, as with Osric's similar foundation at Gloucester.[52] Double houses of men and women, presided over by an abbess, were common at this time and it has been assumed that Bath was one such. However, Osric's preamble states his intention to found separate houses for men and women. In the past this has thrown doubt upon the authenticity of the preamble, but scholars now recognise the influence of Archbishop Theodore, who signed the charter. He disapproved of double houses.[53]

Osric's preamble also explains that his primary purpose was to found a diocese, according to synodal decree. This must refer to the synod of 672, which had proposed more bishoprics.[54] The idea would be welcome to the Hwicce, who had presumably been swept into the orbit of the newly-created see of Mercia in 656.[55] In 679 the Hwicce did receive their own bishop, based at Worcester.[56] The cathedral there was dedicated to St Peter, as was the convent founded at Gloucester by Osric.[57] Presumably the convent at Bath was also St Peter's, like the abbey that came after it. Was there a message here? St Peter was a symbol of the papacy. If the Hwicce had earlier come within the British Church, transition to the Anglo-Saxon Church would be eased by a demonstration of loyalty to Rome.

Also interesting is the Frankish name of the first abbess – Berta. At this time high-born Anglo-Saxon girls were educated at houses like Chelles, near Paris, known for their learning. Or the nuns could come to them. Chelles supplied nuns and books for teaching and the foundation of convents in England.[58] Berta may have returned to France after establishing the convent. A charter in 681 granted land to the Abbess Bernguida (Beorngyth, an English name) and Folcburg (Frankish). Apart from a spurious charter to Bernguida copied from this one, there are no more charters to abbesses in the Bath cartulary.[59]

Offa's Abbey

The patronage of Bath later belonged to the Bishop of Worcester. However, there is no charter granting Bath to the see, unless we count Osric's hopeful preamble in 675. So the bishop was helpless in the face of a dubious claim by Offa of Mercia (757-96). Offa argued that the see was wrongly holding the inheritance of his kinsman King Æthelbald of Mercia (d.756), including ninety hides in Bath. The dispute was resolved at the Synod of Brentford in 781, when Bishop Heathored 'restored' to Offa and his heirs 'that most famous monastery at Bath'. In addition to the ninety hides claimed as Æthelbald's (presumably the 100 hides granted to Berta), the bishop granted thirty hides near Bath on the south side of the Avon, which the bishopric had 'bought at a proper price from Cynewulf, King of the West Saxons [757-86] '.[60]

A puzzling entry in the Bath cartulary may be a mangled record of that purchase. It purports to be a charter of 808 by Cynewulf, King of the Saxons, granting North Stoke to the brethren of the monastery of St Peter in Bath, witnessed by Offa and Archbishop Cuthbert (d.758).[61] Clearly the date should be 757 or 758. But a more serious problem is that North Stoke was not in Wessex. Probably a genuine grant by Cynewulf was later reworked to legitimise the Abbey's tenure of North Stoke.[62] The monks attributed the grant to King Cenwulf of Mercia (796-821),[63] and presumably added the spurious date. If the reference to the brethren was from a genuine charter of Cynewulf, then it is the first record of Bath as a masculine house. Gloucester Abbey also changed from convent (or double house) to monastery after the death of the Abbess Eafe in 757.[64]

Why was Offa anxious to gain control of Bath? The Avon was the dividing line between the rival powers of Wessex and Mercia.[65] The mighty Offa had subdued other Anglo-Saxon kingdoms and could call himself King of all the English. From his time the Hwiccian dynasty, never truly independent of Mercia, were termed under-kings or *ealdormen*.[66] Wessex however showed fight. Offa had defeated Cynewulf in 779,[67] but he may have felt it prudent to guard his borders. The acquisition of Bath would put a frontier post under his direct control. From then until after the Conquest, Bath Abbey was a royal *eigenkloster*. Offa even gained papal dispensation for his ownership of several monasteries of St Peter, which he had acquired or erected.[68] Probably priests administered the estates as part of the royal demesne. That was a pervasive pattern at the time.

But while Bath lost its independence, it might hope to gain from royal interest. Offa had the means and the vision to build on a grand scale. A substantial monastery at Bath would provide useful accommodation for a royal household constantly on the move. Offa was apparently there in 793.[69] Certainly in the months after Offa's death in July 796, his son held court at the monastery in Bath.[70] So there seems no reason to doubt the word of William of Malmesbury that Offa built St. Peter's, although he was writing centuries later.[71] William was probably relying on information from the last Saxon monks at Bath. Major benefactors would be remembered in the prayers of the community and possibly in inscriptions on the fabric, so the monks could have been entirely reliable. In 957 Bath monastery was described by King Edwy as 'marvellously built'.[72] By that time stone churches were no longer so rare in themselves as to excite such comment, so we must suppose that Bath's was exceptionally fine. The architecture may have impressed simply by the reuse of Roman materials, but it is possible that Offa actually revived Roman building methods in emulation of Carolingian work. He certainly matched Charlemagne in striking coins in Roman style. Offa was the greatest of English kings before Alfred and his dealings with Charlemagne betray a conscious rivalry.[73]

Apart from the church itself, there was probably only a loose grouping of cells for the priests and some communal buildings. But where was Offa's monastery? Saxon burials spread over a wide area south of the present Abbey Church are clearly linked with the abbey. Finds in this area include a

38

3. Tenth-century lead cross with inscription to 'Eadgyvu ... a sister of the community'. (*Photograph by courtesy of the Institute of Archaeology, Oxford*)

tenth-century lead cross inscribed 'Eadgyvu ... a sister of the community' (fig.3). This has been interpreted as a re-interment of one of the seventh-century nuns, but seems more likely to record a benefactress of the monastery. (Patrons had burial rights.) Recently the footings of a substantial Saxon wall have been discovered south of this cemetery, which must be part of the abbey.[74]

Alfred's Borough

Thus far, although Bath continued to be called a town, we may imagine it more as a modest set of baths, presided over by a monastery. It was another great king who made Bath a true town once more. One of the most familiar stories in English history is how Alfred the Great was overwhelmed by Viking marauders at Chippenham in January 878 and had to take refuge in the Somerset marshes.[75] But the outcome still astonishes. By 886 (on the most recent dating) Alfred had built a chain of fortresses around Wessex.

Bath of course was over the border in Mercia, but that had become an academic point. Mercia had been taken by the Danes. Burgred was the last King of Mercia to hold court at Bath. In 864 he was there with Queen Æthelswith (the sister of Alfred), attended by his nobles and bishops.[76] Just ten years later he was driven out and replaced by a puppet king. Alfred supported a rival Mercian leader, Æthelred, who married Alfred's daughter Æthelflæd. So Bath was a natural link in the chain of defence. The city was protected on two sides by the curve of the Avon and had at least remnants of its Roman defences.[77] The city wall would have been about 600 years old by Alfred's day. Even a century and a half earlier the author of 'The Ruin' saw a sadly dilapidated structure:

> Wondrous is this masonry, shattered by fate.
> The stronghold has burst open; the handiwork of giants is mouldering.
> The roofs have fallen, the towers are in ruin;
> The barred gate is roofless; there is rime on the mortar.[78]

Although the poetic style is impressionistic, these lines appear to refer to the city walls. The image conjured up is a late Roman wall, with roofed gate-towers.

Alfred generally built in earth and timber for rapid security. A timber barricade, apparently Saxon, was found outside and parallel to the northern city wall in 1980. The length of this timber outwork would correspond more closely than that of the stone wall with the assessment of Bath in the *Burghal Hidage*, the list of Alfred's fortresses now thought to date from 886.[79] Alfred perhaps threw this outwork around Bath at speed; within its shelter the stone wall could be repaired at greater leisure. With the city full of Roman ruins, the masons would not have far to go for materials. Early antiquaries visiting Bath were fascinated to discover chunks of Roman carving embedded in the upper part of the city wall.

Such repair-work could scarcely date from much later than Alfred. He and his son can be credited with such a thorough re-organisation of the town that Roman ruins would not be much in evidence thereafter.

Although some of Alfred's forts were no more than that, Bath was one of a string of *burhs* created by him and his children.[80] The charter of Worcester demonstrates their twin purposes. Æthelred and Æthelflæd stated that, having ordered the borough at Worcester built for the protection of the people, they now granted to St Peter's half their rights in the market and borough, including the tax levied for repair of the borough wall.[81] A successful market town would generate revenue and pay for its own defence. As a river crossing on the Foss Way, Bath was in a good trading position.

The Roman street pattern would have been lost under the debris, so the town had to be laid out afresh (fig.4). Alfred's *burhs* follow a standard pattern. A broad main street running between the city gates housed the market. Then lanes ran out from that at fairly regular intervals to join a street circling the city, which gave easy access for those defending the walls.[82] In Bath the Saxon street plan was later disrupted by the Norman cathedral priory and bishop's palace. These changes need to be mentally peeled away to discern the Saxon pattern beneath. It was logical to suppose initially that the main Saxon artery ran straight down from the North Gate to a Saxon south gate on the site of the medieval Ham Gate,[83] but it is now clear that it had to make a detour around the abbey. The northern part – High Street – is still there. The market was there in the medieval period and probably from the first.[84] The southernmost part became a lane from the priory gate to the Ham Gate in the medieval period. In the middle the street swung west around the abbey. Part of it was apparently adopted as the boundary between the Norman bishop's close and priory.[85] It would have simplified Norman planning to lay out the close between two Saxon streets, so another Saxon street probably underlies Stall Street.

Westgate Street was part of another important thoroughfare, which probably continued eastwards to the East or Lot Gate (OE *ludgeat* = postern). That would have led out to the town mill. Bath Abbey had a mill at Domesday, probably in the same place as the later Monk's Mill. Mills tend to remain on the same site, however often they are rebuilt. (The medieval lane to the mill made a detour around the Norman priory cemetery, shifting the East Gate to its present position.)[86] Today the eastern arm of Westgate Street is Cheap Street. Although it sounds convincingly Anglo-Saxon (OE *ceap* = market), it is actually quite a late name. Before 1399 it was Sutor (shoemaker's) Street, which was considered undignified, so the citizens requested a name change.[87]

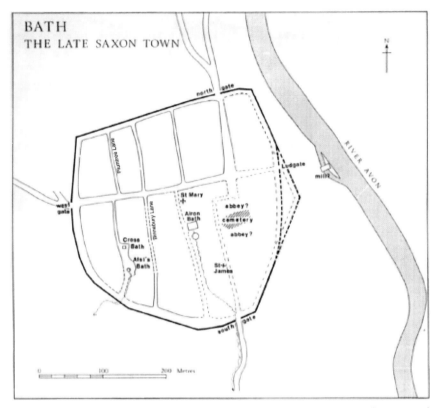

4. Bath, the Late Saxon Town. Alternative lines are shown for the mid-section of the east city wall. That furthest east is the medieval wall. The Roman and Saxon wall either followed that line or lay further west and was demolished to create more space for the Norman cathedral. (*Adapted with his kind position from a plan by Barry Cunliffe. Alterations are the responsibility of the present author*)

Still today there are remnants of Saxon planning in the blocks of property along the two main streets. Standard burgage plots can be discerned behind the modern map, with narrow houses facing the street and long gardens and yards behind. Merchants and artisans would have been encouraged to settle in this permanently built-up area, while land in the back lanes was probably left open to make camp sites. Then if danger threatened, the villagers around could take refuge within the walls.[88] This may explain the name Binnebury for the south-west quarter of the city. OE *binnan burh* meant within the fortified place.[89] Originally Binnebury (now Bilbury) Lane ran north to Westgate Street. A short section of Saxon

42

street along the route has been excavated.[90] On the north side of Westgate Street back lanes survive today, though their names have changed. Bridewell Lane was *Plumtreow strete* or *twichen* in the thirteenth century.[91] Here the Old English spelling of 'tree' had been retained, as well as *twicen*, meaning a place where two roads meet. One can picture a plum tree as a landmark on the corner.

If Bath was not already a functioning *burh* by the time of Alfred's death in 899, then it became one soon afterwards, for his son Edward the Elder established a mint there in the early years of his reign.[92] Mints were confined to *ports*, -which were market towns, both coastal and inland. Essentially they were synonymous with the *burhs*, but the emphasis was on their trading function, which the mints supported (fig.5).

5. *Above*: the first coin of the Bath mint was issued by Edward the Elder. It bears his name (left). On the reverse (right) is BAÐ, meaning Bath. *Below*: Edgar issued the first coin of the Bath mint to bear a royal portrait. (*Photographs by courtesy of the British Museum*)

Edward ordered that all buying and selling should be done in a *port*, with a reeve as witness, partly to hinder the sale of stolen property.[93] The reeve or portreeve was the royal official in charge of a market town. The first known reeve of Bath was one Alfred, whose death in 906 was noted in *The Anglo-Saxon Chronicle*.

The Domesday survey of 1086 shows just how successful Alfred's policy was. The mint was still flourishing and Bath had become the largest town in Somerset, taxed as the equivalent of twenty hides and with 178 burgesses. While sixty-four of them paid rent to the king and twenty-four to Bath Abbey, ninety were 'burgesses of the king's barons'.[94] As with other royal boroughs, Alfred or his successors had involved their nobles in Bath's development. Grants of borough land would encourage them to build there and use the market.[95] Some of the lords of Somerset manors had houses in Bath, either for their own use or for rent.[96] Centuries later we have a clue to one of their purposes. Walter Hussey of Swainswick leased part of his property in Bath c.1220, with the proviso that he and his heirs could lodge there in time of war.[97]

Lords with a town house might build a chapel for themselves and their tenants, just as they did on their own manors. The evolution of such chapels into parish churches accounts for the high number of churches in towns with Roman or Saxon origins.[98] Of Bath's medieval churches within the walls, only St Peter's (with St Mary of Stalls) had a cemetery before 1400.[99] The lack of a cemetery is a strong indication that St Michael Within, All Saints in Binnebury[100] and St Mary Northgate sprang from domestic chapels, either late Saxon or Norman. From the thirteenth century the Champney family held the advowson of St Mary Northgate and rents in Bath along with their manor of Wilmington.[101] Possession of the advowson indicates that they or their predecessors had founded the church. The origin of the first church of St James is more intriguing. It lay beside the main Saxon street and was swallowed up by the Norman bishop's close. Burials have been found on the site. Since the bishop would scarcely permit burials in his courtyard, they are thought to be Saxon.[102] The advowson was part of the royal estate in Bath.[103] So it is possible that Alfred or Edward the Elder built the first church of St James for the people of the new *burh*.

The fact that Edward established a mint in Bath early in his reign shows that the city had been permanently transferred to Wessex. (Mercia, regained from the Danes, was controlled by Edward's brother-in-law Æthelred until the latter's death in 910).[104] The transfer was to have long-term implications for the city. As the shire system crystallised, Bath fell into Somerset, not Gloucestershire. The see of Somerset (based at Wells) was created in 909, so Bath also changed diocese. Evidently for ease of administration the lands owned by Bath Abbey in Alfred's time were embraced by the see and county of Somerset.

The Reform of the Abbey

Alfred's descendants inherited the patronage of Bath Abbey. Athelstan and several of his successors arranged for the Abbey to celebrate the anniversaries of their deaths by the gift of alms to the poor.[105] In 1535 that custom was laconically noted as 'alms distributed to various paupers and lepers ... from the endowment of Kings Athelstan, Edgar, Ethelred and Edwy and many other founders',[106] which is probably the source of the misconception that Athelstan founded a leper hospital in Bath. Athelstan did give several books to the Abbey, including a copy of *The Acts of the Council of Constantinople*, inscribed 'King Athelstan gave this book to God and to the holy mother of Christ and to the saints Peter and Benedict in the monastery of ... Bath'.[107]

The dedication to St Benedict is curious at this date, suggesting that Bath had already adopted the Rule of Benedict, but it may simply be that this note was added a few years later. A stricter form of monasticism was reviving across the Channel, but in England it had a mixed reception by the Crown. In 944 King Edmund granted refuge in Bath Abbey to Flemish monks expelled from St Bertin for refusing to live to rule.[108] Edmund did appoint the reformer Dunstan Abbot of Glastonbury, but Dunstan was exiled by Edmund's son Edwy.[109] The young King Edwy held *witans* close to Bath in 956 and 957, which drew his attention to local affairs and produced a spate of charters.[110] His reaction to the city crept into them: one refers to the hot springs and another to the 'marvellously built' monastery.[111] Under Edwy, Bath remained a royal *eigenkloster*, ruled by his chaplain Wulfgar. However, Edwy's brother Edgar admired and supported the reformed monasticism. On his accession he recalled Dunstan, who became Archbishop of Canterbury in 961.

Dunstan brought the monastic revival to England, encouraging the adoption of the Rule of St Benedict, with its emphasis on poverty, chastity and communal living.[112] In the following years Bath Abbey was presumably reorganised on Benedictine lines, with communal buildings around a cloister and the monks ruled by an abbot. William of Malmesbury tells us that Edgar, delighted by the grandeur of the place, enlarged it 'after his manner'.[113] It was probably not designed for a huge community; in 1077 there were eighteen monks including the abbot.[114] Saxon cross-fragments found in various places in Bath (fig.6) probably date from around this period.[115]

The early years of the reformed monastery were not without problems, some mercilessly recorded by the biographer of St Ælfheah (Elphege).

6. The head of a Saxon cross discovered in Bath. (*Photograph by courtesy of the Royal Commission on the Historical Monuments of England, © Crown Copyright*)

Ælfheah left Deerhurst monastery for a hermit's cell near Bath, where he attracted followers much against his will. Once a monastery large enough to house them was built, he withdrew again to a solitary life and provision for the community was delegated to a suitable prior, presumably Æscwig, Abbot of Bath in 965 and 970. However, lapses in discipline all too often required Ælfheah's personal attention. He had to chastise those slipping out at night for drunken revels, or reluctant to forsake all personal property. This may explain why Ælfheah was also styled as Abbot of Bath over the same period as Æscwig.[116] Ælfheah was later appointed Archbishop of Canterbury, but his name was long remembered at Bath. 'St Alphege's Well' on Lansdown, just north of Upper Weston, may be a clue to the location of his hermitage.[117] Centuries later Bath Priory was still giving ten bushels of wheat a year to their tenants in Weston, 'called St Alphegis grist as hath been used in tymes past',[118] perhaps the saint's recompense for their kindness to a hermit.

The reformed abbey had powerful supporters. On one of Dunstan's rounds of encouragement and exhortation, he visited the 'place where hot springs burst forth from their hiding place in the abyss in steaming droplets, a place which the inhabitants call *Bathum* in the vernacular.'[119] Edgar was a generous patron of the monastery, as were some of those close to him,[120] and in 973 he chose Bath Abbey as the setting for his splendid coronation by Archbishops Dunstan and Oswald.[121] But on 8 July 975, Edgar died suddenly and was succeeded by his young son Edward. Resentment of Edgar's generosity to the monasteries emerged into the open. Ælfhere, Ealdorman of Mercia, disbanded several monasteries within the diocese of Worcester. According to Leland, he expelled the monks of Bath for a time. Since Bath was in Wessex by then, that seems unlikely. In any case anti-monastic feeling gradually wore away after the accession of Ethelred in 979.[122]

Saxons Beleaguered

It was in Ethelred's reign that the Vikings returned, more organised, more disciplined, more formidable than before. By 1009 the Danish army had rampaged over every shire in Wessex, so it is not surprising that Ethelred chose to hold a *witan* that year in the relative safety of Bath.[123] St Ælfheah, by then Archbishop of Canterbury, was captured in 1012 and murdered when he would not allow himself to be ransomed, but this was not part of a widespread attack on the Church. The Vikings were Christian by this time, so when King Sweyn of Denmark advanced on Bath during his campaign of conquest in 1013, he is unlikely to have sacked the abbey. In fact *The Anglo-Saxon Chronicle* speaks of nothing more violent than his camping at Bath, where he received the submission of the ealdorman and thanes from the west. However, there are clues that Bath put up some resistance. A memorial rune at Navelsjo, Sweden, presumed to date from this period, says 'Gunnar, son of Rode, was buried by his brother Helge in a stone coffin in Bath'.[124] A broken tenth-century sword found in the city ditch outside the North Gate (fig.7) could have been simply thrown away, but the position hints at an assault on the city.[125]

If Sweyn's son Cnut paid any attention to Bath during his reign, we know nothing of it. Only when the English monarchy was restored do royal charters to Bath Abbey resume.[126] Edward the Confessor and Queen Edith acted as witnesses to a lease of land by Abbot Ælfwig of Bath to Archbishop Stigand.[127] The queen had a particular interest in Bath; it was

7. Part of a Viking sword found in the city ditch beside the North Gate. The inscription was intended to read ULFBERHT ME FECIT (Ulfberht made me) but was inaccurately copied. It was probably made in an Anglo-Scandinavian workshop in England. (*Photograph by courtesy of the Institute of Archaeology, Oxford*)

part of her dower. She held it until her death in 1075, so the advent of the Normans had little immediate impact on the city, except for one curious episode. From 1061 to 1084 Abbot Wulfwold held the abbeys of Bath and Chertsey, Surrey, in plurality. Chertsey must have been his preferred house, for a second abbot was needed actually to run Bath. In 1066 Sæwold had not long taken over this post from Abbot Ælfwig.[129] His fear of the Normans was such that at the Conquest he fled to Arras, taking with him many books from the Bath Abbey library.[130]

Happily these did not include the Anglo-Saxon gospels (fig.8) which now belong to Corpus Christi College, Cambridge.[131] The four gospels are written in different hands, each on a separate quire; probably four monks worked on the book simultaneously. The scribe of Matthew inserted a colophon, giving his name as Ælfric and saying that he wrote the gospel in the monastery at Bath and gave it to the prior Brihtwold.[132] That is a clue that Bath was between abbots at the time. Blank pages were then used to record solemn undertakings 'here sworn on this Christ's book', of which the earliest

8. CCCC 140, f.45v: The final page of the gospel of St Matthew, on which is written (in Latin): 'I Ælfric wrote this book in the monastery at Bath and gave it to the Prior Brihtwold. May he who writes this live in peace in this world and the age to come and be granted eternity by whomsoever reads it.' (*Photograph by courtesy of the Master and Fellows of Corpus Christi College, Cambridge*)

is a manumission by Abbot Sæwold,[133] so the gospels were probably finished just before his appointment. Ælfric was still among the monks in 1077.[134]

The self-exiled Sæwold was replaced by Abbot Ælfsige, who seems to have been an industrious and worthy man. Alsi's Bath (later the Hot Bath) was presumably named after him; he perhaps built a Saxon bath there to replace the ruined Roman one.[135] He allowed a number of the slaves on the Bath Abbey estates to purchase their freedom, or that of their children, and freed two for the good of his soul.[136] He made an inventory of the abbey's huge collection of relics. Most were together in the shrine, but relics of St Barbara belonged to the altar of St Mary.[137] That may have been within the church of St Peter, or in a Saxon predecessor of St Mary of Stalls.

Under the dowager Queen Edith and Abbot Ælfsige, Bath remained essentially Saxon. In 1077 all the monks still had Saxon names.[138] The same is true of the witnesses to Ælfsige's transactions, except for the portreeves. The end of Saxon Bath really came on the deaths of William I and Abbot Ælfsige in 1087. In the upheaval that followed, Bath was sacked, but emerged anew as the cathedral city of Somerset.[139]

Notes

1   B. Cunliffe, 'Saxon Bath', in J. Haslam, ed., *Anglo-Saxon Towns in Southern England* (Chichester, 1984), pp.345-58.
2   M. Aston, 'The Bath region from late prehistory to the Middle Ages', *Bath History*, Vol.I (Gloucester, 1986), pp.73-8; A.J. Keevil, 'The Barton of Bath', *Bath History*, Vol.VI (Bath, 1996), pp.26-7.
3   B. Cunliffe, *Iron Age Communities in Britain: an account of England, Scotland and Wales from the seventh century BC to the Roman conquest,* 3rd ed. (1991), pp.170-5.
4   The Roman geographer Ptolemy listed *Aquæ Calidæ* as a town of the Belgæ, but he was working from limited information. H. Petre, ed., *Monumenta Historica Britannica,* Vol.I (1848), pp.xiv-xv; A.L. Rivet and C. Smith, *The Place-Names of Roman Britain* (1979), pp.121, 256; B. Jones and D. Mattingly, *An Atlas of Roman Britain* (Oxford, 1990), p.50 and maps 3:2, 5:11.
5   K. Dark, *Civitas to Kingdom: British Political Continuity 300-800* (Leicester, 1994), chaps.2-3.
6   N. Higham, *The English Conquest: Gildas and Britain in the fifth century* (Manchester, 1994), chaps.2, 5, 6.
7   N. Higham, *Rome, Britain and the Anglo-Saxons* (1992), pp.94-5.
8   A. Young, Avon Archaeological Unit, personal communication.
9   D. Eagles, 'The archaeological evidence for settlement in the fifth to seventh centuries AD' in M. Aston and C. Lewis, eds., *The Medieval Landscape of Wessex,* Oxbow Monograph 46 (Oxford, 1994), pp.23-4.
10   *Gildas, The Ruin of Britain and Other Works,* ed. and trans. W. Winterbottom (1978), pp.26-28.
11   T. and A. Burkitt, 'The frontier zone and the siege of Mount Badon: a review of the evidence for their location', *Somerset Archaeology and Natural History (SANH),* Vol.134 (1990), pp.81-93.
12   Higham, *English Conquest,* chap.4; Dark, Appendix 1.
13   S.C. Hawkes, 'The early Saxon period' in G. Briggs *et al*, eds., *The Archaeology of the Oxford Region* (Oxford, 1968), p.67.
14   *Gildas,* p.28.
15   R. Hodges and B. Hobley, eds., *The Rebirth of Towns in the West AD 700-1050,* Council for British Archaeology Research Report No. 68 (1988), pp.2, 8-15.
16   Dark, pp.21-5, 168-9, fig.40.
17   *The Anglo-Saxon Chronicle,* trans. D. Whitelock *et al* (1961).
18   P. Sims-Williams, *Religion and Literature in Western England 600-800* (Cambridge, 1990), p.23.
19   Found in the excavation of Bathampton meadows by Bath Archaeological Trust in 1994 (P. Davenport, personal communication).
20   Sims-Williams, *Religion and Literature,* fig.2.
21   N.J. Higham, *An English Empire: Bede and the early Anglo-Saxon kings* (Manchester 1995), pp.74-111.
22   Bede, *The Ecclesiastical History of the English People,* ed. J. McClure and R. Collins (Oxford, 1994), p.193.
23   D. Hooke, *The Anglo-Saxon Landscape: The Kingdom of the Hwicce* (Manchester, 1985), pp.8-10; P. Sims-Williams, 'St Wilfred and two charters dated AD 676 and 680', *Journal of Ecclesiastical History,* Vol.39, part 2 (1988), p.169.

24   C. Thomas, *Christianity in Roman Britain to AD 500* (1981), pp.253-71; Hooke, p.10; C. Heighway, 'Saxon Gloucester' in Haslam, p.375.

25   R.S.O. Tomlin, 'Voices from the Sacred Spring', *Bath History,* Vol.IV (Bath, 1992), pp.16-17.

26   Dark, p.37.

27   Aston, 'The Bath region', p.73 and fig.4.

28   F. Weaver, ed., *Wells Wills* (1890), p.178.

29   Dark, pp.20, 59-63.

30   A. Woodward and P. Leech, *The Uley Shrines: excavation of a ritual complex on West Hill, Uley, Gloucestershire 1977-79* (1993), pp.70-1, 321.

31   B. Cunliffe and P. Davenport, *The Temple of Sulis Minerva at Bath, Vol.1: The Site* (Oxford, 1985), pp.68-75, 114.

32   J. Manco, 'The Cross Bath', *Bath History,* Vol.II (Gloucester, 1988), pp.49-50. At that date the cross had not supplanted the chi-rho as the dominant symbol of Christianity, so the first cross from which the bath took its name must have been erected later.

33   Woodward and Leech; R. Leech, 'The excavation on Lamyatt Beacon, Somerset', *Britannia,* Vol. 17 (1986), pp.259-328.

34   Cunliffe and Davenport, pp.100, 118, figs. 118, 121.

35   Cunliffe and Davenport, p.179.

36   R.Coates, *Toponymic Topics* (Brighton, 1988), pp.24-37.

37   Also the genitive form *Achumanensi. Two Chartularies of the Priory of St Peter at Bath,* Somerset Record Society (SRS), Vol.7 (1893), chartulary 1, nos.23-24; catalogued by P.H. Sawyer, *Anglo-Saxon Charters: an annotated list and bibliography* (1968), nos.735, 785; W. de Gray Birch, *Cartularium Saxonicum,* Vol.3 (1899), no.1185 (Sawyer no.808).

38   *The Anglo-Saxon Chronicle; The Chronicle of Æthelweard,* ed. A. Campbell (1962), p.55.

39   A. Mawer and F.M. Stenton, *The Place-names of Bedfordshire and Huntingdonshire,* English Place-name Society, Vol.3 (1926), pp.1-2.

40   Cunliffe and Davenport, pp.68-75.

41   J. Morris, ed. and trans., *Nennius* (1980), pp.40, 81; present author's translation. The fact that 'Nennius' places Bath in the country of the Hwicce may simply be his own clarification for a ninth-century audience and so cannot be taken as firmly dating the original after c.600.

42   B. Cunliffe, 'The earth's grip holds them' in B. Hartley and J. Wacher, eds., *Rome and her Northern Provinces* (Gloucester, 1983), p.79; B. Cunliffe, *Roman Bath Discovered,* 2nd edn (1984), chap.5.

43   Dark, p.68.

44   *Two Chartularies,* chart.1, no.7 (Sawyer no.51).

45   *The Anglo-Saxon Chronicle,* Chronicles and Memorials of Great Britain and Ireland During the Middle Ages, published under the direction of the Master of the Rolls (Rolls) (1861); *Two Chartularies,* introduction, appendix 1, chart.1, nos.4, 9, 15, 17, 19, 27, 29, 31; J.M. Kemble, ed., *Codex Diplomaticus Aevi Saxonici* (1839-48), nos.171, 290; D. Hill, 'The Burghal Hidage: the establishment of a text', *Medieval Archaeology,* Vol.13 (1969), pp.84-92; L.V. Grinsell, *The Bath Mint: an historical outline* (1973); D. Whitelock, ed. and trans., *Anglo-Saxon Wills* (Cambridge, 1930), nos.8-9; *Memorials of St. Dunstan, Archbishop of Canterbury,* ed. W.Stubbs, Rolls (1874), p.46; J. Earle, *A Handbook to the Land-charters and Other Saxonic Documents* (Oxford, 1888), pp. 268-71.

46 Bede, pp.9, 361; J. Campbell ed., *The Anglo-Saxons* (Oxford, 1982), pp.40-1.

47 R.F. Leslie ed., *Three Old English Elegies* (Manchester, 1961), pp.34-6, 50-2; present author's translation.

48 A post-Roman channel was cut in the wall between the Sacred Spring and the circular bath (P. Davenport, personal communication.)

49 J. Manco, 'References to the King's Bath drain' in P. Davenport ed., *Archaeology in Bath 1976-1985* (Oxford, 1991), microfiche 1:E3-4.

50 'Vita Merlini' in P. Goodrich ed., *The Romance of Merlin; an anthology* (New York, 1990), p.87; Bath Record Office, Ancient Deeds, bundle 1, nos.13-15 and bundle 2, no.84; transcribed in *Ancient Deeds Belonging to the Corporation of Bath*, trans. C.W. Shickle (Bath, 1921). *Alrone* was probably intended as a Latin ablative.

51 This charter survived as a copy in the twelfth-century cartulary of Bath Priory: *Two Chartularies*, chart.1, no.7 (Sawyer no.51). It is accepted by H.P.R. Finberg, *Early Charters of the West Midlands* (Leicester 1961), pp.172-4, and P. Sims-Williams, 'St Wilfred'. The latter gives the correct dating. H. Edwards, *The Charters of the Early West Saxon Kingdom*, British Archaeological Reports, British Series, Vol. 198 (1988), pp.210-227, argues that this charter has been almost entirely rewritten and does not apply to Bath. That would remove the major obstacle to her preferred view of Bath as a West Saxon foundation, but she fails to explain why in that case Bath came into the possession of the Bishop of the Hwicce.

52 C. Heighway, 'Saxon Gloucester' in Haslam, pp.365-6, 370-1.

53 Finberg, pp.173-4; K. Harrison, 'The annus domini in some early charters', *Journal of the Society of Archivists*, Vol.4 (1970-3), p.553, and *The Framework of Anglo-Saxon History to A.D.90* (Cambridge, 1976), pp.67-9; P. Sims-Williams, 'Continental influence at Bath monastery in the seventh century', *Anglo-Saxon England*, Vol.4 (1975), p.8, 'St Wilfred', pp.163-74 and *Religion and Literature*, pp.120-1.

54 *Councils and Ecclesiastical Documents relating to Great Britain and Ireland*, ed. A.W. Haddon and W. Stubbs (Oxford, 1839-48), pp.3, 210.

55 Bede, p.145.

56 *The Chronicle of Florence of Worcester*, trans. T. Forester (1854), pp.27-8, 423; Finberg 'The Princes of the Hwicce' in *Early Charters of the West Midlands*, pp.161-71.

57 Sawyer, nos.70, 74, 77.

58 Sims-Williams, 'Continental influence', pp.1-10.

59 *Two Chartularies*, chart.1, nos.6, 8 (Sawyer nos.1167-8).

60 *English Historical Documents*, Vol.1, ed. D. Whitelock (1961), p.466.

61 *Two Chartularies*, chart.1, no.19 (Sawyer no.265).

62 I am indebted to Dr M. Costen for this suggestion.

63 *Two Chartularies*, chart.2, no.808, referring to King Cenwulf, father of St. Kenelm, i.e. Cenwulf of Mercia, alleged father of the saint.

64 Finberg, p.161.

65 *Æthelweard*, p.52.

66 Sims-Williams, *Religion and Literature*, p.33.

67 *The Anglo-Saxon Chronicle*.

68 W. Levison, *England and the Continent in the Eighth Century* (Oxford, 1946), pp.29-31.

69   *Mattaei Parisiensis, Monarchi Sancti Albani, Chronica Majora,* ed. H.R. Luard, Rolls (1872-83), Vol.1, p.356.

70   J.M. Kemble, ed., *Codex Diplomaticus Aevi Saxonici* (1838-48), no.171; no.170 seems to be a poor copy of 171, substituting town for monastery (both Sawyer no.148).

71   *Willelmi Malmesbirienses, Monarchi, de Gestis Pontificum Anglorum,* ed. N.E.S.A. Hamilton, Rolls (1870), p.194.

72   *Two Chartularies,* chart.1, no.18 (Sawyer no.643).

73   R. Hodges, *The Anglo-Saxon Achievement* (1989), pp.126-9.

74   B. Cunliffe, 'The abbey and its precinct' and D.Hinton 'Saxon finds' in B.W. Cunliffe, ed., *Excavations in Bath 1950-1975* (Bristol, 1979), pp.90, 138-40; R. Bell, 'Bath Abbey: some new perspectives', *Bath History,* Vol.VI (Bath, 1996), pp.14-5, fig.4.

75   *The Anglo-Saxon Chronicle.*

76   Kemble, no.290 (Sawyer no.210).

77   The city wall was largely demolished in the eighteenth and nineteenth centuries, but its line is marked on several earlier maps. Excavations of parts of it have demonstrated a Roman origin. T.J. O'Leary, 'Excavations at Upper Borough Walls, Bath, 1980', *Medieval Archaeology,* Vol.25 (1981), pp.1-30; B.Cunliffe, *Roman Bath, Reports of the Research Committee of the Society of Antiquaries of London,* No.24 (Oxford 1969), pp.173-5; A Roman ditch was found in 1995 by Bath Archaeological Trust outside the East Gate (Peter Davenport, personal communication).

78   R.F. Leslie, ed., p.51.

79   C.A. Ralegh Radford, 'Later pre-conquest boroughs and their defences', *Medieval Archaeology,* Vol.14 (1970), pp.83-103; O'Leary, pp.22-23; R.H.C. Davis, 'Alfred and Guthrum's frontier', *English Historical Review,* Vol.97 (1982), pp.807-9.

80   M. Biddle and D. Hill, 'Late Saxon planned towns', *Antiquaries Journal,* Vol.51 (1971), pp.70-85; D. Hill, *Atlas of Anglo-Saxon England* (Oxford, 1981), fig.235.

81   *English Historical Documents,* Vol.1, p.498.

82   Biddle and Hill, 'Late Saxon planned towns', p.70.

83   Cunliffe, 'Saxon Bath', pp.351-52; P. Greening, 'The origins of the historic town plan of Bath', *A Second North Somerset Miscellany,* Bath and Camerton Archaeological Society (Bath, 1971), p.14. On the site of Ham Gate, J. Manco, 'The buildings of Bath Priory', *SANH,* Vol.137 (1994 for 1993), p.82, corrects W.Wedlake, 'The City Walls of Bath', *SANH,* Vol.110 (1966), p.97, Fig.5B.

84   A deed of 1319 mentions 'Northgate Street [an earlier name for High Street] where the market is situated' (Shickle, *Ancient Deeds,* bundle 2, no.83).

85   Manco, 'Bath Priory', pp.80-82.

86   Manco, 'Bath Priory', pp.78, 94-5. Excavation outside the East Gate has dated the medieval lane as post-Norman (P. Davenport, personal communication.)

87   Shickle, *Ancient Deeds,* bundle 3, no.66.

88   M. Aston and J. Bond, *The Landscape of Towns* (1976), p.69.

89   A.H. Smith, *English Place-Name Elements* part 1, English Place-name Society Vol.25 (1956), pp.26, 58.

90   P. Davenport, 'Excavations at Bath Street, Bath', *Avon Past,* Vol.16 (1993), p.14.

91   Bath Record Office, Ancient Deeds, bundle 5, nos.60-61.

92   The style of the coin was modelled upon his father's coins from Exeter and Winchester; Edward's coins from 910 are in a different style. C.H.V. Sutherland, *English Coinage 600-1900* (1973), p.28; Grinsell, pp.10-11.

93   Campbell, ed., pp.130-1, 176.

94   *Domesday Book*, gen.ed. J. Morris, Vol.8: *Somerset*, ed. C. and F. Thorn (Chichester 1980), section 1, no.31; section 7, no.1 and p.313.

95   F.M. Stenton, *Anglo-Saxon England*, 3rd ed. (Oxford, 1971), pp.530-2.

96   *Domesday Book, Somerset*, section 1, no.28; section 5, nos.20, 30, 66; section 40, no.1; section 41, no.1

97   Shickle, *Ancient Deeds*, bundle 1, no.19.

98   J. Schofield and A. Vince, *Medieval Towns* (1994), p.147.

99   Manco, 'Bath Priory', p.80.

100   Shickle, *Ancient Deeds*, bundle 4, no.88; bundle 6, no.43.

101   *Feet of Fines for the County of Somerset*, ed E. Green, SRS, Vol. 6 (1892), pp.253-4; Vol.12 (1898), p.137; Vol.17 (1902), pp. 82-3; British Library Egerton Charters nos.260, 336; *The Registers of ... Bishop[s] of Bath and Wells 1518 ... [to] 1559*, SRS, Vol. 55 (1940), no.496.

102   Manco, 'Bath Priory', pp.80-82; Davenport ed., *Archaeology in Bath*, pp.104, 109, 116, fig.91.

103   Sold to Bishop John de Villula c.1090 and re-acquired by the Crown in 1193. In 1274 the advowson was held to be part of that estate. *Rotuli Hundredorum*, Vol.2 (1818), p.123.

104   *The Anglo-Saxon Chronicle*; Davis, 'Alfred and Guthrum's frontier'.

105   *Two Chartularies*, chart.2, no.808.

106   *Valor Ecclesiasticus*, Vol.1 (1810), p.177.

107   S. Keynes, 'King Athelstan's books' in M. Lapidge and H. Gneuss, eds., *Learning and Literature in Anglo-Saxon England* (Cambridge, 1985), pp.159-64.

108   *English Historical Documents*, Vol.1, p.318.

109   E. John, 'The age of Edgar' in Campbell, ed., p.185.

110   At Cheddar, Somerset, in November 956 and Edington, Wiltshire, in May 957. S. Keynes, *The Diplomas of King Aethelred 'The Unready' 978-1016* (Cambridge, 1980), pp.59-61, 67.

111   *Two Chartularies*, chart.1, nos.5, 18 (Sawyer nos.610, 643).

112   *The Anglo-Saxon Chronicle; English Historical Documents*, Vol.1, nos.234, 238.

113   *Willelmi Malmesbiriensis de Gestis Pontificum*, p.194.

114   *Two Chartularies*, chart.1, no.4; trans. D.A.E. Pelteret, *Catalogue of English Post-Conquest Vernacular Documents* (Woodbridge, 1990), no.78.

115   Hinton, 'Saxon finds' in Cunliffe, ed., *Excavations in Bath 1950-1975*, pp.140, 180.

116   'Vita Elphegi' in [Warton, ed.], *Anglia Sacra* (1691), Vol.2, pp.122-42; D. Knowles *et al, The Heads of Religious Houses 940-1210* (Cambridge, 1972), p.28.

117   Aston, 'The Bath region', pp.80-81.

118   British Library Harl Ms 3970, f.31; *Calendar of Patent Rolls: Elizabeth*, Vol.5 (1966), p.358.

119   *Memorials of St. Dunstan*, p.46; Leslie, ed., p.23.

120   *Two Chartularies*, chart.1, nos.20, 23-25 (Sawyer nos.694, 737, 777, 785); *Anglo-Saxon Wills*, nos.8, 9 (Sawyer nos.1484-5).

121   *The Anglo-Saxon Chronicle; The Historians of the Church of York and its Archbishops*, ed. J. Raine, Rolls, pp.436-38.

122   E. John, 'The return of the Vikings' in Campbell,ed., p.192; *Itinerary of John Leland*, ed. L. Toulmin Smith (1907-10), Vol.1, p.143; Keynes, pp.169-72.

123   *English Historical Documents*, Vol.1, no.45, n.4.

124   S.B.F. Jansson, *The Runes of Sweden* (1962), pp.52-53.

125   T.J. O'Leary *et al*, 'A Viking period sword from Upper Borough Walls, 1981' in Davenport, ed., *Archaeology in Bath 1976-1985*, pp.1-3.

126   *Two Chartularies*, chart.1, no.28 (Sawyer no.1034).

127   *Two Chartularies*, chart.1, no.15 (Sawyer no.1426).

128   *Domesday Book, Somerset*, see under section 1, no.26.

129   Knowles, p.28.

130   Sims-Williams, *Religion and Literature,* pp.205-06, 208, n.141.

131   This book was acquired at the Dissolution of the Monasteries by Archbishop Matthew Parker, along with many other manuscripts from monastic libraries, and donated to Corpus Christi College.

132   M.R. James, *A Descriptive Catalogue of the Manuscripts in the Library of Corpus Christi College, Cambridge* (Cambridge, 1912), Vol.1, no.140; N.R. Ker, *Catalogue of Manuscripts Containing Anglo-Saxon* (Oxford, 1957), no.35.

133   J. Earle, *A Handbook to the Land-charters and other Saxonic Documents* (Oxford, 1888), p.271.

134   *Two Chartularies*, chart.1, no.4; translated in Pelteret, no.78.

135   Shickle, *Ancient Deeds*, bundle 5, nos.66-78; *Medieval Deeds of Bath and District*, section 1, nos.47-8. The name Alsi's Bath occurs from c.1200 to 1366, when the Cross and King's Baths were identified as such, so it must be the Hot Bath.

136   Earle, *Handbook*, pp.268-271; translations of most of these by Pelteret, pp.90-5.

137   *Two Chartularies*, pp.lxxv-lxxvi; calendared by Pelteret, p.90.

138   *Two Chartularies*, chart.1, no.4; translated by Pelteret, no.78.

139   Manco, 'Bath Priory', p.77.

Acknowledgements

My greatest debt is to Peter Davenport for the years of discussion and debate that stirred my interest in the subject. I would also like to thank Stephen Clews, Dr. Michael Costen and Professor Barry Cunliffe for their careful reading of the first draft of this paper. Helpful comments on etymology were also made by Dr. Oliver Padel, who directed me to Professor Richard Coates, who in turn kindly sent me his work on *Acemannesceastre*.

SCIENCE LECTURING AT BATH, 1724-1800

Trevor Fawcett

Early in May 1724 some eleven to twelve hundred curious visitors travelled to Bath to observe a total eclipse of the sun. Among them came Dr J.T.Desaguliers, F.R.S., perhaps the most active and well-connected science lecturer in London, who in the run-up to the eclipse explained the coming event to thirty or forty three-guinea subscribers. Some of the audience on this occasion were surely freemasons, since Desaguliers, in his other character of deputy grandmaster of the Grand Union Lodge, used his visit to receive into Bath's fledgling Queen's Head Lodge several new members, including Viscount Cobham, Lord Hervey and Beau Nash.[1]

At this date public instruction in astronomy or any other branch of 'natural philosophy' (i.e. the experimental and natural sciences) was still a novelty outside the select confines of the Royal Society and the universities, or the handful of London coffee houses and academies where lecture courses were periodically held. Desaguliers' explanation of the eclipse not only marked the start of scientific education at Bath, it helped initiate the practice of itinerant lecturing more generally. From the 1720s and 1730s onwards scientific demonstrators would increasingly take to the road on extensive provincial tours, advertising and delivering series of paid experimental lectures as they went. Even though a growing genre of popular science books and periodicals also contributed to public enlightenment, the itinerant 'philosophers' were perhaps the chief means by which scientific knowledge, new discoveries, and technological improvements were communicated and disseminated. Furnished with an imposing array of scientific instruments, mechanical devices and working models, they were able to convey abstract principles through vivid practical demonstration and to enact experiments directly in front of their audience. Public educators at large, they were at the same time skilled performers, providers (in their own words) of 'rational entertainment'. Since they depended on science for a living, they had to rouse public curiosity, attract subscribers, and then put on a good show. Most lecturers were practical men (often instrument-makers themselves), largely self-taught, and of ambiguous social status – to some extent bearing a similar class relationship to the elitist fellows of the Royal Society as an apothecary (the general practitioner of his day) did to a contemporary university-educated physician.[2] Some enjoyed long careers, gradually modifying their syllabus of lectures as the field of science and technology developed from its early domination by Newtonian physics, optics and astronomy (an essentially mechanical view of the universe), through to the mid-century excitements about the phenomenon of electricity, the development of chemistry (and a new understanding of gases) from the 1770s, and the rising interest in biology, geology and, once again, astronomy in the final decades. Not infrequently it was the stimulus of visiting and resident lecturers that led to the formation of local science societies up and down the country. The establishment of the Bath Philosophical Society in 1779 is arguably a case in point.

After his 1724 début Desaguliers may have lectured regularly at Bath, where his chief patron, the Duke of Chandos, began financing a set of superior lodging houses to John Wood's design in 1727. Certainly he delivered courses in 1729 and 1730:

> Bath, Septem.3 [1730]. This Day Dr. Desaguliers came here in order to have Courses of Experimental Philosophy during the Season: He has brought down, besides the common Apparatus usual in his Courses of Experiments, several new Machines for the Entertainment of his Subscribers. He will have his Lectures at Mr. Harrisons Room, where he was last Year, at the same Price of three Guineas, one Guinea at Subscribing, and the other two the first Day of the Course. Subscriptions are taken in by Mr. Leake, Bookseller in Bath.[3]

References to the 'Season' and Harrison's Assembly Room suggest that Desaguliers was directing his publicity more at visitors than Bathonians, and we know that Viscount Percival for one was among the subscribers to this typically expensive series.[4] But the encouraging reference to 'Entertainment' did not imply any lack of didactic rigour. While not taxing his listeners (women among them) with difficult mathematics, Desaguliers did expect their close attention, common sense and just a little arithmetic, as he launched into proving a chain of axioms through experiments and demonstrations.[5] Disciple of the late Sir Isaac Newton, he was also a convinced Baconian, believing – like his fellow-freemasons – in the application of scientific knowledge to bettering the world. The apparatus he had specially carried down from London included therefore not only measuring and optical instruments, prisms to split light, an air pump, a device to simulate the motions of heavenly bodies, and other laboratory equipment, but also levers, model engines and machines,

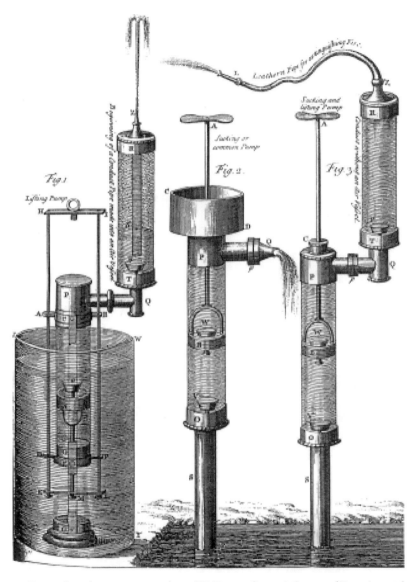

1. Examples of water pumps from J.T. Desaguliers, *A Course of Experimental Philosophy* (1734), Vol.2, plate 15. Desaguliers would explain the theory and applications of such devices in his lectures, a topic of some relevance at Bath where the hot mineral waters had to be pumped from underground sources for drinking in the appositely named Pump Room.

the visible evidence of 'natural philosophy' in action. Much engaged himself in practical projects, from curing smoky chimneys to improving water supply, Desaguliers was impressed at Bath by Ralph Allen's horse-cranes and innovatory tramway, and subsequently published accounts of both.[6]

Documentation of his courses in the 1730s remains patchy, but he undoubtedly performed at the spa in 1731 and 1737-8 as well as adding Bristol and Worcester to his West Country circuit. In fact he recorded in verse the tender-hearted incident at one of the 1731 lectures when Prince William's governess, Amanda Smith, unable to bear the gradual suffocation of the experimental fish during a trial of the air pump, had them rescued and thrown back into the nearby Avon.[7] In 1737, on top of his standard demonstrations of the principles of mechanics, hydrostatics and optics, he expounded the phenomenon of tides with a brand-new piece of clockwork, and illustrated the solar system on an improved planetarium – probably the costly 4-foot apparatus he devised with the instrument-maker George Graham.[8]

Before Desaguliers' death in 1744, another itinerant Newtonian philosopher had arrived on the West Country scene. Benjamin Martin's agenda too had a serious ring. His lecture course was far from being 'a Shew, for Amusement only; but is intended as a Science to exhibit a just Idea of the true Nature, Reason, and State of Things, as far as they can be known'.[9] While still a Chichester schoolmaster Martin had published a *Philosophical Grammar* and embarked on instrument making, and by summer 1743 his touring equipment included an orrery (for explaining the solar system), a cometarium, celestial globe, reflecting telescope, air pump, a 'very precise' baroscope, various other measuring devices, and models of a forcing pump and marine depth-gauge.[10] No electrical machine figured in the list, nor did Martin rush to add electricity to his lecture syllabus in the following years despite, as the *Gentleman's Magazine* put it in April 1745, the recent discovery of phenomena 'so surprising as to waken the indolent curiosity of the public ... who never regard natural philosophy but when it works miracles'. The discovery of the electrical capacitor or Leyden jar turned curiosity into a craze. Everyone wished to see the sparks igniting a dish of alcohol or watch a line of people jump as they felt the transmitted shock. Yet Martin's two successive courses at the Bath Assembly Rooms in late 1744, and others in autumn 1745 and spring and autumn 1746, seem to have ignored electrical phenomena altogether and concentrated on traditional useful science, both theory and practice. In these lectures:

the true System of the *World*; the various Properties, Affections, and appearances of *Natural Bodies*; the Principles and most considerable Machines in the *Mechanical* and *Philosophical Arts* and *Sciences*, are Exhibit'd, Explain'd and Illustrated, by a very large and curious Apparatus of Instruments, and a great Variety of Instructive and Entertaining Experiments, accommodated to the various Uses of Life, and easy to be understood by all Capacities.[11]

Privately, however, Martin conducted his own electrical trials, employing a variant of Monnier's machine, and convinced himself it was all explicable in terms of Newtonian effluvia. But though his *Essay on Electricity*, published at Bath in October 1746, outlined 42 'capital' experiments, it appears he still refrained from showing them in public.

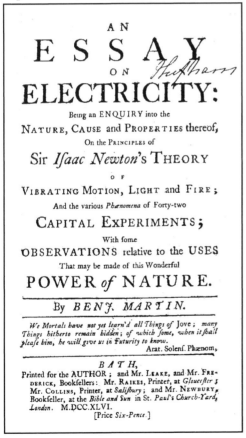

The appetite for electrical drama was met instead by a visiting instrument-maker from London, one Smith, who in September 1746 hired a room at the *Queen's Head* accessible to all 'Judges of Experimental Philosophy' and guaranteed a showman's performance: 'Electrical Commotions to be felt by every Person in the Room, and the Fire to come out of any Part of the Body'.[12]

Martin knew the dangers of playing the magician or indulging in quack showmanship. Even Desaguliers, who unlike Martin had Royal Society credentials and rich backers, had sometimes met hostility

2. Title-page from one of Benjamin Martin's works published in 1746 during his residence at Bath.

and misrepresentation. The difficulty for peripatetic professionals like Martin, whose income depended on attracting customers (and on promoting sales of textbooks and instruments), lay in achieving a balance between high-minded science, popular education and cheap trivialisation. In attempting to reveal the wonders of natural phenomena they were also open to the theological criticism that prying into divine creation was itself a blasphemous act. Electricity was a high-risk topic in both respects, as Martin learned to his cost in the sudden polemic that blew up in the autumn of 1746 with John Freke, F.R.S. and London surgeon, who not only castigated itinerant lecturers as mercenary 'Country ... Showmen' but attacked the very basis of electrical research, arguing that to release this mysterious life spirit in casual experiments was literally and metaphorically to play with fire.[13] Hence the ensuing war of words had deeper meaning for both contestants than simply the morality of lecturing for money or the authority of a Fellow of the Royal Society against a mere pretender, for it pitted a particular Pietist view of divine creation against the usual argument of natural theology that scientific investigation, far from being sacrilege, actually heightened the sense of religious awe and led the mind, in Pope's often-quoted phrase, 'through Nature up to Nature's God'. In sharp contrast Freke and his fellow Pietists (who included the novelist Samuel Richardson and the recently deceased Bath physician George Cheyne) believed that profane enquiry had its limits, and that the phenomenon of electricity belonged in the spiritual, not the scientific, domain. Martin responded by labelling his opponent a scientific Don Quixote, but the controversy between them must have rumbled on for some time at Bath, especially in the circles of James Leake's bookshop and at Prior Park.[14]

By now Martin was living at Bath off the north side of Orange Grove, his 'Experimental Room' in Orange Court becoming the new site of his public demonstrations. His announcement of a course beginning January 1748, though firmly emphasising '*Newtonian*' philosophy and his rich new equipment, still made no overt reference to electricity, and the same went for further series a year later which did however touch on chemistry and magnetism. Between these dates he delivered a course of uncertain content which may possibly have broached the topic at last.[15] Unable to manage by lecturing at Bath alone, he also undertook tours – the summer of 1750, for example, being spent on a sweep through East Anglia. Otherwise he probably continued working on scientific instruments while his wife took in lodgers and ran a haberdashery business across the Grove in Wade's Passage. Here in November 1751 she significantly had on sale James

3. An engraving of Benjamin Martin (1704-82), based on an earlier portrait and printed posthumously in the *Gentleman's Magazine* (1785), Vol.55, part 2, p.583.

4. James Ferguson (1710-76) in an engraving of 1776, with his hand apparently resting on a sidereal globe. His passion for astronomy helped to enthuse William Herschel.

Ferguson's 'Portable CARD-DIALS' and 'LUMINARIUM', an almanac device.[16] Since Ferguson likewise lectured for a living, it must be assumed that Martin was allowing him to take over, and indeed within a year or two Martin removed to London (his wife selling off in Wade's Passage early in 1753) to concentrate on publishing and setting up what proved a successful Fleet Street instrument shop.

Ferguson may first have lectured at Bath around Christmas 1747, though it has been suggested this initial sortie was more to do with his alternative occupation of Indian ink portraiture.[17] A self-taught Scot, Ferguson specialised in astronomy which for Martin had been only a component topic in a much broader curriculum. His five-lecture, five-shilling courses at Wiltshire's Assembly Rooms in the autumns of 1750 and 1751 were wholly astronomical, meaning in effect that they covered the solar system in some detail but almost ignored outer space, which until Herschel's vast improvements of the telescope was little studied or known. Ferguson's key piece of equipment was therefore an elaborate orrery of his own making which could represent the movement of Sun, Moon and planets, and help to explain the calendar and the causes of eclipses and tides. He had this and other apparatus on daily view at his lodgings, where during his stay he also gave private lessons and made ink drawings on vellum at 12s.6d. – perhaps still his mainstay activity.[18]

Whatever his success at Bath, Ferguson did not return until the 1760s, leaving the field mainly to William Griffiss who included the spa in his lecturing tours of 1752 and 1755-6. Griffiss is a less familiar figure than most of the itinerant natural philosophers, yet he travelled assiduously, covered all the physical sciences except electricity, and owned a considerable quantity of apparatus. His first Bath series (following nine at Bristol and one at Pensford) opened at the *Pineapple*, Orchard Street, in April 1752 – once he had attracted a minimum of thirty subscribers (at a guinea each) through his printed prospectus of experiments and his comment: 'N.B. Subscribers are free to propose any Questions, and the Apparatus being finished with the latest Improvements on Instruments, is allowed to be the compleatest and most extensive in Britain'. Returning in December 1755 for Bath's burgeoning winter season, Griffiss more ambitiously hired Wiltshire's Assembly Rooms and now required at least forty names on his list. In ten sessions he would then cover natural philosophy in general ('to illustrate and confirm Sir Isaac Newton's Principles'), mechanics, hydrostatics and hydraulics, pneumatics, chemistry, the useful applications of science, optics, military architecture ('illustrated by a large Model of a fortified Town'), geography, and astronomy.

> In these Lectures, besides the usual Experiments, will be explained (by Models) the Nature and Construction of the most considerable Engines now in being, with their Application to the various Purposes of Life. What Opinion the greatest Men have had of these Lectures, is well known to those who have heard Professor Bradley, of Oxford's Recommendation of them. – This Course consists of all the most curious and entertaining Parts of Philosophy ... being particularly calculated for such Gentlemen and Ladies as would chuse to be acquainted with the more rational and sublime Parts of Knowledge, in the most expeditious and familiar Manner, with the least Expence.[19]

And because such a packed programme demanded much pre-planning, 'Mr. GRIFFISS hopes none will take it ill if they are not personally waited on, as he will be greatly engaged on Account of the necessary Preparations'. The course went well, however, and Griffiss advertised a repeat performance with a reminder of how 'exceedingly beautiful as well as accurate and compleat' all his equipment was, and how up-to-date his information. He welcomed the attendance of women, but seemed to be angling too for more technologically-minded subscribers – 'the Quality and Gentry expressing great Satisfaction with the Variety of Experiments which are universally allowed by all who have seen them, to be not only highly entertaining, but extremely useful to all Sorts of Persons, especially those well read or employed in Mechanicks, &c.'.[20] This fairly broad public appeal suggests that the predominantly gentry composition of the audience before 1750 was beginning to include subscribers from the professional and commercial classes, even plain middle-class tradesmen and their families. Later in the century some of the more theatrical performances were certainly directed at the general public, though not yet specifically at artisans who would have to await the rise of mechanics' institutes in the 1820s.

In spring 1756, having meanwhile lectured in Ireland, Griffiss travelled through the West Country for the last time, giving a final series at Bath on the eve of the Seven Years' War which, causally or not, was to coincide with a general dip in the market for science lectures.[21] Locally the dearth lasted even longer, for even a claimed lecturing visit by James Ferguson in 1763 has not been substantiated.[22] He did turn up at Christmas 1766, however, on a trip arranged by his bookseller Andrew Millar to promote a reissue of the popular *Lectures in Mechanics* and *Astronomy Explained*. Ferguson, now a F.R.S., had extended his range and probably had with him many working models of cranes, wheel-carriages, mills, pumps, and other mechanical devices besides his faithful orrery. At the start of his second twelve-lecture course he offered an evening course, presumably for people with daytime occupations, before gradually packing his apparatus for the London waggon. His final session with the orrery touched on the seasons, eclipses, and 'Saturn's Ring', and ended on a dramatic note: 'The Year of our SAVIOUR's Crucifixion will be Astronomically ascertained, and the Darkness at the Time of his Crucifixion proved to have been out of the common Course of Nature'. Astronomy was still Ferguson's strongest suit with the public, for two months later a proposed dozen lectures employing his full battery of model machinery had to be abandoned in favour of a further short course on the solar system.[23] Only once more was he recorded at Bath, when in April 1774 he ran a double series of twelve lectures. Then aged 64, he still had the curiosity to calculate the weight of air in the ballroom of the new Upper Assembly Rooms and to determine it would keep 900 people alive and 100 candles burning for just 23 hours 49 minutes.[24]

A new generation of lecturers dominated the last third of the century at Bath, notably John Arden (who settled for a time there), Benjamin Donn (or Donne) of Bristol, John Warltire, Henry Moyes, Walker junior, and John Lloyd. Expounding science was now a reputable activity and took place against a surge of fresh discoveries and interest in astronomy, electricity, the chemistry of gases, geology and botany. British skills in inventions and instrument-making – which had already produced Knight's artificial magnets, Dollond's achromatic lens, Ramsden's scale-divider and Harrison's chronometer – remained unsurpassed, and before 1780 Bath had acquired its own specialist 'optical, philosophical and mathematical' instrument-makers in Ribright & Smith. The scientific public was expanding. In a growing market for popular instruction, women were specially targetted in publications like the *Lady's Diary*, and children too in the *Museum for Young Ladies and Gentlemen* (which passed through fifteen editions by c.1800), Benjamin Martin's *General Magazine of Arts and Sciences* (1755-65), and the miniature *Newtonian System of Philosophy adapted to the Capacities of Young Gentlemen and Ladies* (1761).[25] Fringe activities such as the ballooning craze (1783-4), electric medical therapy, and the vogue for Mesmerism (from the 1780s) stirred further interest, while at Bath popular adult education was stimulated by public lectures on topics other than science, ranging from elocution, literature and the visual arts to medicine, veterinary science and dietetics.

John Arden and Benjamin Donn both sought a Bath audience from the late 1760s. Arden, with much experience of teaching and lecturing in the North and Midlands, first tried his luck in winter 1768-9 with two successive long courses covering physics, astronomy and geography, in which he promised to make the experiments 'as plain and intelligible as possible, even to those who have not applied Time or study this Way' and with the aid of an extensive apparatus incorporating 'the latest Improvements'. For twenty lectures he charged one guinea, where Desaguliers had once asked three. Arden's custom would be more middle-class, and he could exploit his stay besides by giving private lessons to young people on elementary astronomy and geography: 'Attendance for one Hour in a Day, for ten Days, or a Fortnight, is sufficient', he noted. His subsequent visits in late 1769 and early 1770 kept to the same pattern.[26]

Meanwhile Donn had also started to lecture. Stemming from a gifted family of Bideford mathematics teachers, he moved to Bristol about 1759-60, becoming assistant at the King Street Library and later opening a mathematical academy geared in part to Bristol concerns in navigation and shipping. At Bath he advertised a first course in December 1769 together with details of his academy and publications (including his important *Navigation Scale Improved,* and excellent maps of Devon – for which he won a Society of Arts award – and of 11 miles round Bristol). It is uncertain whether this course ran, but next spring he offered another 'whereby any one with only common Sense and a moderate Degree of Attention' could easily grasp the principles involved:

> The *First Lecture* will contain some some introductory Theorems in Geometry – Of Matter, its Divisibility – Laws of Motion – Composition and Resolution of Forces – Attraction of Cohesion – Solution of Bodies in Mediums – Rise of Water in Capillary Tubes, Vegetables, &c. // The *other Lectures.* The Attractions of Magnetism and Gravity – Laws of falling Bodies – Nature of Pendulums – Centre of Percussion, Expansion of Metals – Mechanic Powers, and compound Machines – Equilibrium and Pressure of Fluids – Properties of the Air – Some Electrical Experiments – The Nature of Vision, Origin of Colours – Geography, with the sublime Science of Astronomy, more fully explained than is commonly done, &c. &c.

Provided he had thirty subscribers by the first lecture, he would undertake the course and furthermore, given encouragement, would mount a course at Bath every Christmas. Enough support must have been forthcoming since he returned in December and tentatively began with three discourses on astronomy, hoping it would swell into a full series.[27] The regular Christmas series never materialised, however, and Donn left the spa alone until spring 1773 when he seems to have lectured at both the *Queen's Head* in Cheap Street and the Ladies' Coffee Room beside the Pump Room, sometimes twice a day.[28]

About this time Joseph Priestley arrived in Calne to look after the Earl of Shelburne's Bowood library, and the Bath music master William Herschel purchased Ferguson's *Astronomy Explained* and some months later obtained from 'a Quaker resident at Bath, who had formerly made attempts at polishing mirrors, all his rubbish of patterns, tools, hones, polishers, unfinished mirrors, &c ... '[29] Both events had major scientific consequences. Over the next few years Priestley took a huge stride in the understanding of atmospheric and other gases; he isolated 'dephlogisticated air' (oxygen), explained plant and animal respiration, and hinted at medical uses for the new pneumatic chemistry. Herschel, doubtless further enthused by Ferguson's lecture courses at Bath in 1774, was meanwhile labouring to build the powerful reflecting telescopes that would reveal the planet Uranus and penetrate the night sky as never before. Bath in the late 1770s stood near the frontier of scientific research.

Benjamin Donn's series on experimental philosophy at the Upper Assembly Rooms in June 1776 (thirteen plus an extra three lectures) included electricity but nothing yet on gases – which it aptly fell to John Warltire to introduce.[30] 'Aptly' because Warltire was in the forefront of recent discoveries in this area. He had collaborated with Priestley, obtained pure chemical samples for him, worked with him at Calne, and continued to pass on his personal observations – which in January 1777 came close to proving the chemical constituents of water.[31] An experienced lecturer with close links to the industrial Midlands, Warltire reached Bath about the end of August 1776. He announced courses of 'New Experiments upon Air' at the Lower Rooms, each of three meetings, at 5s. for the course or 2s.6d. a meeting, which he was called on to repeat at least four times. Systematically he dealt with atmospheric gases, artificial gases, and the actions of gases in organic life and industrial processes, repeating each 11 a.m. 'discourse' at 7 p.m. to suit different audiences.

> Mr.WARLTIRE flatters himself these Experiments claim attention the most of any discoveries since the introduction of *Experimental Philosophy*; because they are highly interesting to the ladies as well as gentlemen, and are the most entertaining, and the easiest understood of any in the circle of Philosophy – besides, they are quite new discoveries, and the chief part of them never yet published ... The discourses open precisely at the above times – and it is requested that no part of the apparatus may be moved, and that the company will not require gold to be changed.[32]

There can be little doubt the topic must also have appealed to medical practitioners, some of whom would in the 1790s try out carbon dioxide and nitrous oxide in treatments. More immediately the discoveries were relevant to the spa's literal source of wealth, the effervescent hot waters whose potency had always been agreed to be greatest when drunk straight from the pump before their vital gases had evaporated. Deploying their limited knowledge of chemistry, local and visiting physicians and apothecaries had often – and controversially – analysed the springs, but Priestley's discovery of dissolved carbon dioxide ('fixible air') in the waters made it possible not merely to reconstitute Bath water gone flat but, more threateningly, to produce artificial waters from scratch.[33]

Warltire's success at Bath induced him to come back in October 1777 to give another state-of-the-art series, this time with four lecture-demonstrations in which he undertook to manufacture each gas as his audience watched (with an entire session on nitrous oxide and another partly devoted to acid compounds). Nodding invitingly towards the recently formed Bath [and West] Agricultural Society he proposed further lectures that would treat the still embryonic science of agricultural chemistry. It is likely John Arden attended Warltire's lectures. After some years' absence he had settled at Bath and in late 1776 resumed lecturing to select audiences of a score or more at his own house in St James's Street. By next April he was already into his third course when he had to recruit replacements for subscribers leaving Bath early, with lectures still to come on electricity and magnetism, mechanics, hydrostatics, astronomy, optics, and – a first venture onto Warltire's ground – the properties of air. Later in the year that advance was more definite as he offered sixteen lectures 'in the course of which will be exhibited Dr. Priestley's new experiments upon different kinds of air. Such Lectures will require about one hour and half attendance and no more'.[34]

Early in 1778 competition was keen. Arden's third winter series clashed directly with Donn's six lectures 'on the most entertaining Parts of NATURAL PHILOSOPHY' (astronomy, pneumatics and electricity) which he would repeat in a separate evening course to 'accommodate People in Business'. And Warltire that April, facing a rival course on the genius of Milton and another one forthcoming – in French – on the the humanities and sciences, seasoned his five lectures at a room on George Street with a few novelties. In addition to many experiments he would reveal 'an application to the doctrine of fossils, minerals, &c' and display an opaque solar microscope, 'an instrument of an entire new construction' capable of explaining many recent discoveries.[35] The somewhat cryptic reference to fossils and minerals is noteworthy in view of the specific local interest in geology[36] and its rising significance as a science. Ancient shells, corals, sea urchins, belemnites ('thunderbolts') and spectacular ammonites ('snakestones') abounded in the nearby lias and oolite quarries, and several Bath residents made collections – including Edmund Rack, secretary not only of the Agricultural Society but of the new Bath Philosophical Society whose formation in late 1779 may well have been precipitated by John Arden's latest course of lectures. On 22 December

Rack noted in his 'Disultory Journal' that he had begun attending

> a Course of Philosophical Lectures on Electricity – the Air, Chemistry, Astronomy, Hydrostatics, & the Globes – these Lectures are given by Wm [actually John] Arden of this City, a very Ingenious Man, & who has a Noble Apparatus of the best Instruments. Entertainments of this kind are the most truly Rational & instructive of any that can Employ the Human mind. And a few Lectures explaind by experiments convey more lasting instruction than many volumes of theory. We have them read here all winter. At these Lectures were many Men of great scientific Knowledge ...[37]

---

150   EXPERIMENTS with

SECTION II,

ENTERTAINING EXPERIMENTS PERFORMED BY MEANS OF THE LEYDEN PHIAL.

NO electrical experiments anfwer the joint purpofe of pleafure and furprize in any manner comparable to thofe that are made by means of the Leyden phial. All the varieties of electrical attraction and repulfion may be exhibited, either by the wire, or the coating of it; and if the knobs of two wires, one communicating with the infide, and the other with the outfide of the phial, be brought within four or five inches of one another, the electrical fpider above mentioned will dart from the one to the other in a very furprifing manner, till the phial be difcharged. But the peculiar advantage of the Leyden experiment is, that, by this means, the electrical flafh, report, and fenfation, with all their effects, may be increafed to almoft any degree that is defired.

WHEN the phial, or the jar, is charged, the fhock is given through a perfon's arms and breaft, by directing him to hold a chain communicating with the outfide in one hand, and to touch the wire of the phial, or any conductor communicating with it, with the other

THE LEYDEN PHIAL.   151

other hand. Or the fhock may be made to pafs through any particular part of the body without much affecting the reft, if that part, and no. other, be brought into the circuit through which the fire muft pafs from one fide of the phial to the other.

A GREAT deal of diverfion is often occafioned by giving a perfon a fhock when he does not expect it; which may be done by concealing the wire that comes from the outfide of the phial under the carpet, and placing the wire which comes from the infide in fuch a manner in a perfon's way, that he can fufpect no harm from putting his hand upon it, at the fame time that his feet are upon the other wire. This, and many other methods of giving a fhock by furprize, may eafily be executed by a little contrivance; but great care fhould be taken that thefe fhocks be not ftrong, and that they be not given to all perfons promifcuoufly.

WHEN a fingle perfon receives the fhock, the company is diverted at his fole expence; but all contribute their fhare to the entertainment, and all partake of it alike, when the whole company forms a circuit, by joining their hands; and when the operator directs the perfon who is at one extremity of the circuit to hold a chain which communicates with the coating, while the perfon who is at the other extremity of the circuit touches the wire. As all the perfons who form this circuit are ftruck at the fame time, and with the

L 4   fame

---

5. The Leyden jar as vehicle of popular entertainment, from Joseph Priestley's widely read treatise, *The History and Present State of Electricity*, first issued in 1767 and reproduced here from the 3rd edition of 1775.

Several days later Rack was approached by Thomas Curtis, one of the Hospital governors, and together they drew up a list of prospective members for what was to be in effect a rather distinguished, scientific gentlemen's club. Most of them had probably frequented lectures at Bath, Arden was himself a lecturer, and another member, Benjamin Smith, was about to make his début. Smith was the junior and probably active partner in a firm dealing in optical, scientific and mathematical instruments, Ribright & Smith, which in 1780 removed to a fashionable address in Bath's [Old] Bond Street. As well as hiring out and selling electrical machines, they installed one on the premises for treating cases of rheumatism, paralysis, spasm, deafness and other complaints 'by Shock, Spark, or passing the Electric Matter through the human frame locally or generally'. Partly because of this kind of medical promotion, electricity was in vogue again and in spring 1781 Smith charged 2s.6d. a time for regular lectures on the subject after shop hours. Arden, however, abandoned lecturing at Bath after 1780 except for a long return visit in 1786-7 when, with Smith's co-operation, he gave three lecture courses while seeking a buyer for his scientific library and apparatus.[38]

The 1780s and 1790s resembled earlier decades in the unpredictability of offerings on scientific topics. Smith seldom lectured, other than to publicise a solar microscope in 1784 and to explain the considerable apparatus he had on permanent display. Donn came intermittently from Bristol (1781, 83, 85, 95-6) with a syllabus adaptable to any current vogue, so that one lecture in December 1783 for example, at the height of the Montgolfier craze, was partly devoted to making 'inflammable air' (i.e. hydrogen) 'wherewith AIR BALLOONS are filled'. Otherwise it depended mainly on the chance arrival of itinerant performers. Warltire's tours brought him back to the spa in 1786 and 1788, on the second occasion to focus on the useful applications of modern chemistry.[39] Chemistry was similarly the theme of the blind lecturer Henry Moyes when he proposed an extraordinarily long course of 28 one-hour lectures (four per week) for a mere guinea in 1781. This was still early in his career, before his American tour, but the amiable Moyes was already an impressive performer. Priestley in 1783 considered him superior even to most sighted lecturers – 'and tho' he cannot himself make many experiments, he gets them made for him by an assistant, so that none of his hearers ever complain on that account'.[40] Priestley also thought well of the London lecturer, Adam Walker, who had begun by purchasing William Griffiss' famous equipment in 1766 but had greatly supplemented it since, notably by his 'Eidouranion', a huge transparent orrery. This his son William brought to Bath in 1783 for

6. A mechanical orrery used to display the relative motions of planets and satellites about the Sun. This example, built by the instrument-maker George Adams the younger, was advertised in his *Astronomical and Geographical Essays* (1789), plate 17. The same work (p.542) pays generous tribute to Adam Walker's more spectacular, large-scale orrery, the Eidouranion, demonstrated at Bath in 1783.

an almost theatrical demonstration of astronomical phenomena. The fifth and final scene in what Walker junior called a daring imitation of 'the sublime and awful simplicity of nature' showed 'every planet and satellite in annual and diurnal motion at once; a comet descends in the parabolic curve from the top of the machine, and turning round the sun, ascends in like manner; its motions being accelerated and retarded according to the laws of planetary motion'. Moreover, he told the Bath public, all Herschel's recent discoveries would be woven into the exposition, not forgetting 'the georgian or new planet', Uranus.[41]

The Eidouranion set a fashion. With Benjamin Smith's technical assistance, Abraham Didier, a former actor with Bath's theatre company, constructed a small, glass 'Lilliputian orrery' or 'Aetheroides'. Claiming the mechanism created an unparalleled illusion of 'suspended Orbs' and had an 'inconceivably smooth' movement, he used it – and two similar glass globes, the 'Tellurium' and 'Cometarium' – in lectures to small groups in 1788 and late 1789. His temporary monopoly was challenged, though, in autumn 1788 by John Lloyd, a well-known metropolitan lecturer, who likewise explained the solar system by means of a model, much larger than Didier's, the so-called 'New Eidouranion'. But Didier promised most. His exhibition was 'a Theatre on which Astronomical Talents may be fully exercised, whilst the eye is gratified with a truly pleasing spectacle', yet it was 'neither tedious, nor grave enough to make a Lady yawn', might even at times be interspersed 'with apt and approved Poetic Passages', and was well within the comprehension of children.[42]

There was a perennial risk of confusing the wonders of real science with its showy trappings. What, for instance, was the status of Mr Bradberry's travelling exhibition of Newton's philosophical experiments – 'with a variety of deceptions' – in 1787? How should the curious react to the expensive tuition offered by John Holloway and his local disciple John Giles in 1790-1 on the contentious subject of 'animal magnetism' or Mesmerism, in which its mysteries and medical effectiveness would be divulged, in the strictest secrecy, during five-guinea lectures lasting eight hours over two days? No wonder that before soliciting subscriptions a Mr Burton, a new face at Bath, felt obliged to flourish a testimonial from Priestley stating that he had an elegant set of apparatus, spoke well, came of good family, had suffered from the late American war, and deserved patronage.[43]

Even such established lecturers as Henry Moyes grew more cautious in the 1790s as paranoia about radical subversion intensified and the whole Enlightenment project of disinterested science was at times called into question for introducing Illuminist doctrines and undermining Christian faith.[44] Assisted by his nephew, and always giving generous value of around twenty lectures for a guinea, the blind Moyes was now the most constant of the visiting lecturers at Bath. Several times at the Lower Assembly Rooms in 1793, 1796 and February 1798 he repeated his wide-ranging series on the relatively safe theme of 'natural history', in which he discussed celestial bodies, the Earth's geography, the plant and animal kingdoms, and the natural economy and health of humans. But in February and December 1797, switching to chemistry, he must have felt it prudent to cover himself with a pre-emptive defence in the local press, signed 'B', pointing out that he avoided all 'cabbalistic jargon' and addressed his audience in plain language:

7. In the later eighteenth century lecturers paid increasing attention to geology as a branch of natural history and at Bath helped to inspire fossil-collecting. This common ammonite from the Bath and Keynsham district was engraved for a Bath publication of 1779, Joseph Walcott's *Descriptions and Figures of Petrifactions found in Quarries, Gravel-Pits, &c. near Bath*, plate 40.

> When science is administered in such delightful vehicles, it cannot fail to produce the most rational of all amusements, and at the same time it improves the understanding and amends the heart. How different is this system to that of modern scepticism ...

Later in the year he encountered a different sort of sceptic who took the mild Moyes heatedly to task after one lecture, telling him that heaven was in the Sun and that Newton was quite mistaken on many points.[45]

Astronomy was nevertheless the subject most capable of evoking feelings of sublimity and religious awe and (next to electricity) the one most suitable to dramatic presentation. Both John Lloyd, from the stages of the Lyceum and Royalty Theatre in London, and William Walker, from the Haymarket Theatre Royal, paid return visits to Bath as the century closed. In 1799 and 1800 Lloyd was accompanied by his *pièce de résistance*, the 'Dioastrodoxon', a huge transparent orrery 21 feet in diameter and 'richly decorated with appropriate scenery', on which to demonstrate in a course of three lectures 'the sublime Economy of the SOLAR SYSTEM'.

> In this awful and animated transcript of creation, the *mind* contemplates scenes beyond the ken of *mortal eye*, divinely winged; shakes off the cumbrous lumber of contracted worlds, and 'soars through Nature up to NATURE's GOD!'

The whole complex apparatus, which by 1800 permitted over forty scene changes had, Lloyd intimated, cost him more than £500, was expensive to transport and set up, and naturally deserved liberal support. That year he hired Potter's large auction room in Monmouth Street, dubbed it the 'Theatre of Astronomy' and delivered four 3-day courses, morning and evening, probably to a hundred or more subscribers a time. Later in the year Walker, whose current Eidouranion measured a mere 15 feet across, went one better by taking the Theatre Royal itself, which besides admitting a bigger audience enabled him to heighten his effects with staging, curtains, and the aetherial strains of a celestina. This was science lecturing turned into polished, mannered, self-conscious performance.[46]

Yet the more everyday style was also represented at Bath in 1800, when Dr Raphael Gillum, a physician from the Bath Dispensary, provided the first public botanical course at the spa, a month-long series on the Linnaean system and its applications, held at the Agricultural Society's rooms.[47] The very existence of this Society dedicated to agricultural innovation, plus the revival of the Philosophical Society in late 1798[48] and the fact that Gillum borrowed specimens for his lectures from an eminent local apothecary's botanic garden, all point to the continued presence of scientifically inclined, improvement-minded people in and around Bath.

Mentha rubra common red Mint.

8. The Bath apothecary William Sole ran a botanical garden, arranged on Linnaean principles, which furnished specimens for Dr Raphael Gillum's lecture series in 1800. Sole's important book systematising the mint family, *Menthae Britannicae* (Bath, 1798), included many fine plates by the local artists Thomas Robins junior and William Hibbert.

While the place was no Birmingham, Manchester or even Bristol, humming with manufacturing enterprise, it was no stranger either to industry and technology, despite the guidebooks' pretence otherwise.[49] And the fact that local financial investment went into buildings, leisure and transportation rather than factories did not rule out commercial, let alone cultural and intellectual, curiosity about scientific progress and applications.[50] The hot springs alone made it a congregating ground for medical practitioners whose calling required the exercise of close observation, rational deduction and practical trial, but scattered evidence indicates an active interest in science well beyond the health profession and quite widely spread among both residents and visitors. Admittedly few were quite so obsessive as the natural philosopher depicted in *Bath Anecdotes and Characters* (1780) who valued an antediluvian bone more than a fine woman:

> He lets fall a guinea and a feather in an air-pump. His room is hung with glasses which invert, enlarge, and diminish ... [and] furnished with mattrasses [flasks], alembics, crucibles, and cucurbits [distillation vessels]; in one corner halfpence are dissolving in aqua fortis; in another, guineas in aqua regia; while the spaces are filled up with thermometers, barometers, globes, and a thousand curious baubles and nicknacks.[51]

But nor on the other hand can most of those attending science lectures have been quite so obtuse as the ageing Mrs Thrale (later Mrs Piozzi) suggested after attending a course by Dr Clement Archer, chemist to the Agricultural Society, in 1806:

> Doctor Archer has been trying to teach us Chymistry by Lecture, this Season at Bath; but I learned nothing except that where the Sphere of Attraction ceases, the Sphere of Repulsion begins ... We had much Talk ... concerning Oxygen, & much Talk concerning the Analogy between our Animal & Vegetable Kingdoms ... A Lady at ye Lecture ask'd me if ye 3 Kingdoms Dr Archer talked so of were England Scotland & Ireland.[52]

Lecturers deserved better than that. Over some eighty years they presumably found Bath worth cultivating for the lucrative returns alone, but their efforts at painless popular instruction were not simply mercenary. Often experimenters and instrument-makers themselves, they were practised communicators in touch with every latest development. Enthusiastic, entertaining, competitive and professional, they kept the spa *au fait* with scientific and technological advance through successive generations.

Notes

1 Printed letter from Bath, 11 May 1724, in *Weekly Journal or British Gazetteer*, 16 May 1724. The Queen's Head Lodge, founded 1723, was the first outside London to come under the Grand Union: see George Norman, 'The masonic lodges of Bath', *Transactions of the Somerset Masters Lodge, No.3746*, Pt.3 (1919).

2 Desaguliers and, eventually, James Ferguson were among the few itinerants who became Fellows of the Royal Society (F.R.S.).

3 *Gloucester Journal*, 9 Sep 1730. According to *The Dictionary of National Biography* the Newcastle lecturer John Horsley visited Bath in 1727, but there is no evidence he lectured there.

4 Hist. MSS. Comm. Rpt 63, Egmont, Diary of Viscount Percival, Vol.1, 14 Sep 1730.

5 See J.T. Desaguliers, *A Course of Experimental Philosophy*, 2nd ed., 2 vols. (1745); Vol.1, p.xi for his basic expectations.

6 *Ibid.*, Vol.1, pp.283-8, pls.12 and 21-2.

7 See Larry Stewart, *The Rise of Public Science* (Cambridge, 1992), p.131.

8 *Gloucester Journal*, 20 Sep 1737. J.F. von Bielfeld describes the planetarium in action during a London lecture in 1741 in *Letters of Baron Bielfeld*, trans. Hooper, 4 Vols. (1768-70), Vol.4, pp.83-6.

9 *Gloucester Journal* 26 Apr 1743. The key publication on Martin is John R. Millburn, *Benjamin Martin: Author, Instrument-Maker, and 'Country Showman'* (Leyden, 1976), with its *Supplement* (1986).

10 *The Oracle or Bristol Weekly Miscellany*, 6 Aug 1743.

11 *Bath Journal*, 29 Oct 1744.

12 *Ibid.*,10 [misdated, actually 8] Sep 1746. Meanwhile another metropolitan instrument-maker, John Bennett, put on electrical displays at Bristol, followed by Thomas Wilks: *Bristol Oracle*, 20 Sep, 4 Oct and 27 Dec 1746. Electrical showmanship is discussed in Simon Schaffer, 'Natural philosophy and public spectacle in the eighteenth century', *History of Science* (1983), Vol.21, pp.1-43.

13 The episode is discussed in Simon Schaffer, 'The consuming flame: electric showmen and Tory mystics in the world of goods', *Consumption and the World of Goods*, ed. John Brewer and Roy Porter (London and New York, 1993), pp.489-526. See also Benjamin Martin, *A Supplement Containing Remarks on a Rhapsody of Adventures of a Modern Knight-Errant in Philosophy* (Bath, 1746).

14 Leake, one of Martin's publishers, was after all Richardson's brother-in-law and a former intimate of Dr Cheyne. All three had been guests of Ralph Allen, whose protégé and Richardson's arch rival, Henry Fielding, nevertheless introduced a slightly mocking mention of Freke into *Tom Jones* (Book 4, ch.9), just then being penned.

15 *Bath Journal*, 11 Jan and 26 Sep 1748, 23 Jan 1749.

16 *Ibid.*,18 Nov 1751. In *ibid.*,12 Dec 1748, Martin explained the circumstances following the death of a lodger.

17 John R. Millburn, 'James Ferguson's lecture tour of the English Midlands in 1771', *Annals of Science* (1985), Vol.42, p.400.

18 *Bath Journal*, 22 Oct and 12 Nov 1750, 18 and 25 Nov 1751. In 1750 he also showed a model pile-driving engine.

19   *Bath Advertiser*, 27 Dec 1755. Dr James Bradley, F.R.S., was Savilian professor of astronomy at Oxford and also Astronomer-Royal.

20   *Bath Journal*, 5,19 and 26 Jan, 2 Feb 1756.

21   *Bath Journal*, 3 and 10 May 1756. The dip was also evident in London where some established lecturers gave up: A.Q.Morton, 'Lectures on natural philosophy in London, 1750-1765', *British Journal for the History of Science* (1990), Vol.23, pp.411-34. At Bath the number of visitors dropped in the war years, but it would be hard to prove an exact correlation between the prevalence of science lecturing and the statistics of visitors.

22   According to Nicholas Hans, *New Trends in Education in the Eighteenth Century* (repr.1966), pp.145-6, he made £100 on a 6-week tour to Bath and Bristol in spring 1763, but no lectures were advertised in the Bath press.

23   Millburn, 'James Ferguson', *op.cit.*, p.406. *Bath Chronicle*, 22 Jan,12 Feb, 26 Mar, 16 and 23 Apr 1767.

24   *Ibid.*, 31 Mar 1774. Calculation from Ferguson's 'Common Place Book' communicated by J.R.Millburn, now in Bath Central Library clippings file under 'Martin, Benjamin'. In 1774 Ferguson had 118 subscribers at Bath and c.90 at Bristol: J.R.Millburn, *Benjamin Martin, op.cit.*, p.52.

25   Patricia Phillips, *The Scientific Lady* (1990); Marina Benjamin, ed., *Science and Sensibility: Gender and Scientific Enquiry, 1780-1945* (Oxford, 1991); James A. Secord, 'Newton in the nursery', *History of Science* (1985), Vol.23, pp.127-51.

26   *Bath Chronicle*, 1 and 29 Dec 1768, 5 Jan, 23 Nov 1769, 22 Feb 1770. For Arden see Holburne Museum, *Science and Music in Eighteenth Century Bath* [exhibition catalogue by A.J.Turner *et al*] (Bath, 1977), pp.83-6.

27   *Ibid.*, 28 Dec 1769, 5 Apr and 6 Dec 1770. For Donn see also Hans, *New Trends, op.cit.*, pp. 99-100; Eric Robinson, 'Benjamin Donn (1729-1798), teacher of mathematics and navigation', *Annals of Science* (1963), Vol.19, pp.27-36.

28   And also possibly at the *Christopher Inn*: *Bath Chronicle*, 4 Mar, 29 Apr, 6 and 13 May 1773.

29   *The Herschel Chronicle*, ed. C.A. Lubbock (Cambridge, 1933), pp.59-60; Mrs John Herschel, *Memoir and Correspondence of Caroline Herschel* (1876), p.35; and for Herschel's Bath setting see Holburne Museum, *Science and Music, op.cit.*, and W.J.Williams and D.M.Stoddart, *Bath – Some Encounters with Science* (Bath, 1978). Priestley's eagerness to publicise his discoveries through lectures, etc. is shown in Jan Golinski, *Science as Public Culture: Chemistry and Enlightenment in Britain, 1760-1820* (Cambridge, 1992).

30   *Bath Chronicle*, 16 May, 3 and 27 Jun, and 28 Nov 1776 for more astronomical lectures.

31   Douglas McKie, 'Mr Warltire, a good chymist', *Endeavour* (1951), Vol.10, pp.46-9. The composition of water was finally proved by Cavendish in 1784.

32   *Bath Chronicle*, 5 Sep 1776.

33   Trevor Fawcett, 'Selling the Bath waters', *Somerset Archaeology and Natural History* (1990), Vol.134, pp.193-206.

34   *Bath Chronicle*, 23 Oct 1777 (Warltire), 19 Dec 1776, 3 and 10 Apr, 13 Nov, 25 Dec 1777 (Arden).

35   *Ibid.*, 1 Jan (Arden and Donn), 26 Feb (Arden's fourth course), 2, 9 and 16 Apr 1778 (Warltire *et al*).

36   H.S.Torrens, 'Geological communication in the Bath area in the last half of the eighteenth century' in *Images of the Earth*, ed. L.J.Jordanova and R. Porter (Chalfont St Giles, 1979), pp.215-47.

37   Edmund Rack, 'A Disultory Journal of Events &c at Bath, 1779-80', Bath Central Library, MS. B920. Arden advertised in *Bath Chronicle*, 18 Nov 1779.

38   *Ibid.*, 6 Jan, 3 Feb, 6 Apr, 16 Nov 1780; 3 May 1781; 26 Oct, 16 Nov, 28 Dec 1786; 1-29 Mar 1787.

39   *Ibid.*, 17 Jun 1784, 14 Jan 1790 (Smith); 8 Mar 1781, 9 Jan and 25 Dec 1783, 6 and 13 Jan 1785, 31 Dec 1795, 7 and 14 Jan 1796 (Donn); 7 Sep 1786, 6 [misdated, actually 7] and 21 Mar 1788 (Warltire).

40   *Ibid.*, 13 Dec 1781; J.A.Harrison, 'Blind Henry Moyes', *Annals of Science* (1957), Vol.13, pp.109-25.

41   *Bath Chronicle*, 2 and 9 Jan 1783.

42   *Ibid.*, 1 Nov 1787, 21 Feb, 28 Mar, 10 Apr, 10 Jul, 13 Nov 1788, 3 Dec 1789 (Didier); 20 and 27 Nov 1788 (Lloyd). It is uncertain whether this is the John Lloyd who belonged to the Bath Philosophical Society.

43   *Ibid.*, 5 Apr 1787 (Bradberry); 5 Aug and 23 Sep 1790, 6 Jan 1791 (Lloyd, etc.); 25 Nov, 8 Dec 1791 (Burton). On the cult of Mesmerism see Roy Porter, 'Under the influence: Mesmerism in England', *History Today* (Sept 1985), pp.22-9.

44   The Unitarian Priestley was particularly suspect: e.g. John Robison, *Proofs of a Conspiracy against all the Religions and Governments of Europe*, 4th ed. (1798), pp.482-6.

45   *Bath Chronicle*, 14 and 21 Nov 1793;1 Dec 1796, 26 Jan, 16 Feb (when Moyes requested that dogs be not brought into lectures), 30 Nov and 14 Dec 1797; 8 Feb 1798.

46   *Ibid.*, 18 and 25 Apr, 2 and 16 May 1799; 6, 13 and 20 Feb 1800 (Lloyd); 16 and 23 Oct, 6 Nov 1800 (Walker).

47   *Ibid.*, 15 May 1800. The botanical garden referred to in the next sentence was William Sole's, just off the London road. Sole was a recognised authority on British grasses and mints.

48   Hugh Torrens, 'The four Bath philosophical societies', *A Pox on the Provinces*, ed. Roger Rolls and Jean and John R. Guy (Bath, 1990), p.183.

49   Trevor Fawcett, 'Mechanical enterprise in eighteenth-century Bath', *BIAS Journal* (Bristol Industrial and Archaeological Society, 1998), No.30, pp.8-10.

50   The close link between the earlier science lecturers and practical projects has been highlighted in Larry Stewart, *The Rise of Public Science, op.cit.*

51   *Bath Anecdotes and Characters*, by the Genius Loci [Dr Henry Harington] (1782). For real examples of Bath philosophers see Rack, 'A Disultory Journal', *op.cit.*

52   *Thraliana: the Diary of Mrs. Hester Lynch Thrale (later Mrs. Piozzi)*, ed. K.C. Balderston, 2 vols. (Oxford, 1942), pp.1073-4.

Acknowledgements

I am indebted to Dr. Hugh Torrens for commenting on a draft of this article and for helpful information, and to Dr. Brenda Buchanan for her constructive editorial advice.

GENTEEL WIDOWS OF BATH

I – MRS MARGARET GRAVES
AND HER LETTERS FROM BATH, 1793-1807

Hilary Arnold

In November 1792 Mrs Margaret Graves (1727-1808), the wealthy widow of Admiral Samuel Graves,[1] moved into the newly built house at 15 Lansdown Crescent. Over the next fourteen years she wrote regularly to her great niece Eliza Simcoe. Her letters not only describe some of Bath's social events, her concerns about servants and the cost of living, and contemporary reaction to events in France, they also reveal some of the problems and pleasures of moving into a new house in Bath.[2] In particular they provide evidence of the use of rooms and garden which is slightly different from other recent interpretations, for it shows that Mrs Graves and her staff were the sole occupants of the house, and that the planting was for fruit rather than flowers.[3]

Margaret Spinckes was baptised on 16 March 1727 in the parish church of All Saints at Aldwinkle, Northamptonshire, youngest daughter of Elmes Spinckes who owned the manor. She married the widower Admiral Samuel Graves on 15 June 1769. After the death of her sister Mrs Elizabeth Gwillim, in September 1762, Margaret helped her mother to rear her orphaned niece, Elizabeth Posthuma Gwillim, and then took the six year-old child to her new home, Hembury Fort House at Buckerell, near Honiton, in Devon (fig.1). Fourteen years later, Elizabeth met and, on 30 December 1782, married Admiral Graves's godson, Colonel John Graves Simcoe.[4]

1. Hembury Fort House, Buckerell, Devon.

The Admiral died in March 1787 and his nephew Captain Richard Graves inherited Hembury Fort House. Mrs Graves first moved to stay with the Simcoes in their new mansion, Wolford Lodge, at nearby Dunkeswell

2. Wolford Lodge, Dunkeswell, Devon.

(fig.2). In 1791 Colonel Simcoe was invited to become the first Lieutenant-Governor of Upper Canada (now Ontario). He and his wife eventually decided to accept and set sail for Canada taking the two younger children (Sophia and Francis) and leaving the four older girls (Eliza, Charlotte, Harriet and Caroline) at Wolford Lodge with Miss Hunt acting as governess and her mother Mrs Hunt as housekeeper. Soon afterwards Margaret Graves moved to Bath (fig.3).

Lansdown Crescent was being constructed by various speculative builders between 1789 and 1793 but the unified façade was the design of the architect John Palmer. Margaret Graves was the first occupant of No.15. She wrote to Eliza in January 1793:

I like my house extremely, 'tis a very handsome one, but I have been much inconvenienced by my best chairs not having been sent which, with the want of a carpet, at present make my Drawing Room of no use to me ... I have had surprising luck in the moving of my furniture as there is little or no damage to them. The leg of the black Sopha is broke of[f], but as it was one of the hind legs, 'twill be of no other consequence than the expence of repairing it. The books, which were the material things, are all of them come safe. My Drawing Room is seven and twenty feet by two and twenty,

3. 15 Lansdown Crescent, Bath, Margaret Graves's home from 1792 until her death in 1808.

and fifteen high. The picture of Hero and Leander and yours is over the chimney. Captain Saunders and Captain Richard are on each side of them ... The Admiral's picture hangs over the chimney in the front Dining Room, and your Grandmother's in the Summer Dining Room and vastly well they look. My books are not yet put up, and the workmen here are particularly tedious.

Her books were important to her. She proudly told Eliza in 1797 that she had added many more books to her Library, and she asked General Simcoe to 'lay out' £100 in new books in 1803. Those named in her letters include Plutarch's *Lives*, the *Revolution in Portugal*, a book of American sermons, Hannah More's *Strictures on Female Education*, Livy in translation and Dugdale's *Baronage*. Her will reveals that 'Hero and Leander' was painted by Rubens, but makes no reference to the portrait of the Admiral mentioned above.[5]

In May 1794 Mrs Graves wrote to Eliza inviting her, with her sisters and Mrs and Miss Hunt, to Bath for a fortnight's holiday. 'You need not bring your Cribbs with you, for I can dispose of you all without any trouble of that sort. Mrs and Miss Hunt shall have Mrs Doughty's Room.' Mrs Doughty must have been the companion who had left. 'She is a very great loss indeed and I am quite melancholy and dull without her ... You shall have the bed you used to occupy put into Darney's Room for it is too large to be carried up my small staircase.' Darney was probably the housekeeper. 'I have fitted up the Northern room or large Garret. There Charlotte and Harriet shall lie and little Caroline shall have the smallest of the Duchess Beds in their room. I have no bed now in the Dining Room Apartment. I moved that into Mrs Doughty's Room and her bed into the Garret ... and set the top and bottom chairs in my Closet.' Duchess beds were made up of two low padded bergère chairs forming the head and foot with a padded stool between.

It is thus possible to reconstruct the layout of Margaret Graves's Lansdown house and the use of the rooms (fig.4). We have no information about the basement with its kitchen and servants' quarters. There were two dining rooms on the ground floor, the one for summer use being on the north side. The second floor was given over to chambers (bedrooms) with that of Mrs Graves and her closet facing south and probably two on the north side – Mrs Doughty's and Darney's. Above lay the north and south garrets in the roof space.

The fine house in Lansdown proved less than waterproof on the night of 7 January 1802 when 'the present thaw' occurred and 'the water was

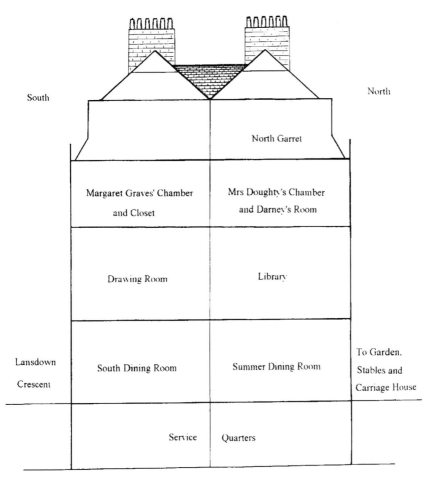

South

North

North Garret

Margaret Graves' Chamber
and Closet

Mrs Doughty's Chamber
and Darney's Room

Drawing Room

Library

Lansdown
Crescent

South Dining Room

Summer Dining Room

To Garden,
Stables and
Carriage House

Service   Quarters

4. Section across 15 Lansdown Crescent during Margaret Graves's occupancy, 1792-1808, with suggested use of the rooms.

pouring down in the best garret at an amazing rate, the people were running about for to get tubs to receive it in ... I slept very quietly until the morning when I had the mortification to find the snow, or water proceeding from it, had found its way into the chamber next to my own. A Crack in the ceiling just over the Bed gave it way and it has dirtied my clean white Bed, the quilt etc.'

There was a garden behind the house with a coach-house and stables. These are marked on the first large-scale Ordnance Survey map of 1886 (fig.5).

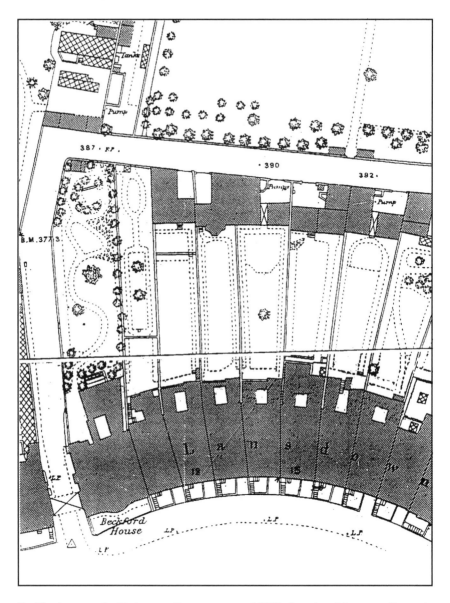

5. The large-scale Ordnance Survey map of 1886 showing Margaret Graves's house, 15 Lansdown Crescent, facing south, with her garden stretching northwards to the stables and carriage house along the back access road. (*Reproduced by courtesy of Bath Central Library*)

The layout of her garden is similar to that of the reconstructed Georgian garden behind the Circus, but most of the plants mentioned were for food. Margaret Graves wrote on 7 October 1794:

> I have just had a great quantity of strawberries planted in my Garden that when I have the pleasure of seeing you and your sisters again you may have still more fruit to pick. But the wind was so high on Sunday night that all I had put in my Garden was very near being demolished. It blew down four foot of the Coach House and Stable Walls the whole length of the building and, had the ruins not tumbled into the Garden, the poor Horses would have been demolished and carriage broke to pieces. It made a dreadful crash when it fell.

By 10 November, 'My Garden is put in order again though it cost me £2.8s. to repair it. The gardener was purloining all my strawberries into the bargain, but I happened to see the gentleman at his work and sent down and forbad his carrying them away for you know when you and your sisters come to Bath again it will be very pleasant for you to pick strawberries for your supper.'

Eliza had received some seeds of a sweet-scented fern and Mountain Tea from Canada (fig.6).[6] Mrs Graves suggested, 'If you have a great quantity of it pray send me a little. I think I should like prodigiously to drink some of your Brother's Tea', but the following year wrote again, 'I have altered my mind concerning them for I think my Garden is so small that were they to grow with me, they would only encumber the place instead of beautifying it.' There are more clues as to what she had planted. In June 1795 'The season is so backward that I have not one single rose in bloom in my Garden not so much as one Honeysuckle. The fruit trees too make a very moderate appearance. I doubt when you and your sisters come here that we shall not be able to gather currants and cherries for Puddins as we did last year.' But in September 'My Apricots were and are very fine tasted ... for I have a tart or dumplin of them every day'.

6. Mountain Tea or Wintergreen which was sent by the Simcoes to Devon but rejected by Margaret Graves in favour of fruit trees.

Alterations to the garden layout occurred. 'I have pulled up my gravel walk and covered it in turfs which in a good measure prevents the reflection that used to render my Library unpleasant during the bright months.'

Mrs Graves's comments on servants are of interest. In July 1800 she wrote, 'Last week my stables were in the night broken open and William, who was too lazy to bring his cloaths into the house, was robbed of his new livery and his next best coat, 2 very good waistcoats, 3 pocket handkerchiefs and several other things. They got clear off with their booty.' In December 1801 she wrote,

> Poor Smith, who went from me in September to the low marshy village of Bridstock in Northamptonshire for the benefit of her health, has recovered surprisingly since she got into her native air, but I have no means to supply her loss. The Lady-looks of this city undertake everything and perform nothing, nor do they seem to have the excellent respect for the interest of their employer. My footman too, John Thergold, who had long been too great to wear a livery, left me a fortnight after I came from Devonshire. He had got a situation he told me would bring in £40 a year upwards. It was bookkeeper to the Stone Masons Company. There he went for one week, and was turned out the next for not being sufficiently versed in accounts. He now plays to a French Dancing Master's scholars and at servants' clubs and things of that sort ... I have got a sad awkward stupid fellow in his room.

The letters list a number of people whom she had met or visited. In September 1794, 'Mrs Porteous, sister to the Bishop of London, is come to live in the wing belonging to Lansdown. She resides with a Mrs Fairfax, an American lady. I like these both very much.'[7] 'Mr Randulph, who preaches at the Octagon, preaches better than any man since the times of the blessed Apostles, it seems is an acquaintance of your father', she wrote with irony in February 1797. He visited her and explained that, 'If there had been a bishop of Upper Canada, Col. Simcoe would have appointed him'. Mrs Graves was probably a well-preserved old lady, as she makes a number of derogatory remarks about other people's looks worthy of Jane Austen's Sir Walter Elliott – 'Lady Graves seems pritty well in health but appears as old as if she had taken a sail in the Ark with Noah', and 'Miss St. John is such a martyr to ill health as makes her appear more like the sister than the daughter of her mother'. She admired other older ladies like Mrs Rose Drew who 'has kept herself in a marvelous preservation, her teeth as white, her eyes as bright as when she and her aunt used to be of our parties at Bath before your mother married'.

There are occasional glimpses of popular entertainment in Bath.

> You cannot think how I wished on Thursday the 25 [October 1798] to have had you and your sisters with us for this whole city was illuminated. There was an abundance of transparencies and other devices, some very elegant ones. Those that pleased me most was Hibernia fallen and a Ruffian going to destroy her, but Britannia held forth her protecting shield and saved her from his fury. There was another transparency of Hibernia lamenting over her burning towns and slaughtered people and Warren pointing to his fleet to comfort her. Lady Elizabeth Noel had a very pritty one of the French fleet surrendering and in coloured lamps was wrote, God gave the Word and Nelson struck the Blow. Pickwick had transparencies of Lord How, Lord St. Vincents, Lord Duncan and Warren and the device was These are my faithful Friends spoken by the King, who was looking at and pointing to them with great delight. Crowns, Anchors and ships in coloured lamps were innumerable and the houses so decorated with laurels that Bath now seems less like a City than a Laurel Grove. However the joy showed on the occasion was very temperate and proper; the people were wonderfully pleased but very civil; there was neither riot nor bustle in any part of the town.[8]

On 3 February 1802,

> I designed to go last night to see the Phantasmagoria. It was exhibited at the Theatre. The house was crowded, the lights extinguished and every door fast locked, the noise of the galleries very disagreeable enveloped in darkness. They uttered abject fear and vulgar impatience with shrill whistles and loud screams. The first appearance was an imitation of the forked lightning too dull to be terrifying. Then skeletons came forwards and one figure seemed in pain. They receded and grew less as they left the stage, a yellow light flowing round them had a good effect. These gave place to Lord Nelson's crowning by Fame and ended with a figure of his Majesty ushered in by the old loyal tune of God Save the King.

Three weeks later she visited Millardet's Automatons and wrote a detailed description of the figures which she saw writing in French and English, drawing, fortune-telling and performing acrobatics, along with a mechanical spider.

Margaret Graves has far less to say about visits to more usual plays at the Theatre. In April 1806 she wrote,

> Master Betty has come to Bath and all the inhabitants of this city are mad to see him act. I design going to the Theatre to see his Duglass on Thursday next, but I had the prudence to refuse a place for tomorrow, as the crowd was so great that some ladies fainted away in the box-lobby in only endeavouring to bribe Bartley to secure them places. I had no mind to die. I shall leave the whole management to my friends. If they get me a place I shall accept it with pleasure. If not I shall be very well satisfied for my eyes are too bad to judge of his countenance.

Margaret Graves would have approved of Jane Austen's view of contemporary drama expressed in *Mansfield Park* by Fanny Price and Sir Thomas Bertram, upset by the choice of the German play *Lovers' Vows* for amateur theatricals. Mrs Graves states,

> I used to love plays amazingly and thought them not only entertaining but instructing to auditors ... but now one meets in German pieces profaneness, the vulgar pert manners of our own ... they are only calculated for a village wake and should be acted in a Barn for the Dramatis Persona are footmen, abigails [lady's-maids], cheats, barbers and apothecaries. I am literally too much of an aristocrat to be the least entertained with the conversation of those underbred gentry.

Eliza had attended Lady Porchester's rout in 1803 and Mrs Graves commented, 'Amusements at these meetings are always the same – casino, whist, quadrille, and so likewise are the refreshment – cakes, ices, lemonade. The company at Bath, tho' not so brilliant as London, is yet very respectable. Royal personages have we none, Stars and Garters some but very few.' However she poured scorn on the royal family in July 1796.

> The Prince of Wales has been to Bath to visit his brother, the Duke of York. He was extremely well received here and great crowds of people assembled wherever he went in order to see him ... so they would have done if his Pandemonium Majesty had appeared with any degree of splendour. I was most pleased with little John Smith, who was beyond measure eager to see the Prince of Wales. At last his friends got him a full view of the Prince. The child burst out acrying, rolled himself in the street and said aloud, 'That's not the Prince, it's a man.'

Fear of the French is a theme which recurs in the correspondence. The Simcoe girls were anxious to receive letters from their parents in Canada. Margaret Graves explained in a letter of 1794,

> Not hearing so frequently as you used to do, is owing I believe to those vile French monsters, who I am sorry to say, take abundance of our ships ... I have just heard that those wretches ... the French ... have murdered the Dauphine by mixing slow poison in strong wine which was the only liquor they allowed him to drink. Happy for him, poor child, that he is now released from their tyranny ... I hope at last it will please God to destroy those impious persons who renounce his authority and trample on his laws, profane his sanctuaries and act with more than savage cruelty by humankind.

Four years later (May 1798) she reported, 'This city is rejoicing from one end to the other for the escape of Sir Sydney Smith', who had thwarted Napoleon's plans in Syria. She was rather surprised,

> for he brought neither peace nor victory ... the Pump Room, the Public Gardens, every place of amusement where the people can get a glance of him is crowded. When he enters the Theatre the people clap him as they do the Royal Family. The people who have benefits beg leave to mention on their bills that he will honour the Theatre with his presence and they are thought to gain at least £50 a night by his complying with their request.

Fears of the French revolutionaries were replaced by fears of Napoleon. He was rumoured to be preparing for a landing in June 1801. Eliza's father, now General Simcoe, had been placed in charge of the defence of south-west England. Mrs Graves wrote to Eliza in July 1803,

> You are very good to invite me [to Wolford Lodge] ... by telling me how quiet Buonaparté remains on the other side of the water ... I cannot but look upon his present quietness as that awful stillness which precedes the thunderstorm, before it roars tremendous and scatters fire and death amongst the sons of man. ... But it appears to me ... that one great means of our preservation will be owing to your father's scheme of arming the whole mass of the population. They talk of it here. And of teaching them to load and fire quick and to shoot at a mark, but if the Government does not send arms and ammunition

and appoint people to show their mark-firing, they may plan schemes of defence when England will be no more ... The mass cannot furnish themselves with ammunition and, had they sufficient for that purpose, they are more likely to spend it on strong liquors than on gunpowder.

Rising prices worried her. In 1799,

> Everything is so expensive that one hardly knows how to get along. However the poor are well supplied, for the Corporation have allowed the use of their kitchen and likewise their Cook and a subscription has been raised for them among the rich to purchase provisions for them, so that any poor person who can raise three halfpence may have a quart of soup, a small piece of meat and a few potatoes and take it home to their families or eat it there as they choose.

Margaret Graves's payment of the Poor Rate is recorded in the Returns for the parish of St. Stephen's (fig.7). She had also paid 'about eleven pounds' in Income Tax at this time. In 1800 she had heard, 'Mr Pitt intends putting a tax on carriage horses. If that Gentleman continues ... I must lay down my carriage, quit my house, and take a smaller one in a more central part of Bath which would not be so agreeable.'

It is Margaret Graves's attitude towards the inequality of the sexes in contemporary society which is the surprising part of her letters. After the Simcoes had returned from Canada a second son, John Cornwall Simcoe, was born. She wrote to Eliza, 'Not that I like Boys better than Girls for I do not love them half so well; for in general I think them a dominating set of beings, strutting and boasting and making a noise about trifles ... these are boisterous and turbulent times, ill-suited to the delicacy of women'. In 1800 a third son was born, Henry Addington Simcoe, and Mrs Graves wrote,

> I was happy to find ... that your mother had given you a Brother and not another Sister; for, as you observe, there is girls enow ... I don't rejoice because I like Boys better than Girls, ... but they can struggle through difficulties better than Girls ... By being brought up to professions they can acquire fortunes for themselves or better those they have. Girls have none of those advantages and can scarce gain (with their utmost industry and pricking their finger to the bone) a single Shilling a day. Gentlemen's Daughters are too often an unfortunate set of beings. Brought up in affluence, used from their cradles to tenderness and delicacy, in maturer age are often left to

9	Sharpless	1 10	
10	A M Cooban	1 16	
11	Charles Worthington	1 18	
12	Blanch Woollaston	1 18	
13	Charles Coxe	1 18	
14	Mary Shinner	1 18	
15	Margaret Graves	1 18	
16	Mary Hickey	1 18	
17	Charles Arthur	1 18	1 18
18	Edith Frankland	1 10	
19	Christopher Irving	1 10	
1	John Lowder	2 2	
2	~~Edward Thales~~ King	1 5	
3	Henry Bosanquet	1 5	
4	E S French	1 1	
5	Henry Best	1 1	
6	Grace Blackwood	1 1	
		27 7	1 18

7. Poor Rate Returns for the Parish of St. Stephen's, Walcot for August 1802 showing that Margaret Graves, living at 15 Lansdown Crescent, paid £1.18s. (*Reproduced by courtesy of Bath Record Office*) disappointment and distress. The appearance and manners of Gentlewomen taught them from infancy, they cannot support, and their present narrow circumstances rendered bitter to them by the remembrance of their former happy situation in Life.

Margaret Graves had enjoyed wealth and comfort all her life, so these observations must have been based on such women she met in Bath. She might have been describing Jane Austen's characters like Miss Bates and Jane Fairfax in *Emma*. In October 1799 she wrote again in this vein. 'I think every woman should be taught the worth of things and how to make the best of them. Economy is not only amiable in a woman, but absolutely necessary. The custom of our country to give so large a part of the fortune to the son, as but too often, leaves the girls in an uncomfortable situation.' When in 1801 the Simcoes bore another daughter, Katherine, Margaret Graves wrote to Eliza, 'I by no means rejoice that your relation is a Sister and not a Brother. The present times are awful ... distressful and turbulent ... poor helpless girls are ill-calculated to struggle with the impending difficulties of the present times.'

By April 1807 Mrs Graves was renovating her whole house.

> The more I wish to economise, the more I spend. The paper I had bespoke for the rooms was too small in quantity by at least one third. I was obliged to have a new lock to the Door and they are breaking pains [panes] ... that I have to replace. I have been sleeping on two Sophas in the great Drawing Room for this month past and when I shall have the comfort to repose on a Bed again I cannot exactly say. I do sit in my Library again but at the hazard of my health for it stinks of pain[t] like poison.

This was the last letter she wrote to Eliza so maybe the paint did indeed contain poisonous fumes. Naval records state that the widow of Admiral Graves died in November/December 1808. There is however no mention of her death in any Bath newspapers, nor her burial at Walcot Parish Church in Bath. Perhaps her will of October 1806 gives the reason. She wrote,

> I do desire that my corpse shall be carried to the grave without any show or parade, no hearse, mourners, no scarfs, hatbands or gloves, no pall or covered coffin, but carried by six poor men to the churchyard and there buried without entering the church, which properly is a place of prayer for the living and not a receptacle for the dead.

She made a few small bequests and then ordered that her house with all its contents should be sold and the money divided amongst her five older nieces – Eliza and her sisters. Margaret Graves had made sure that 'those young ladies' had sufficient income for the rest of their lives.

Notes

1 Admiral Samuel Graves (1713-1787) pursued an unspectacular naval career until promoted in 1774 to be commander of the North America station, where he attempted to enforce the Boston Ports Act. Having no firm orders on how to deal with colonists' attacks on British shipping, he was goaded into a retaliatory assault on Falmouth (now Portland), Maine. This so incensed the Americans that George III recalled him. Graves's request for a courtmartial was disregarded, so he withdrew to Hembury Fort House where he died in 1787. Margaret (with a supposed fortune of £30,000) was annoyed at being turned out of her house, which he bequeathed to his nephew. (Information from Mr C.T. Cooper of Tor Point, 1988)

2 The letters are in Devon Record Office, Exeter. Ref 1038M/F 1/117-176.

3 See The Building of Bath Museum at The Vineyards, The Paragon, Bath, and the handbook by Christopher Woodward, *The Building of Bath* (Bath Preservation Trust, n.d.), especially pp.38-9. Also the Georgian Garden, 4 Circus, Bath, discovered and restored by Bath Archaeological Trust.

4 Many biographies of General and Mrs Simcoe have been published in Canada. The most recent is Mary Beacock Fryer, *Elizabeth Posthuma Simcoe* (Dundurn Press, Toronto and Oxford, 1989).

5 The fate of the portrait of 'The Admiral' is not known, but hopes were raised by a sale at Sotheby's in November 1988. It has however been confirmed that this painting by Gainsborough was of Admiral Thomas Graves (1725-1802), a cousin of Samuel, who commanded the British fleet in the American War of Independence, and was later created Baron Graves of Gravesend.

6 Mountain Tea or Wintergreen needs to be fermented to yield any flavour. It was used by native Americans and colonists as a medicine. (*Information from Sue Kershaw, London, Ontario*)

7 Mrs Sally Fairfax and her husband were lifelong friends of George Washington. After her husband's death she moved to 109 East Wing, Lansdown, the name by which the present Lansdown Place East was known.

8 The celebrations were occasioned by the quelling of an uprising in Ireland and a mutiny in the navy, and by victories over the French, Dutch and Spanish fleets.

GENTEEL WIDOWS OF BATH

II – 'A PERSECUTED RELATION': MRS LILLINGSTON'S FUNERAL AND JANE AUSTEN'S LEGACY

Deirdre Le Faye

On 11 July 1804 Mrs Willielma Johanna Lillingston, widow, of No 10 Rivers Street, Walcot parish, Bath, made her Will.[1] She was aged sixty-three and living alone, save for her little dog Malore, in her small house in a quiet but highly respectable street on the northern edge of Bath. She was attended by her maid Molly Stowe, her faithful man-servant Francis Varley, and a succession of not-so-faithful cooks; and as her nearest relations had in recent years brought lawsuits against her, she now cut them completely out of her Will and instead divided her possessions in the minutest details amongst nephews, nieces, cousins and friends, not forgetting her household staff. Most of these legatees were elderly ladies of her own generation, but two were much younger – the Misses Cassandra and Jane Austen, daughters of the Revd George Austen, rector of Steventon in Hampshire but living in retirement with his family in Bath since 1801. Mrs Lillingston further appointed Mr Austen's brother-in-law, her old friend Mr James Leigh-Perrot, to be her chief executor and residuary legatee; Mr Leigh-Perrot, an efficient and conscientious man, kept until his own death all the documents relating to the settlement of Mrs Lillingston's estate.[2] From these and other sources, including Jane Austen's own letters, the outline of Mrs Lillingston's life, and the full details of her ceremonial departure from that life, can be ascertained, providing a complete picture of the social and economic requirements for the funeral of a Bath dowager of the Regency era.

Mrs Lillingston, born Wilhelmena Johanna Dottin in 1741,[3] came from West Indian planter family stock – the Dottins of Grenada Hall, Barbados, who had intermarried with the Alleynes of Barbados, who in turn were connected with the Walter family of South Baddesley, Hants. At some time probably in the late 1760s she had married Mr Luke Lillingston of Ferriby Grange, North Ferriby, Yorkshire, a man considerably older than herself. When he made his Will in November 1771 at the age of fifty-three, they had but the one child, Elizabeth Mary Agnes, and Mr

Lillingston specified that as she was his heiress, whoever married her should then assume her name.[4] Elizabeth inherited Ferriby Grange in her childhood, as her father died in 1778. The first of the surviving documents relating to Mrs Lillingston's probate affairs is a balance-sheet of the Ferriby estate presented to Miss Elizabeth by the bailiff or steward, Robert Dunn, and dated August 1794. The balance-sheet also shows that in 1793 and 1794 the Grange had been advertised for lease. Presumably as soon as a tenant had been found, Mrs Lillingston and her daughter moved south and met the Spooner family, *nouveaux riches* ironmasters from Birmingham, who had recently purchased Elmdon Hall near that mushrooming industrial town and also owned a house in Bath.[5] Elizabeth became engaged to the eldest son, Abraham, and they were married at St Mary's, Kensington, London, on 19 August 1797.[6] Mr Leigh-Perrot was one of the parties involved in the marriage settlement drawn up a few days beforehand, whereby the Ferriby Grange estate passed to the joint trusteeship of the bridegroom's uncle Lord Calthorpe and the bride's cousin Mr Abel Rous Dottin.[7] On 22 August 1797 Abraham Spooner, now signing himself Spooner-Lillingston in accordance with the terms of his late father-in-law's Will, acknowledged having received from his mother-in-law 'all the Plate belonging to the late Luke Lillingston Esq., & all his Writings – & Tittle [*sic*] Deeds'.

For the next three years no further documents survive, and no trace of any lawsuit involving Mrs Lillingston can now be found; but on 26 July 1800 her London lawyer Mr C. Coulthurst of Bedford Row informed her:

> Your Cause was heard yesterday & I am happy to add that the Chancellor has dismissed so much of the Bill as seeks to set aside the Release saying there was not the least Pretence for it, and that the Bill was filed from Spleen and ill Humour, but he thought that as you had executed the Deed of August 1797 which from the Purport of it might be so construed as to induce a Belief in the Husband that no Debt was due from the Daughter to you, the Chancellor thought that you was not from the Words of that Deed intitled to call upon the Plaintiffs for any money due at the Time of the Marriage – the Chancellor and every one present were perfectly satisfied with the Purity of your Conduct & the general opinion was that the Bill was a most unjust and unnatural one.

This would seem to imply that the young Spooner-Lillingstons were suing Mrs Lillingston over money matters dating back to the time of their marriage in 1797, an implication strengthened by the fact that in the interim Mrs Lillingston's nephew Abel Rous Dottin had relinquished his position as trustee to the marriage settlement and had been replaced by William Spooner, younger brother of Abraham.[8] From this time evidently dated the breach between Mrs Lillingston and her daughter, a breach never to be repaired during the remainder of the older lady's life.

The next information regarding Mrs Lillingston is in 1801, when she is mentioned in Jane Austen's correspondence. The Revd George Austen had decided late in 1800 to retire from active parochial duties at Steventon, and the spring months of the next year were spent in packing up the Austen family home at the rectory there. At the beginning of May 1801 Mrs Austen and Jane arrived in Bath, and stayed with Mr and Mrs Leigh-Perrot in No 1 Paragon to do some house-hunting while Mr Austen made a trip to Kent. Mrs Lillingston immediately called on them, and the Austens returned her call a few days later. Jane wrote to her sister Cassandra, then staying at Up Hurstbourne, near Andover, giving her unenthusiastic comments on the placid trivia of Bath life: 'We met not a creature at Mrs. Lillingstone's [sic] & yet were not so very stupid as I expected, which I attribute to my wearing my new bonnet & being in good looks'. On 21 May Mrs Leigh-Perrot gave a 'tiny party' at the Paragon, the guests being Miss Edwards and her father, Mrs Busby and her nephew Mr Maitland, and Mrs Lillingston. On 25 May the Austens visited the Holders for tea, and met Mrs Lillingston

1. Silhouettes of James Leigh-Perrot (1735-1817) and his wife Jane (1744-1836), Jane Austen's uncle and aunt. They may have been cut in Bath by Mrs Harrington or her assistant Mrs Collins, perhaps c.1780. (*Reproduced by courtesy of The Jane Austen Memorial Trust, Chawton*)

2. (*left*) 'L'aimable Jane': silhouette believed to be of Jane Austen in her youth, as it was found this century pasted into a copy of the second (1816) edition of *Mansfield Park*. (*Reproduced by courtesy of The National Portrait Gallery, London*) (*right*) Silhouette of Cassandra Austen in later life. (*Reproduced by courtesy of The Jane Austen Memorial Trust, Chawton*)

again there: 'My evening visit was by no means disagreeable. Mrs. Lillingston came to engage Mrs. Holder's conversation, & Miss Holder & I adjourned after tea into the inner Drawingroom to look over Prints & talk pathetically.'[9]

Jane provides no further information regarding Mrs Lillingston, but it is evident that the Austens must already have met her before 1801, as otherwise Jane would have mentioned her to Cassandra as a new acquaintance. The Leigh-Perrots had regularly stayed in Bath for the season for many years past, and the Austens had on occasion visited them there, so the contact with Mrs Lillingston probably arose in this way and may have dated back almost to Jane's childhood. How the Leigh-Perrots themselves came to know Mrs Lillingston is uncertain – it may have been their common West Indian background (Mrs Leigh-Perrot, née Jane Cholmeley, had been born in Barbados), or a friendship formed in earlier years by neighbourly contact in the Humberside area (Mrs Leigh-Perrot was sent home as a child from Barbados to be reared in England by the senior branch of the Cholmeleys in Lincolnshire, not far from North Ferriby), or it may have been a friendship formed only in later years in Bath society. Although the Austens continued to live in Bath until the spring of 1806, there is no further mention of Mrs Lillingston in Jane's correspondence, either before or after that date. Though Jane and Cassandra may privately have found the old lady dull, she evidently viewed the sisters with affection, as is proven by the fact that she remembered them in her Will.

Two more lawyers' letters are preserved amongst Mrs Lillingston's papers, dating to the summer of 1803, which seem to imply that either the earlier lawsuit was still dragging on, or that the Spooner-Lillingstons had made a second attempt to sue her. Mr Coulthurst acknowledged his £10 fee: 'I am truly glad that my Exertions in your Cause have given you satisfaction & I assure you that having Justice on our side was alone the Cause of our success – I hope the Time has arrived or will soon arrive when the Persons alluded to will be convinced (as every other impartial Person has been) of the Purity & Rectitude of your Conduct' – and a local Yorkshire lawyer, Mr William Iveson, also sent his congratulations: 'I am very happy to find the troublesome contentions you have so long been engaged in, are at length terminated to your satisfaction ... proceedings which I considered so very unjust ... I truly sympathise in the satisfaction you must feel in having at last overcome difficulties & trials that must have required the exercise of all your fortitude & patience.'

A year later Mrs Lillingston made her last Will and Testament, and although by now she had two grandsons (Isaac-William, born 6 June 1802 and Charles, born 25 April 1804), not even their existence could heal the breach between herself and their parents, and they also were omitted from her choice of legatees. She made a point of leaving token gifts to those who presumably had sympathised most strongly with her during her legal battles – her cousins Mrs Charlotte Senior and Mrs Lucy Hannah Rugge were each to have twenty guineas 'as a triffling [sic] Remembrance of a persecuted Relation'; her niece by marriage Mrs Dorothy Dottin, her younger cousins Mr John and Miss Ann Walter, and her friend Mrs Leigh-Perrot, were each to have five guineas to buy mourning rings as 'a remembrance of a persecuted Relation & Friend'. Miss Sarah Rous, maternal aunt of Abel Rous Dottin, was to have Mrs Lillingston's 'Red Cornelian Seal set in Gold, device a Dove and Serpent motto Innocence Surmounts'. Other relations and friends were to have varying sums of money, and it is here that the names of Jane and Cassandra Austen appear, to receive £50 apiece – unfortunately in their case no comment is made or reason given for the bequest. Other valuable effects were also distributed – her friend Mrs Caroline Habersham, who kept a School for Young Ladies across the road at No 1 Catherine Place, was to have a plated tea-urn and a silver cream jug and £200 as well; her very young cousin Miss Charlotte Fuller, granddaughter of Mrs Senior, was to have all the silver spoons; and her old Yorkshire friends the Misses Constance and Evereld Hustler, of Acklam Hall in the North Riding, were to have her two old-fashioned formal dress suits of point lace and Devonshire Brussels lace.[10] Her library was likewise a treasured possession, to be individually bequeathed: 'I also request that my Books and other things which may have a label of my own hand writing in them may be given to the different persons as thereby described'.

Her three servants, provided they were still in her employment at the time of her death, were each to have a suit of 'decent mourning' in which to attend her funeral, plus other suitably graded bequests. The maid Molly Stowe was to have £90, a wide selection of the lesser household effects, and was requested to take care of 'my Favourite Little Dog Malore ... Faithful Companion through all my sufferings'. Francis Varley, 'for his long & faithful service', was to have £220, all his bedroom furnishings (comprising bedstead, white cloth hangings, bed, bolster, two pillows, blankets, rug, two chairs and a table), and Mrs Lillingston's old black mare Sissy, 'requesting she shall never be Road worked or Shod but enjoy the same Indulgences she has done the last eight years of her life'. The current cook, whoever she might be, was to have a bonus of one year's wages. Her servants were to live on at No 10 Rivers Street for a month after her decease, with their expenses paid from the estate.

The executors were to be Mr Leigh-Perrot and her nephew Abel Rous Dottin, each of whom was to have £100 for his pains; the Rivers Street house and all other effects were to be sold to provide the money for the bequests and necessary expenses; and she was to be buried at Charlcombe (a pretty little village some two miles north of Bath, much favoured for smart funerals) in the 'plainest manner', the cortège to consist of nothing more than the hearse with one pair of horses, followed by only one mourning coach and pair, no other carriage or horsemen to attend. She evidently suffered from the fear, fairly common at that period, of being buried alive, and so specified that her coffin was not to be closed until a week after her death was presumed to have occurred.

Mrs Lillingston lived for another eighteen months, but not even the birth of a third grandson, Alfred, in November 1805, produced any reconciliation with her daughter or any codicil to her Will. The *Bath Journal* for Monday 3 February 1806 reported: 'On Thursday night [30 January] died, at her house in Rivers-street, Mrs. Lillingston; a lady of exemplary benevolence'; and Mr Leigh-Perrot moved promptly to fulfil his duties as executor. James Howe, the parish clerk of Walcot, had been instructed to toll the passing bell and ring the knell, for which he later received a fee of 17/6d. The servants were equipped with their 'decent mourning' – Francis Varley had a hat from Messrs

Harding & Frankham of Borough Walls, a suit and two under-waistcoats from the tailor Samuel Sims, and other smaller items from Messrs Ballans & Bradley, linen-drapers and undertakers, of 14 Bond Street. Molly Stowe and the cook, Mary Howse, had their complete mourning attire supplied by Ballans & Bradley. The interment took place at Charlcombe a week later, as Mrs Lillingston had wished, on 8 February, with the cortège provided by Eleazar Pickwick, Coach-Master, of 17 Westgate Buildings. Ballans & Bradley then presented Mr Leigh-Perrot with their detailed four-page account of expenses for this 'plainest manner' funeral (see pp.98-101).

No 14 Bond St. Bath Feby 8th 1806

The Exec^{rs}.

To Ballans & Bradley
for the Funeral expenses of the late Mrs Lillingston

To a fine Calico Winding Sheet		1 10 -
To a fine Calico Pillow	3/-	- 3 -
To 2 ys White Ribbon for the Cap of the Corpse	9d	- 1 6
To a Quilted Mattrass of fine W^t Calico		1 1 -
To a Stout inside Coffin lined with fine Calico		1 11 6
To a Stout Outside D° Cover'd with fine Black Cloth 2000 Brass nails & 4 Pair best gilt Handles		7 7 -
To a Brass breast Plate engraved		1 5 -
To 5 Hatbands & Scarves for Rev^d Mr Morgan Rev^d Mr Sibley Mr Tickell Mr Hay & Undertaker 5³/4 each is 28³/4 ys Rich Black Satin	12/-	17 5 -
To 10 ys Satin Ribbon for D°	10d	- 8 4
To 5 Pair Black Shamay Gloves for D°	3/6	- 17 6
To 2 Hoods & Scarves Maid Servts 5³/4 ea is 11¹/2 ys Black Mode	6/-	3 9 -
To 4¹/2 ys Ribbon for D°	8d	- 3 -
To 18 Hatbands for 2 Mutes 2 Coachmen 4 Pages 8 Bearers Clerk at Charlcombe & Featherman 2¹/4 each is 40¹/2 ys Blk Mode) 4/6		9 2 3
To Ribbon for D° each	6d	- 9 -
Carr^d forward		£44 13 1

Apart from Ballans & Bradley's own employee, the other four gentlemen being provided with mourning hatbands, scarves, ribbons and gloves were the incumbents of the two parishes involved, the Revd Mr Morgan of Charl-combe and the Revd Mr Sibley of Walcot, and Mrs Lillingston's apothecaries, Mr Tickell of Queen Square and Mr Hay of Bladud's Buildings. Mrs Shipton the nurse was not one of Mrs Lillingston's servants, and had presumably been called in by the apothecaries to attend at the last, and so received the standard token acknowledgement of mourning.[11] The black fabrics worn by attendants or used as drapes all had matt finishes, in order to give

Am'. Bro'. forward			44 13 1
To 18 Pair Black Gloves	18d		1 7 -
To 11½ ys Black Mode for 2 Mutes Poles & Feathermans Scarf	4/6		2 11 9
To 16 ys Ribbon for D°	8d		- 10 8
To 1 Crape Hatband Man Servant			- 5 -
To the Use of the best Velvet Pall			1 1 -
" of 2 Mutes Dresses	2/6		- 5 -
" of 1 Cloak Mourner			- 2 6
" of 2 Box Coats Coachmen	2/6		- 5 -
" of 17 Black Coats	18d		1 5 6
" of 4 Caps 8 Truncheons & 4 Page Rods	6d		- 8 -
" of a Rich Sett of Feathers & Velvets for a Hearse & four			2 16 -
" of a Rich Sett of Feathers & Velvets for a Coach & four			1 5 -
" of the Plume			1 1 -
" of 2 Velvet Hammer Cloths	5/-		- 10 -
			£58 5 6
To Cash Paid for a Hearse & four & Coach & four to Charlcombe			4 7 -
To Cash Paid for 2 Mutes Horses	4/6		- 9 -
To D° Paid the Featherman	4/-		- 4 -
To D° Paid 8 Bearers & 4 Pages each	2/6		1 10 -
To D° Paid Coachmen for Driving	4/-		- 8 -
To D° Paid the Fees at Charlcombe			4 4 -
To D° Paid the Fees for the Monuments			3 3 -
To D° Paid the Mortuary Fees at Walcot			- 17 6
Carrᵈ. forward			£15 2 6

a lustreless, dead-black, sooty appearance. Crape was a crimped silk gauze, alamode or mode a lightweight silk, and lovehood or love-ribbon was a transparent silk ribbon for bonnet-trimmings and favours. Bombazine was a mixture of silk and wool, and bombazet was a cheaper mixture of wool and cotton – hence Molly Stowe, the lady's maid, has her mourning dress of the former, and Mary Howse, the cook, of the latter. The marble monumental tablet was made by William Reeves & Son and the cost of ten guineas included its carriage to Charlcombe and erection there. It still exists (though possibly not in its original location) on the south wall of the church (see opposite).[12]

Am¹. Bro¹. forward		15 2 6
To Cash Paid for Bran		- 2 6
To D° Paid the Fine for Burying in Linen		2 10 -
To D° Paid the Carpenters Bill for Removing Seats		1 0 6
To D° Paid Lansdown Turnpike		- 3 6
To D° Paid for a Marble Monument		10 10 -
		£29 9 0
Mourning for Man Serv¹.		
To Cash Paid M᷑ Sims for a Suit of Mourning as pr Bill		6 - -
2 Squares Muslin for Cravats	4/3	- 8 6
2 Pair Worsted Hose	6/-	- 12 -
2 Mourning Handkerchiefs	3/3	- 6 6
1 Pair Gloves		- 2 6
To Cash Paid M᷑ Frankham for a Fine Hat & Stamp		1 6 -
		£ 8 15 6
for Mrs Stow		
20½ ys fine Bombazine	4/6	4 10 -
1 - Fine Brown Lawn	2/3	- 2 3
1 Pair Blk Silk Gloves	7/-	- 7 -
1 yd Jacconet Muslin	6/6	- 6 6
3 - ¼ Black Crape	5/6	- 16 6
1 Barcelona Handkerchief	6/-	- 6 -
2½ ys Black Jacconet	4/6	- 11 3
2 Mourning Handkerchief	3/6	- 7 -
2 Pair Worsted Hose	4/3	- 8 6
4¼ ys Black Mode	7/-	1 9 9
3¼ - Lining D°	3/-	- 9 9
2½ - Ribbon	6d	- 1 3
		£9 15 9

Sacred to the Memory of
WILHELMENA JOHANNA LILLINGSTON
Relict of the late LUKE LILLINGSTON Esq[r]
of *Ferriby Grange* near *Hull Yorkshire*
she died at *Bath* January 30th 1806
in her 66th Year.

12 ys Black Bombazett	2/4	1 8 -
1 - Jacconet Muslin	5/6	- 5 6
1 Barcelona Handkerchief	5/-	- 5 -
3 ys ¼ Black Crape	5/6	- 16 6
4 - ½ Ell Mode	6/-	1 4 -
3 - Lining - D°	3/-	- 9 -
1 Pair Woms. Black Gloves	3/3	- 3 3
1 Pair Woms. Worsted Hose	3/3	- 3 3
1 yd Brown Irish	18d	- 1 6
2½ Ribbon	6	- 1 3
2 Squares Muslin	2/6	- 5 -
		£ 6 2 3
1 Pair Black Kid Gloves for	3/3	- 3 3
2 ys Love Ribbon M[rs] Shipton 6d		- 1 -
		£ - 4 3
To Amount of Funeral as stated to M[r]. Dottin		58 5 6
To amount of Cash Paid by B & B		29 9 -
To am[t]. of Man Serv[ts]. Mourning		8 16 6
To D° of M[rs]. Stows D°		9 16 9
To D° of Maid Servants D°		5 2 3
To D° of. Nurse		- 4 3
		£111 12 3

3. Transcript of Messrs Ballans & Bradley's account to Mr Leigh-Perrot.
Hampshire Record Office, 23M93/51/1-18.

The sale of Mrs Lillingston's household goods was then advertised:

> To be sold by Auction by C. Trimnell On the Premises, on Tuesday the 18th of March inst., and following day, at eleven, all the household furniture, linen, etc. of a lady deceased, at No. 10 Rivers Street, Bath, comprising four post and field bedsteads, with cotton hangings; goose feather beds; hair mattresses; counterpaines, quilts, and blankets; mahogany articles in wardrobe, double chest, dining and card tables, chests of drawers, night-tables, chairs, etc.; pier and dressing glasses; Wilton and Scotch carpets; a bracket clock, smoke jack, good kitchen utensils, table and bed linen, etc. etc. To be viewed Monday March 17th; when catalogues may be had at the place of sale, and of the Auctioneer, No. 13 Westgate Street.

Paid	£ s d		£. s. d
Proving the Will &c	44:3:6	Brought forward	1434:7:1
Funeral Expences &c	115:12:0	Servants Wages	16:8:6
Legacy to Francis Varley	220:0:0	James &c	32:15:6
Mrs Hindy	200:0:0	Mr Tickell	10:0:0
Mrs Habersham	200:0:0	Mr Day, apothecary	10:0:0
Mrs Maycock	100:0:0	House Bills	23:18:0
Mr Dottin	100:0:0	Daniel, Wine merchant	4:12:0
Mr Leigh Perrot	100:0:0	Christmas, Brewer	2:11:6
Molly Stowe	90:0:0	Skrine, Grocer	2:13:2
Miss Austen	50:0:0	Garthwayte, Chymist	5:7:4
Miss Jane Austen	50:0:0	Taylor, for keeping a Horse	7:9:6
Mrs Senior	21:0:0	Barratt, Bookseller	1:10:0
Mrs Rugge	21:0:0	Bishop, Ironmonger	2:2:10
Mary Stowe	8:6:0	Sheppard, Painter	23:12:0
Mr Walter	5:5:0	Shipway, Carpenter	3:5:7
Mrs Ann Walter	5:5:0	Lanham, Milliner	2:8:6
Mrs Dottin	5:5:0	Carpenter, Schoolmaster	1:8:10
Mrs Leigh Perrot	5:5:0	Sundry small articles	2:16:6
Duty on Legacies	93:3:7	Letters, Stamps &c	2:5:6
Carried forward	1434:7:1		1559:9:7
		Received	£ s d
		Money in the House	154:16:0
		Dividend on 600£ Consols	9:0:0
		Sold 600£ Consols	561:14:0
		House sold for 1300£, Conveyance 14:6 = 1285:14	1285:14:0
		Paid by Miss Corthurst	5:7:6
			1814:7:6

1814:7:6
1589:9:7
224:17:11
10:18:5
235:16:4

4. The balance sheet drawn up by Mr Leigh-Perrot in settling Mrs Lillingston's estate. (*Reproduced by courtesy of Hampshire Record Office, 23M93/51/1-18*)

Mrs Lillingston's investments were sold by agents in London, and the house was sold privately to a Mr Russell. Mr Leigh-Perrot's lawyers, Messrs Watts & Griffith, presented him on 4 March with a bill totalling £23.5s.2d. for their attendance, correspondence and legal documentation in these matters.

Following this liquidation of Mrs Lillingston's assets, Mr Leigh-Perrot settled all other outstanding bills and distributed their bequests to the legatees. He drew up a neat list and balance-sheet for himself, transcribed below. For all his trouble his own residuary legacy only amounted to £235.16s.4d.

Paid	£	S	D		£	S	D
Proving the Will &c	44	3	6	Brought forward	1434	7	1
Funeral Expenses &c	115	12	0	Servants Wages	16	8	6
Legacy to Francis Varley	220	0	0	Taxes &c	32	15	6
Mrs Hendy	200	0	0	Mr Tickell	10	0	0
Mrs Habersham	200	0	0	Mr Hay, Apothecary	10	0	0
Mrs Maycock	100	0	0	House Bills	23	18	0
Mr Dottin	100	0	0	Daniel, Wine Merchant	4	12	0
Mr Leigh Perrot	100	0	0	Christinaz, Brewer	2	11	6
Molly Stowe	90	0	0	Skrine, Grocer	2	13	3
Miss Austen	50	0	0	Garthwayte, Chymist	5	7	4
Miss Jane Austen	50	0	0	Taylor, for keeping a Horse	7	9	6
Mrs Senior	21	0	0	Barratt, Bookseller	1	10	0
Mrs Rugge	21	0	0	Bishop, Ironmonger	2	2	10
Mary Howse	8	8	0	Sheppard, Painter	23	12	0
Mr Walter	5	5	0	Shipway, Carpenter	3	5	7
Mrs Ann Walter	5	5	0	Lanham, Milliner	2	8	6
Mrs Dottin	5	5	0	Carpenter, Schoolmaster	1	8	0
Mrs Leigh Perrot	5	5	0	Sundry small articles	2	16	6
Duty on Legacies	93	3	7	Letters, Stamps &c	2	3	6
Carried forward	1434	7	1		1589	9	7
				Received	£	S	D
				Money in the House	154	16	0
				Dividend on 600£ Consols	9	0	0
				Sold 600£ Consols	361	10	0
1814	7	6		House sold for 1300£			
1589	9	7		Conveyance	14	6	
224	17	11			1285	14	1285 14 0
10	18	5	Final Dividend from	Paid by Miss Coulthurst		3	7 6
235	16	4	Sherlock & C°		1814	7	6

In the spring of 1806 Mrs Austen and her daughters (Mr Austen had
died early in 1805) were on the verge of leaving Bath for good; they
spent most of the summer visiting friends and relations, and did not
settle again until they found lodgings in Southampton in October 1806.
No letters of Jane's survive from this unsettled period of her life, so
there is no information as to whether Mrs Lillingston's legacy came as
a surprise to her or not, or what her feelings were when she learnt of
it. This lump sum of £50 was sufficient to cover her whole year's
expenditure in 1807, and perhaps allowed for some small luxuries as
well.[13] The Austen sisters had evidently not found Mrs Lillingston's
company enthralling, but on the latter's side it may perhaps have been
the grief of the total rift between herself and her daughter which led
her to transfer affection towards two young women very much of her
daughter's age.

When Jane started writing *Persuasion* on 8 August 1815, and set the
scenes so firmly and factually in the Bath she remembered from nine
years before, she cannot have failed to remember also Mrs Lillingston
– perhaps with a touch of remorse that she had not been more interested
in returning the affection of this kind-hearted, rather dull old lady,
living alone with her dog and her books in Rivers Street. She must
have recalled too how her uncle Mr Leigh-Perrot had sold the Rivers
Street house to a Mr Russell; it is therefore probably no coincidence
that Anne Elliot's mother-substitute is Lady Russell who lives in
Rivers Street. Jane sketched in Lady Russell as being ' ... a woman
rather of sound than of quick abilities ... of strict integrity herself,
with a delicate sense of honour ... a benevolent, charitable, good
woman, and capable of strong attachments; most correct in her
conduct, strict in her notions of decorum, and with manners that were
held a standard of good-breeding. She had a cultivated mind, and
was, generally speaking, rational and consistent ... ' even though she
'seemed to love [Elizabeth Elliot] rather because she would love her,
than because Elizabeth deserved it'. Later on, the ungrateful Elizabeth
Elliot tells her sister Anne to ' ... take back that tiresome book she
would lend me, and pretend I have read it through ... Lady Russell
quite bores one with her new publications ... I thought her dress
hideous the other night ... Something so formal and *arrangé* in her air!
and she sits so upright!'

Does Lady Russell owe more to Mrs Lillingston than just her address?
In this character, does Jane pay a belated tribute to the benefactress
unappreciated in past years?

Appendix: A Funeral Procession

5. *A Funeral Procession* by Thomas Rowlandson, c.1805-10. Pen and watercolour over pencil. For details see the exhibition catalogue by John Riely, *Rowlandson Drawings from the Paul Mellon Collection* (1978).

Funerals of the nobility had in the past been organised by the College of Heralds, but by the eighteenth century undertakers had come into being as a profession and had become responsible for arranging funerals for the gentry and middle classes. The mutes with their black-swathed wands or staves, and the featherman carrying a tray of black plumes upon his head, had replaced the line of heralds carrying emblems of nobility. The truncheons and rods carried by the bearers and pages were token defences against bodysnatchers who might attempt to waylay the cortège.

It seems to have been quite usual for people to be interred outside their parish of residence; in some cases this may have been due to some earlier family connection which meant a vault was already constructed there, but in others it may merely have been an excuse for displaying the grandeur of the funeral procession. In Mrs Lillingston's case, it will be noted that although she had asked for only two horses each for the hearse and mourning coach, Eleazar Pickwick had insisted upon four for each vehicle.

Notes

1   Public Record Office, London: PROB.11.1440.

2   Eighteen in all; now owned by his collateral descendants and deposited in the Hampshire Record Office, Winchester: reference 23M93/51/1-18. Unless otherwise specified, all documents mentioned in this article are in this group.

3   Her name is spelt thus in the burial register of Charlcombe church and on her memorial tablet there, but she signs herself 'Willielma' and this spelling appears in Burke's *Landed Gentry* and in other documents.

4   For Mrs Lillingston and her descendants see Burke's *Landed Gentry*, Foster's *Alumni Oxonienses* and Venn's *Alumni Cantabrigienses;* further information on earlier Lillingstons has kindly been provided by the Humberside County Archivist, March 1986. The Walters are mentioned in G.F. Russell Barker & Alan H. Stenning, *The Record of Old Westminsters*, Vol.II (1928).

5   John Pollock, *Wilberforce* (1977), pp.156-57.

6   *Gentleman's Magazine*, 1797.

7   Humberside County Record Office: East Riding Deeds Register, No. 443, ff. 282-286, 14 and 15 August 1797.

8   Humberside CRO: East Riding Deeds Register, No. 200, ff. 134-136, 31 July 1800.

9   Deirdre Le Faye, ed., *Jane Austen's Letters*, (Oxford, 3rd (new) ed., 1995), pp.83, 84, 88, 90.

10   For information on such lace suits, unfashionable by this date but still valuable, see Anne Buck, *Dress in Eighteenth Century England* (1979), pp.19, 65, 157, 163 & 191.

11   For details of burial practices, mourning etiquette and the duties of funeral attendants, see Council for British Archaeology Report No.85 (1993), Vol.1, J. Reeve & M. Adams, *Across the Styx*, and Vol.2, T. Molleson & M. Cox, *The Middling Sort*; M. Cox & G. Stock, 'Nineteenth Century Bath-stone Walled Graves at St. Nicholas's Church, Bathampton' in *Somerset Archaeology and Natural History*, Vol.138 (Taunton Castle, 1995), pp.131-50; Nicholas Penny, *Mourning* (1981); John Morley, *Death, Heaven and the Victorians* (1971), pp.19-31, 63-71; P. Cunnington & C. Lucas, *Costume for Births, Marriages & Deaths* (1972), pp.148-51, 159-63 & 193-97; Lou Taylor, *Mourning Dress* (1983), pp.28-34, 108-19, 126-30, 226-32 & 288-304.

12   The writer's thanks are due to the Revd A. Francis Bell, rector of Charlcombe, for providing this information in 1985.

13   Patrick Piggott, 'Jane Austen's Southampton Piano', in Jane Austen Society *Report* for 1980 (Alton, 1981), pp.6-9. When Jane Austen left Steventon in 1801 her pianoforte was sold for eight guineas, and it seems that she did not buy another until she settled in Chawton in 1809. However, in 1807 her expenses for the year amounted to £42.4s.8d., and of this total, amongst other items, she spent £13.19s.3d. on 'Cloathes [*sic*] and Pocket [money]', £6.4s.4d. on 'Presents', £3.10s.3½d. on 'Charity', and £2.13s.6d. on 'Hire Piano Forte'. Something of this expenditure may have been thanks to Mrs Lillingston's legacy.

Acknowledgements

The writer's thanks are due to the collateral descendants of Mr Leigh-Perrot for their kindness in allowing access to the family archive.

EDWARD DAVIS: NINETEENTH-CENTURY BATH ARCHITECT AND PUPIL OF SIR JOHN SOANE

Michael Forsyth

In Regency London surely the most exacting articled training an architect could receive was at the office of Sir John Soane (1753-1837), given his leading professional status, prolific output and personal style – most importantly at the Bank of England – and not least his interest in education. The Bath architect, Edward Davis (1802-52), who spent two years there, said it gave him a 'passport to life', going on as he did to enjoy a successful architectural practice of his own. Soane in 1806 had succeeded his own teacher, George Dance, as Professor of Architecture at the Royal Academy, and delivered his famous lectures there from 1809 until the year before his death.[1] He also took considerable interest in his own pupils' progress, even after they had left his employment, as the correspondence between Soane and Edward Davis shows. Moreover, Soane's office, where his pupils and assistants worked six days a week throughout the hours of daylight, was contained within his own home and museum at 13 Lincoln's Inn Fields. Soane left this fascinating treasure trove of instructive antiquities to the nation provided that nothing be changed, and so it survives today.

Yet surprisingly little is known about Soane's pupils after they left his office, and of the many pupils who passed through his articled training during his long career relatively few went on to develop illustrious and productive practices of their own. Soane was a hard taskmaster and a man of difficult temperament, 'austere, exacting, touchy and neurotic',[2] and more ambitious, less compliant architects may not have stayed the course – (Sir) Robert Smirke (1780-1867) left after a few months. One of the most successful pupils was George Basevi (1794-1845) whose career was cut short by his early death, falling through the belfry floor of Ely Cathedral. Perhaps the most talented was the 'odd and impracticable' Joseph Michael Gandy (1771-1843),[3] among whose few completed buildings is the Greek Revival 'Doric House' at Sion Hill, Bath of 1817, built for the painter Thomas Barker. The handful of others who succeeded as architects in private practice or public service are today little known, and Edward Davis provides a rare example where we can explore the interesting question as to what extent the influence of Soane is evident in a pupil's works. The pared-down classicism of Soane's personal style was almost by definition inimitable, while the idiosyncracy of his work, lying as it did outside the accepted Roman and later Greek classicism practised by his contemporaries, was in Soane's day seen as a criticism.[4]

The architecture of Edward Davis, at least for the first few years of his practice before he developed a secure personal style of his own, reflects the influence of his master, both in architectural detailing and in his ingenuity at planning the building on its site. His buildings, of which the main corpus is a series of Italianate picturesque villas, also represent remarkably early examples of the newly emerging styles of villa architecture as propogated by the publication of numerous and widely read pattern books. In the local context of Bath, Davis's work belongs to a body of architectural works carried out in the early nineteenth century by, or under the influence of, prominent London architects. In addition to Gandy's Doric House these include William Wilkins's Masonic Hall, York Street of 1817 and the Doric portico added in 1806 to the Kingston Assembly Rooms, Decimus Burton's now destroyed Tepid Swimming Bath adjacent to John Wood's Hot Bath, and Partis College, Lower Weston, of 1827 by Samuel and Philip Flood Page.

Edward Davis was born on 9 March 1802,[5] the youngest of five children, and son of a painter, Charles Davis[6] whose own father of the same name was a pastellist. Edward Davis had a brother, Charles, seven years his senior, whose son became the successful later Victorian architect, Major Charles Edward Davis (1827-1902). Major Davis designed many buildings including the Empire Hotel but he is perhaps most notable for having uncovered and excavated the Roman Baths.[7]

Edward Davis became a pupil of Sir John Soane on 25 May 1824, when Soane was already over seventy years old. It is not known how Soane selected his pupils; some are known to have been family friends, but presumably Davis must have displayed promising draughtsmanship, for in 1825 he was awarded a medal by the Society of Arts. On arriving each day the pupils' exact time of arrival was entered into the day books, which survive, together with the projects that they worked on each day. Work began at nine, six days a week, and although the leaving time is not recorded, the working day was possibly governed by the hours of daylight. Christmas Day, Good Friday and Whitsuntide were holidays.

Davis's principal task during his time with Soane was to produce drawings for the Board of Trade and Privy Council Offices, Whitehall, London. He was also much involved with the new Law Courts at the Palace of Westminster, the new dining room at 10 Downing Street (at that time the Chancellor of the Exchequer's house) and with Soane's three late churches. He and the other pupils also spent much time making section drawings of the museum and other rooms at 13 Lincoln's Inn Fields. Davis took occasional leave of absence to visit Bath – one month over Christmas 1824 and two weeks in mid-May 1825 – then on Thursday 18 August we read, 'Davis absent from a *broken leg*'. The cause of the absence is underlined in the book and it is tantalising that we cannot know the circumstances of the accident. It was clearly incapacitating for he next came to the office the following Tuesday when 'Davis received permission from Mr Soane to be absent a month commencing on Thursday 25th'. He returned on 27 September and resumed work on plans and sections of the Cabinet Room at the Foreign Office, but for most of the autumn he drew Soane's museum, breakfast room, study and monk's room for publication. He then worked on miscellaneous projects into the spring, notably the Bethnal Green Chapel, on which the entire office worked for a month during January and February. He spent his final few weeks 'drawing ornaments, etc', plans and elevations of a triumphal arch, and views of the Board of Trade for exhibition. The day books contain little in the way of human insight and rarely humour. However, on his penultimate day, Thursday 13 April 1826 'Davis came last' to which had later been added '... as usual', though next day 'Davis came first'.

Returning to Bath from London he set up in practice at 3 Westgate Buildings, a property that he owned and from where he practised for the remainder of his career. The annual Poor Relief Assessments show both Edward and his brother Charles during the succeeding years to be owners and lessors of several properties in the parishes and the city, and it would appear that their father left them quite well off. Edward himself occupied a house at *Bear Inn*, Wells Road in the early 1830s, and he owned, or by 1836 possibly sublet from another owner, four other properties at the same address. It is reasonable to attribute as an early work by Davis a porch extension to 24 New King Street, Bath, which shows the strong influence of Soane. This has incised pilasters capped by acroteria decorated with anthemia, a very shallow pediment and a Greek key frieze. At the same time the ground floor was rusticated and a round-arch window inserted, the first floor window cills were lowered to floor level (common practice in nineteenth-century Bath) and a balcony added with railings of a swept design derived from Soane's house at 13 Lincoln's Inn Fields. A design dated 1830 for a Toll-House on the London Road near Bailbrook is also by Davis, as may be seen from entries in the papers of the Bath Turnpike Trust. The building is near-octagonal with rusticated ashlar walls, rusticated wings with plain pilasters and a shallow pediment, and a portico of square columns with inset arches supported on brackets, with a simple pedimented attic over the centre (fig.1).[8] It would be intriguing also to know more of his Octagon Temple for Sydney Gardens, Bath. *The Original Bath Guide* notes that 'a very elegant Rustic Temple, erected under the supervision of Mr. ED. DAVIS, Architect, of Bath, and appropriated on Show Days to the Exhibition of The Bath Horticultural Society, presents also a very pleasing and ornamental object'.[9]

The first fully recorded work of Davis was a group of neo-Tudor houses at Entry Hill, Bath, now Entry Hill Drive. The designs were exhibited at the Royal Academy in 1828,[10] the first of several to be accepted during his career, and it is evident that he was indebted to Soane for his help, for Davis wrote to thank him from Bath on 30 April:[11]

> Sir,
> I beg leave to thank you for your very kind and successful pleading to obtain my Drawing an admission in your honorable Academy – Proud am I to have it placed (and by your interest to) in that room which has been so often ornamented by your admirable and instructive Designs – At the same time that I return thanks for the present favor I must not forget the past ones, I allude to those when I had the honor and advantage of studying under your instructions which has raised me above myself and will be a passport to me through life – I intend shortly to pay a visit to London when I hope to have the pleasure of seeing you in health, and the honor of thanking you in person for your abundant favors.
> I have the honor to be
> Sir
> Your most obedient humble servant
> Edward Davis
>
> To
> John Soane Esq RA

Designs for seventeen houses were exhibited at the Royal Academy but only five were built, and although noted in the catalogue as 'now building' their construction was in fact phased and they became occupied between 1829-36.[12] The project was a speculation by a local solicitor Richard Else, who practised in Harington Place, but who possibly occupied the houses progressively as they were finished. The houses are approached from the old Warminster Road up a private road flanked by

- A VIEW of the NEW TOLL-HOUSE on the LONDON ROAD near BAILBROOK-

1. Design for a new Toll-House on the London Road near Bailbrook, dated 1830. (*Reproduced by courtesy of Bath & North East Somerset Library and Archive Service: Bath Central Library*)

vermiculated stone piers. The first to be completed was Entry Hill Villa,[13] which was occupied by April 1829 and purchased by Charles Davis, Edward's elder brother in 1836, followed by Newfield Villa (now Newfield) first occupied by a Lieut. M. Novorelski from 1831. The next was Granville House which was completed by 1835 and, although again Charles Davis was owner, Edward Davis himself lived at the house with his wife and daughter from 1835 until 1841.[14] Curiously the house is symmetrical, with a recessed centre forming the front entrance between flanking projecting wings decorated with tall Tudoresque chimneys and pinnacles. The name is associated with the Civil War royalist general, Sir Bevil Grenville who was defeated and killed at the Battle of Lansdown in 1642 (whose descendents later called themselves Granville) and whose grandson erected a commemorative monument at Lansdown. Edward Davis was commissioned to restore the monument and in so doing removed Grenville's coat-of-arms and incorporated it into the wall of Granville House.[15] The principal edifice on the estate was intended to be Entry Hill House, which was occupied by 1836, an asymmetrical building with mullion and transom windows, an oriel bay window and battlemented parapets. The final house was The Briars, occupied by 1836.

In 1829 Davis applied unsuccessfully for the post of Surveyor to the County of Somerset, and on 16 December 1829 Soane wrote from Lincoln's Inn Fields supporting Davis's appointment:[16]

> Dear Sir,
> The Bearer of this Mr Edward Davis of Bath is a candidate for the vacant appointment of Surveyor to the County of Somerset, in whose success I feel much interest – Mr Davis having been sometime in my office. I can testify to his activity zeal and probity and should you be at liberty to afford him the advantage of your powerful support I shall esteem it a personal favour.
> I am ...
> Yours faithfully
> JS
>
> Copy to:
> Col. Horner
> Sir J. S. Hippersley, Bart.
> Sir Alexr. Hood, Bart.
> G. E. Allen Esq

The same year Edward Davis was commissioned to design the 46-acre Royal Victoria Park, Bath, the history of which is meticulously documented, albeit in a self-congratulatory tone, in the Park Committee's Annual Reports, quoted in Frederick Hanham's *Manual for the Park* which records the species planted.[17] The local architect G. P. Manners had produced a design for the park in 1827, but it was Davis's later design that was carried out. The idea was instigated by a group of local businessmen, who convened a private committee in May and June of 1829 to discuss improvements to the Crescent Fields, land south of the Royal Crescent belonging to Lady Rivers. At their first meeting it was decided to extend the plan to include the Common Fields to the west to provide sufficient land for the ornamental plantations, walks and drives. Davis produced a Plan of the Improvements on the Bath Common Estate and this design was approved on 26 October after an interview, according to the Park Committee's first Annual Report, which was 'conducted in a most friendly manner'. Davis's plan was then submitted to the Corporation who unanimously decided to proceed, while Lady Rivers granted the approach through the Crescent Fields. After a meeting of local residents on 1 January 1830 chaired by the mayor, subscriptions were raised and work started immediately, employing nearly 200 men.

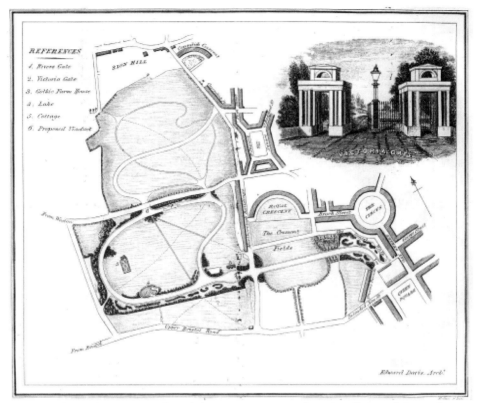

2. Plan of Royal Victoria Park and the entrance screen from Marlborough Lane, from a drawing by Edward Davis engraved by Hollway, printed in the *New Bath Guide*, c.1832. (*Reproduced by courtesy of Bath Central Library*)

Davis's 1831 plan which accompanied the First Report of the Committee follows the principles of landscape design described in the many current books on the subject (fig.2). These notably include Humphrey Repton's *Fragments on the Theory and Practice of Landscape Gardening* of 1816, John Claudius Loudon's *Hints on the Formation of Gardens and Pleasure Grounds* of 1812, and his popular *Encyclopaedia of Gardening* of 1823 that ran to many editions. The plan was in two parts. The eastern part extended from Queen's Parade to Marlborough Lane south of the Royal Crescent, and included the existing Gravel and Subscription walks and the Crescent Fields. The larger part to the west lay between Marlborough Lane and Park Lane. An 'immense plantation' of more than 25,000 evergreens, forest trees and shrubs was formed which 'belted the whole meadow' from the lower end of Marlborough Buildings.

A carriage drive and gravel walk were built through this plantation, with shrubberies on both sides along the South Walk and on the North Walk along the upper boundary. These formed 'agreeable drives' and 'shady promenades', while a 'fish pond' with an encircling gravel walk created a central feature.

The park was open to the public by midsummer, and by the autumn entrances from Queen Square and Marlborough Buildings had been completed. The latter entrance screen, which is in the style of Soane, forms a pair of triumphal arches and owes much to the church of St John's, Bethnal Green, on which Davis was involved in his last few months at Soane's office. The park was officially opened on 28 October 1830 by the Duchess of Kent and her daughter, Princess Victoria, hence the name Royal Victoria Park. The Committee's Report presented at the First Anniversary on 7 January 1831 states that the adjacent Park Farm house, designed as a *cottage ornée*, was also being built. The report is fulsome in its praise:

> The Committee disclaim any participation in that just meed of praise so liberally bestowed – it belongs to Mr. Edward Davis, Architect, who so tastefully laid it out, and to him exclusively. He it was, who has in this instance, so happily blended the luxuriance of nature with the classic proportions of art, as to render the Park at once an ornament to his native city, and a lasting memorial to his own fame.[18]

Edward Davis's next recorded design was another Royal Academy submission in 1832,[19] a 'Design for a Villa intended to be built near to Bath', for which again Davis sought his master's help, for he wrote on 22 April:[20]

> Edward Davis presents his most respectful compliments to Sir John Soane and solicits of him his influence (which he was so kind as to use on a previous occasion) with the hanging Committee of the Royal Academy to obtain an admission of some Drawings which he has sent there for exhibition through his friend Mr Bailey.
> Edward Davis offers many apologies to Sir John Soane for taking so great a liberty but which he trusts he will pardon.

Soane promptly obliged, writing on 25 April from Lincoln's Inn Fields to a Mr. Howard. This time he gives a touching insight into Davis's character:[21]

> Dear Sir,
> Mr. Edward Davis, some years since a pupil of mine, a very modest unassuming young man, and much respected in the County of Somerset,

has sent three architectural drawings to the Royal Academy for the ensuing Exhibition which he is given to understand have all been rejected – may I request that you will have the goodness to take the trouble to arrange that they may again be brought before the Committee in the hope that in further consideration some of them at least may be admitted. Yours faithfully

The identity and form of this villa are unknown, but the core of Edward Davis's work over the next few years was a series of Italianate picturesque villas all containing near-identical repeated elements, but each demonstrating inventive planning and an awareness of the uniqueness of the site. The villas are remarkably in tune with the architectural pattern books that were being published contemporaneously. These books portray an image of Tuscany as seen through the paintings of Claude, with towers and campaniles, picturesque asymmetry, loggias and French windows opening directly onto terraced gardens. The style built on the cult of the Picturesque, a movement initiated at the end of the eighteenth century through the writings of Richard Payne Knight, Uvedale Price and Humphrey Repton. Their publications reacted against the artificial landscapes of Lancelot 'Capability' Brown and developed a new taste for naturalistic, uncontrived landscape, together with an interpenetration of internal and external space. The most popular of the architectural pattern books were J. M. Gandy's two principal publications of 1805, *The Rural Architect* and *Designs for Cottages, Cottage Farms and Other Rural Buildings*, Buonarotti Papworth's *Rural Residences* of 1818, J. G. Jackson's *Designs for Villas* (1828), his teacher Robert Wetton's *Designs for Villas in the Italian Style of Architecture* (1830), Francis Goodwin's *Rural Architecture* (1835), and notably Charles Parker's *Villa Rustica*, published in parts between 1833 and 1841 with a second edition in 1848. The last-named was the first to introduce an Italianate style of house with shallow-pitch roofs and deeply projecting eaves penetrated by tall chimneys, round-arch and tripartite windows, of a type that was to be widely adopted by suburban housebuilders later in the nineteenth century.

Davis's villas belong to this style, yet are remarkably early examples of the genre. The first was precisely contemporary with Parker's initial publication, and for the most part the villas predate similar designs published in Loudon's popular *The Suburban Gardener and Villa Companion* of 1838 and the *Encyclopaedia of Cottage, Farm and Villa Architecture* of 1846. Davis's villas also substantially predate Henry Edmund Goodridge's Tuscan villas of a similar type with projecting eaves, the semi-detached Casa Bianca (originally Villa Bianca) and La Casetta of 1846 and Fiesole of 1848, on Bathwick Hill.

3. Smallcombe Grove (now Oakwood), Bathwick Hill, Bath, with Edward Davis's Italianate extension, c.1833 (left), incorporating Benjamin Barker's original villa (right).

The first of Edward Davis's villas in this style was Smallcombe Grove of 1833, known after 1856 as Oakwood, on Bathwick Hill (fig.3). Uniquely among Davis's villas, the work at Smallcombe Grove was an extension to an existing villa that he radically altered internally and externally to integrate with the new work to form a unified design. The existing house, the first on the upper slopes of Bathwick Hill, had been built by the landscape painter, Benjamin Barker (1776-1838), the brother of the more famous Thomas Barker, nine years his senior, who had commissioned Gandy to design Doric House. Benjamin had bought the land in 1814 jointly with his brother-in-law the flower painter James Hewlett. According to the antiquarian and cartographer John Britten, Barker

> ... painted numerous small landscapes, which were very popular, and readily sold at the exhibitions of the British Institution. He saved money, purchased and possessed a very delightful villa, on the west side of Claverton Down, where his hanging gardens, trout stream, woods, and paintings were calculated to command the admiration, and almost the envy, of his visitors. At this delectable retreat I spent many happy hours, in company with some of the Bath 'Worthies,' amongst whom was James Hewett [sic], a distinguished English flower painter whose sister Barker married.[22]

Barker's biographer Edward Mangin described the place 'as beautiful as time and man could make it'[23] and by 1817 it was evidently locally well known, as Barker was visited that year by Queen Charlotte, accompanied by Princess Elizabeth and the Duke of Clarence.

Barker's address was initially Woodland Cottage, which was possibly an earlier building now incorporated into the existing coach house. Sometime between 1814 and 1833, when Barker retired to Devon, he built for himself a larger but still modest house, perfectly square in plan with an M-shape roof and rendered in Roman cement, which he named Smallcombe Villa.[24] This structure forms the core of the main house today. During his last few years in Bath Barker became increasingly impecunious before he was forced to sell the house in 1833. It is therefore safe to assume that it was the new owner, Thomas Emmerson who commissioned Edward Davis to carry out the new works to transform the existing house into a large Italianate villa, which was renamed Smallcombe Grove.[25]

To Barker's original square house Davis added a wing containing a dining room and main bedroom facing west onto the garden (see fig.3). This has a projecting bay at ground floor and had an open tripartite loggia at first floor (which has now been glazed to extend the bedroom) and a roof of shallow pitch with projecting eaves and a campanile. This wing extends uphill to form an east section, originally containing an art gallery (later used as a billiards room) with servants' quarters and a kitchen, and stables and a coach house beyond. The coach house opening is in the form of a shouldered-arch, and axial to this is a Tuscan watch tower with a shallow-pitch lead roof and projecting eaves. The two sections of the new wing were articulated by a single-storey flat roof (which was infilled to provide additional servants' accommodation in 1871) and connected at bedroom level by a top-lit vaulted vestibule.

Internally the architectural details throughout the house are in the manner of Sir John Soane, several details echoing specifically the projects which Edward Davis is known to have worked on in the office of his master. Davis structured the plan and resolved the natural gradient of the site by forming a north-south circulation axis east of the dining room, linking street level to the drawing room above the garden. A cascading stone staircase descends from the entrance into a shallow-domed ashlar-faced rusticated hall. Beyond is a staircase hall (fig.4) containing a sequence of segmental arches and flanked by arcaded downstand pelmets with finials reminiscent of the Court of Chancery (and of Soane's own dining room and library). The dining room has a shallow groin-vaulted 'starfish' ceiling, Soane's favourite hallmark, which recalls Davis's work on the remodelled dining room at

4. Smallcombe Grove: the staircase hall.

10 Downing Street, and the drawing room has a ceiling similar to that of the dining room and library at 13 Lincoln's Inn Fields. Extensive use throughout the house of segmental arches, clerestory lighting, flush reeded skirtings, recessed architraves, paterae and other antique motifs and a system of incised linear ornamentation, gives a Soanian character.

It is uncertain to what extent Davis developed Barker's garden layout, but several features, including a stone bridge, fountain and balustrading, are of integrated design and form part of the Davis scheme. The reception rooms open onto terraces that overlook a formal parterre and fountain fed by plentiful spring water. This flows into a series of small ashlar-lined lakes linked by cascades, leading progressively to wilderness and views beyond. Because of the significance of the garden and its close relationship with the house it is not unreasonable to suppose that Davis was commissioned because of his interest in landscape design. Davis's work was recorded as built in sales particulars[26] drawn in 1856 by the Bristol architect W. B. Gingell (1819-99) to market the property (it was sold that year) (fig.5).[27] These comprise a single sheet with small but accurate floor plans, a perspective view and a drawn survey of the garden.

In 1836 Davis was commissioned to design a large new rectory near Frome, Somerset. The client was Edmund Boyle, eighth Earl of Cork and Orrery of Marston House, Marston Bigot, and the house was for his youngest son, the Hon. and Rev. Richard Boyle. The isolated parish had a population in 1841 of just 534, and in 1805 the Boyle family had bought the advowson, the right of presenting a clergyman to the living, from the Marquess of Bath for £2,632. Richard Boyle, who had been blinded in one eye by a cricket ball while at Winchester, became curate of Marston Bigot in 1835 and rector the following year at the age of 24.

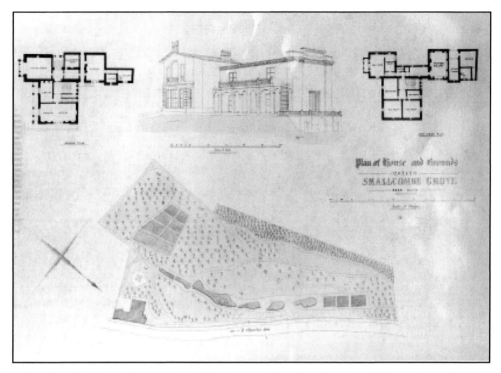

5. Smallcombe Grove: illustrations of the house and garden, drawn in 1856 as sales particulars when the house was placed on the market.

A finely drafted set of Edward Davis's signed watercolour drawings for the design exists, including floor plans, a structural roof plan, elevations, sections and two perspectives, and the completed building remains little altered from the original design (figs.6-7). Again the house is a picturesque assymetrical Italianate villa, with characteristic projecting eaves and tripartite windows, but the interior is Greek Revival. To the left of the south elevation, the main bedroom has an open loggia similar to Smallcombe Grove with a tripartite opening, recessed glazing and a projecting bay to the dining room below. To the right the drawing room has a bay to the ground floor only. The façades here are constructed not of ashlar but rangework with ashlar dressings, presumably because the house was intended to be covered with ivy and wisteria, as indeed early photographs show.

If elements of Davis's façades are somewhat repetitious, he demonstrates originality and skill in the arrangement of the house. The plan is well

6. (above) Rectory, Marston Bigot, near Frome, Somerset, 1836-9, built for the Hon. and Rev. Richard Boyle: watercolour perspective signed by Edward Davis.
7. (below) Rectory, Marston Bigot: rendered elevations and section signed by Edward Davis. (*Both reproduced by courtesy of George H. Boyle, Esq.*)

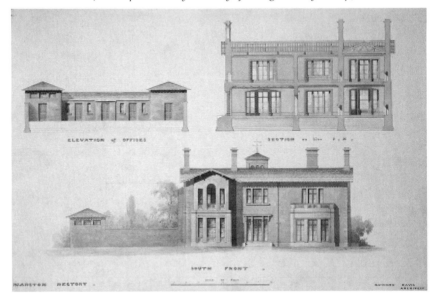

resolved on its site, and is ordered by symmetrical axes that are eroded and overlaid to create an informal, picturesque layout, turning the visitor this way and that. The drawing-room, library and dining room are on the south side facing a terraced formal balustraded Italianate garden with views to wooded hills beyond, while the north side is entirely for circulation. To the west a servants' wing extends north forming an entrance court and a yard with domestic offices and a dairy to the west. On the north elevation the front door, unusually, is in the corner on the left. A stone-flagged entrance hall beyond, with a fireplace, spans the width of the staircase hall which to the right extends the length of the main house. A cantilevered stone stair is contained within an ashlar-clad stairwell (sadly now painted) with Grecian Ionic columns. Over the stairwell the ceiling extends upwards to form a lantern glazed with amber-colour glass. Externally this forms an Italianate tower, suffusing the interior with a rich Soanic glow of yellow light. A sewing room upstairs was recorded in a sketch by Richard Boyle's wife, Eleanor Vere Boyle. It contains a chimneypiece flush with the wall and with incised decoration, with a detached mantleshelf supported on brackets – nearly identical with one also extant at Smallcombe Grove. The house was completed by 1839.[28]

In 1838 Edward Davis exhibited at the Royal Academy two further houses, both said to be 'now building'. One was the north east view of Twerton House, Bath, for Charles Wilkins, a wealthy mill owner,[29] 'his late residence having been taken down by the Great Western Railway Company who required the site in their line between Bath and Bristol'.[30] Wilkins did not remain there long as the house was acquired by the Carr family, another dynasty of mill-owners, after a fire in 1844 and was later known as Wood House. The house was Greek Revival style, with an Italianate west wing containing servants' quarters that survived the fire. Details of the house were recorded in sketches by Peter Coard before the house was demolished in 1965, including the elaborate base to the main staircase (fig.8).[31]

8. Twerton (later Wood) House, Bath, 1838. (*Drawing reproduced by courtesy of Peter Coard*)

The other house exhibited that year, 'now building from designs and under the supervision of Edward Davis', was another asymmetrical picturesque residence known as Barcombe at Barcombe Drive, Paignton, South Devon[32]. The house, built for N. H. Nugent, was possibly the most substantial which Davis built and originally stood alone in its grounds north of the town although it became surrounded by later development. Built in an eclectic Grecian-Gothic-Italianate style, its mixture of styles and asymmetry give the illusion of historical accretion. Unlike the other early nineteenth-century Torbay stucco villas, it was built of red sandstone with Bath stone dressings. The entrance front had shallow Gothic arched windows and doors, combined with a Doric four-column porch, with Doric triglyphs along the cornice. To the left was an Italianate tower with round-arched windows and dentil cornice. The garden elevation contained tripartite windows to the left, a canted bay towards the centre, and on the right the characteristic shallow pitch roof with projecting eaves and a slender campanile. Scandalously not listed by the Department of Environment, the house was demolished in 1989.

The last of this group of Italianate villas is known as Albury at Wrington, Somerset (later renamed le Moigne's but now known by the original name),

9. Albury, Wrington, Somerset, c.1836: detail of the Italianate west elevation with an open loggia to the main bedroom and projecting eaves.

built in the late 1830s for a solicitor. The house is entered from the north side between two nearly symmetrical wings. Each wing has tripartite windows at ground level with cornices supported on consoles and surmounted by acroteria, and round-arched windows at first floor. The west façade has the familiar projecting eaves and tripartite open loggia with recessed glazing to the main bedroom and tripartite windows to the drawing room below (fig.9). Inside, the hall is connected by arched openings to a cantilevered stone staircase lit by round-arched windows with amber glass margins. The staircase detail is similar to that at Wood House. The interior ironwork, joinery and plasterwork contain palmettes and other Greek Revival motifs and the window piers to the drawing room are inset with mirror strips.

Like most other practising architects of his day, Edward Davis carried out some church work. In 1833 he restored Prior Birde's Chapel in Bath Abbey Church, a delightful late medieval gem, and in 1834 published a series of lithographs of the chapel. These were entitled *Gothic Ornaments, etc., of Prior Birde's Oratory* and were made from drawings (now in the RIBA Drawings Collection) by Stephen Burchall (1806-?43) who had been a pupil of Soane from 1823-28, contemporary with Edward Davis. The project appears, however, to have been financially disastrous for Davis, according to the Council Minutes for 16 October 1835:

> Item 11: To consider a Letter from Mr Edward Davis, Architect of this City, respecting the expenses attending the Restoration of Prior Birde's Chapel which considerably exceeds the amount of subscription, soliciting the consideration of this Corpn.

> Mr Ed. Davis's Letter being now read and considered, Resolved: that as he undertook such work upon his own responsibility and as the Corporation were subscribers (amongst others) towards the Expenses upon the understanding that it was not to be commenced until the necessary Sum was raised, no further Contribution be made.

In 1844 Davis extended and altered St. Leonard's Church, Marston Bigot, Somerset, for the Hon. and Rev. Richard Cavendish Boyle for whom he had designed the rectory. It was to be his last work exhibited at the Royal Academy, and was said by the catalogue to be 'now building from the designs and under the supervision of [Edward Davis]'.[33] In 1786 Boyle's grandfather, the seventh Earl of Cork and Orerry had, by Private Act of Parliament, demolished the existing church. This was said to be 'a very ancient Building' but it interrupted his privacy and view from Marston House. He replaced it with a new church built on another site in neo-Gothic style, with three pointed-arch windows on each side of a battlemented parapet. He apparently designed it himself, for the drawings, which exist, are boldly inscribed, 'This plan belongs to me, Cork'. By the 1840s the rector required a chancel to be added to the church for, although the parish population was small, the church had become a popular venue for marriages which by then averaged forty a year. The alteration work which Davis carried out, although to a church of no great age or architectural merit, illustrates the contemporary radical attitude to church restoration, which only gradually disappeared in the nineteenth century. Architects rejected historical congruence and routinely made drastic alterations to churches, removing later additions to obtain a definite unity of style. Davis's chancel was neo-Norman, and the existing church was altered at the same time to be uniform. The windows to the nave and the tower were given round-arch heads, the new chancel was connected to the existing nave by a Romanesque arch, and the south façade of the nave was clad in ashlar. The Romanesque 'beak-head' mouldings to the entrance through the tower are deliberately left unfinished as if the Norman mason had died before he could finish his work.

In 1846 Davis entered a competition to rebuild Llandilo Church in Camarthenshire.[34] Fifty-two competitors entered, and the competition committee, on the recommendation of the Incorporated Church Building Society's surveyor, awarded Edward Davis first prize of fifty shillings. As was common at the time, the designs had to bear a motto that corresponded with the entrants' names in sealed envelopes to ensure anonymity. Davis's design bore the motto *Sic itur ad astra*, while the second prize of twenty shillings went to John Colston of Winchester, whose motto was *Spes*. However, despite Davis's design 'appearing to ... possess the most merit, and to be best adapted for the purposes set forth in the advertisement', the competition came to nothing, and the commission eventually went to Gilbert Scott.

Davis died on 30 April 1852 aged 50, leaving behind him a modest but significant legacy of works.[35] From the correspondence with Sir John Soane he clearly felt indebted to his master, and the 'very modest unassuming young man' is rare among the pupils for carrying forward at the early stages of his career the direct influence of his teacher. Looking forward as well as back, the Italianate villas are very early examples of the type later adopted in Bath by Henry Edmund Goodridge and which later in the century became commonplace with the influence of the *Villa Rustica*, *The Suburban Gardener and Villa Companion* and the *Encyclopedia of Cottage, Farm and Villa Architecture*.

Appendix 1: Projects by Sir John Soane with which Edward Davis assisted, 25 May 1824-14 April 1826

- Privy Council and Board of Trade Offices, Whitehall
- Pelwall Hall, Staffordshire for Purney Silitoe Esq
- New Law Courts, Palace of Westminster: proposed Gothic façade; The Lord Chancellor's Robing Room; Court of King's Bench
- Drawings of Soane's house at Lincoln's Inn Fields: the museum, offices, study, picture rooms, breakfast room
- St Peter's Church, Walworth (pulpit and reading desk)
- House of Lords, Westminster: Committee Rooms and new library
- Bank of England
- Holy Trinity Church, Marylebone
- St John's Church, Bethnal Green
- 10 Downing Street (at that time the Chancellor of the Exchequer's House): alterations including new dining room
- Addition to Sulby Hall, Northants for Rene Payne

Appendix 2: Known architectural works of Edward Davis

1830 (circa)	Alterations to 24 New King Street (attributed)
1828	Houses at Entry Hill, Bath
1830	Royal Victoria Park, Bath
1830	Toll-House on the London Road near Bailbrook
1832	Design for a Villa near Bath
1833 (circa)	Smallcombe Grove (Oakwood from 1856), Bathwick Hill, Bath
1833	Restoration of Prior Birde's Oratory, Bath Abbey Church
1834 (circa)	Restoration of Sir Bevil Grenville's monument, Lansdown
1836	Marston Rectory for the Hon. and Rev. Richard Boyle
1838	Twerton House, Bath, for Charles Wilkins, Esq.,
1838	Barcombe, Paignton, South Devon
1840 (circa)	Albury, Wrington
1844	Extension and alterations to St. Leonard's Church, Marston Bigot, Somerset
1846	Competition entry to rebuild Llandilo Church, Camarthenshire
n.d.	Octagon Temple, Sydney Gardens

Appendix 3: The Davis Family

Charles Davis
Pastellist
(1741-1805)
m. (1) 1764 (St James's Church, Bath)
Hannah Rotten (1726-82)
m. (2) 1792 (St James's Church, Bath)
Miss Townley

Jenny Davis	Charles Davis
m. 1782	painter
(Bath Abbey)	m. 1790
John Langton	(St Andrew's Church, Holborn, London)
	Lydia Winter

Jane	Charles Winter	Louisa	Richard	Edward
b. 1793	b. 30 May 1795	b. 1796	b. 1798	b. 9 March 1802
	architect			d. 30 April 1852
				architect

Major Charles Edward Davis
1827-1902
architect

Notes

1   See David Watkin, *Sir John Soane, Enlightenment Thought and the Royal Academy Lectures* (Cambridge University Press, 1996).

2   Howard Colvin, *A Biographical Dictionary of British Architects 1600-1840* (Yale University Press, 3rd ed., New Haven, 1995), p.905.

3   John Summerson, 'The Vision of J. M. Gandy' in *Heavenly Mansions* (1949).

4   This is quite the reverse of our own century when clients commission prominent architects because they want their building to have the unique style of their architect – Le Corbusier, Mies van der Rohe, Frank Lloyd Wright, etc.

5   Bath Abbey records.

6   The Victoria Art Gallery, Bath has portraits by Thomas Beach of Charles Davis the pastellist, Mrs Charles Davis, Mrs Charles Davis (jnr), and Miss Jenny Davis, and they have biographical information attached.

7   Barry Cunliffe, 'Major Davis: Architect and Antiquarian', *Bath History*, Vol.I (Gloucester, 1986), p.27.

8   James Lees-Milne and David Ford, *Images of Bath* (Richmond-upon-Thames, 1982), no.975, p.348.

9   Meylor and Sons, *The Original Bath Guide* (Bath, 1851), p.53. This is presumably the octagonal building depicted on the Cotterell and Spackman plan of Bath of 1852-54, and identified on the Ordnance Survey Map of 1885 as a 'Refreshments Room'.

10   Algernon Graves, *Royal Academy Exhibitors, 1769-1904* (1905), catalogue no.1130.

11   Sir John Soane's Museum, ref. archives: Private correspondence XV.B.23.1.

12   This and other dates relating to the Entry Hill houses are from the annual Poor Relief Assessments.

13   Known by 1841 as Gothic Cottage, now known via several other names as The Lodge.

14   1841 Census as well as the Poor Relief Assessments; the 1842 Poor Relief Assessments indicate he had vacated the house.

15   R. E. M. Peach, *Street Lore of Bath* (Bath, 1893).

16   Sir John Soane's Museum, ref. archives: Private correspondence XV.B.23.2.

17   Frederick Hanham, *A Manual for the Park; or, A Botanical Description of the Trees and Shrubs in the Royal Victoria Park, Bath* ...(1857), Bath Central Library. See also Robin Whalley, 'The Royal Victoria Park', *Bath History*, Vol.V (Bath, 1994).

18   The 1834 report notes, among numerous other improvements, a new carriage entrance from the Weston Road, which is hoped to be 'creditable to the taste of the architect'. The other architectural feature to be added – during 1837 – was the Victoria Column designed by the City Architect, G. P. Manners. From the reports it is evident that William McAdam, joint surveyor of the Bath Turnpike Trust, became involved from 1835 and that he supervised, without payment, the improvement and maintenance of the drives until 1843.

19   Graves, *ibid.*, catalogue no.1019.

20   Sir John Soane's Museum, ref. archives: Private correspondence XV.B.23.3.

21   Sir John Soane's Museum, ref. archives: Private correspondence XV.B.23.4.

22   John Britten, *Autobiography* (1856), p.225.

23   Edward Mangin, *A Memoir to the Artist* (1843).

24   Barker's house is clearly shown on a steelplate engraving published by John Britton in 1829, *Images of Bath*, no.133.

25   The house has been wrongly attributed in various publications to Henry Edmund Goodridge.

26   Copies in Hunt Collection, Vol.2, p.94 and C. P. Russell, *Maps & Plans of City of Bath*, Vol.2, p.120, both in Bath Central Library. This has led to further confusion that Gingell was connected with extending the building – see Neil Jackson, *Nineteenth Century Bath Architects & Architecture* (Bath, 1991), pp.74-5 (the house also misnamed), p.113 and p.115.

27   The house was acquired by the Dobson family who extended it, first in 1871 to add further servants' accommodation (the 1891 census records eight resident servants) and again in 1896 by the London architect John Brydon, architect of the Guildhall extensions and the Victoria Art Gallery. Brydon designed a substantial new wing to the east of the house on the garden

front in neo-Jacobean style with mullion and transom windows and leaded windows and a projecting bay with a drawing room and further bedrooms. The house was bought by the Aikman family in 1902, and acquired by General Booth of The Salvation Army as a nursing home in 1928. It was known as the Aikman Eventide Home until 1992, when the original villa with its garden was restored as a house by the present writer, and the servants' accommodation made into three self-contained flats.

28　　The rectory is shown on the Marston Bigot Tithe Map of 1839.
29　　On Wilkins's woollen manufacturing business see Nicholas von Behr, 'The Cloth Industry of Twerton from the 1780s to the 1820s', *Bath History*, Vol.VI (Bath, 1996), p.88.
30　　Graves, *ibid.*, catalogue no.1067.
31　　Peter Coard, *Vanishing Bath*, Part 2 (Bath, 1971).
32　　Graves, *ibid.*, catalogue nos.1202 and 1241 (sw view).
33　　Graves, *ibid.*, catalogue no.1147.
34　　*Builder*, iv (1846), p.329.
35　　*Gentlemen's Magazine*, 1852 (i), p.637, though he apparently did not die in Bath (despite belief to the contrary – Colvin, *ibid.*, p.254), as Register Office officials have no record of it.

Acknowledgements

I am indebted to George H. Boyle Esq of Bisbrooke Hall, Rutland; Mr Colin Johnston, Bath City Archivist; Mr Robert Wilton; Mr Michael McGarvie, archivist of Marston House, Frome; the staff of Bath Central Library; and Mr Christopher Woodward and the staff of Sir John Soane's Museum, London.

ISAAC PITMAN
AND THE FOURTH PHONETIC INSTITUTE

Owen Ward

Isaac Pitman was born in Trowbridge on 4 January 1813, the third in a family of eleven children to Samuel, a successful cloth factory overseer and Sunday School Superintendent, and Maria, a sincere and loving mother. He was imbued with his father's sense of purpose but it was tinged by a streak of Spartan eccentricity. From his youth Isaac was fascinated by language, and especially by systems for writing more fluently and quickly than mere words would allow, until in 1837 he was encouraged to improve on existing systems by devising one of his own. His first guide entitled *Stenographic Soundhand* was published late the same year, and he thereafter never ceased to develop and promote the study and use of his 'shorthand'. Isaac Pitman's determination also to rationalise English spelling cost him interminable labour, anxiety and frustration, to the extent that the only known memorial to his phonetic alphabet is the name of Kingston Buildings, painted not long ago, in phonetic characters on the corner of his Fourth Institute, the subject of this paper. Other interests through the years are testified to by modest but regular financial commitments to a number of worthy and ascetic

1. Sir Isaac Pitman (1813-1897). *(Photograph from the Pitman collection, by courtesy of the University of Bath)*

movements. These included the Swedenborgian Local Church in Bath of which he was a devout disciple; the Vegetarian Society, for he was from an early age a vegetarian; Bath Temperance Society, on which principle he was so abstemious as to eschew the drinking of tea and coffee; and perhaps more marginally, Women's Suffrage.[1]

Isaac Pitman's education was limited by family circumstances and he worked as a clerk in Trowbridge, first in Edgell's cloth mill and then from

1829 in that set up by his father. In 1831 his father was able to send him for five months to the Training College of the British and Foreign School Society, from which he emerged at the age of nineteen as a sufficiently qualified teacher to take up an appointment at Barton-upon-Humber in Lincolnshire. Here he married in 1835 a widow with her own income, before moving the following year to Wotton-under-Edge in Gloucestershire, where he eventually started his own school. In 1839 he decided to move to Bath, where he opened a small school at his own residence in 5 Nelson Place. Within four years, the business of preparing and publishing his system of phonography had so expanded that in January 1846 he 'suspended the school, set up a [printing] press in one of the rooms, and used two other rooms for compositors and a bindery'. The building became the First Phonetic Institute. Then, as he later explained in a letter to a friend, 'in January 1851, to obtain more room, I removed to 1 Albion Place, Upper Bristol Road, where the business was carried on, under many inconveniences, in four rooms'.[2]

In 1855 the rented premises of this Second Institute at Albion Place were acquired for the Western Dispensary, and Pitman was obliged at short notice to move once more. He found a spacious room, but it was on the top floor of a block of buildings in Parsonage Lane, 'occupied principally by cabinet makers' although it had once been a brewery. This room became the Third Phonetic Institute, kept according to Pitman in 'apple-pie order', but 'situated in the only filthy lane I have seen in this beautiful city of crescents and squares ... The ground floor is a large gateway leading to a pig slaughterhouse that lies at the back; there is another pig slaughterhouse in front of my office, and a sheep slaughterhouse that does a deal of business, next door.'[3] This building, of c.1810, is now being gutted by developers of the old Wessex Newspapers site.

Pitman longed to build a more appropriate Institute in more salubrious surroundings. From 1859 he was beginning to put money aside for the purpose, but he was as patient as he was determined, and it was not until some fourteen years later that he began in earnest to set his plans in motion. At an early stage in his search (April 1873) he learned of the intention to dispose of the 'handsome' portico belonging to St. Mary's Chapel, on the corner of Queen Square (figs.2 & 3), which was then being demolished to provide better access to what is now known as Green Park Station. He bought the stone of the portico for £20 intending it to be re-erected as an impressive entrance feature to his proposed new building.[4] Until the eventual construction of the Fourth Phonetic Institute, the stones must have been held in store, it is not known by whom. We can see from his bank book that Pitman drew the sum of £20 on 26 April, presumably to pay for the portico, though the purpose is not actually stated.

2. (above) St. Mary's Chapel, Queen Square, as built: a watercolour view of c.1855 by H.V. Lansdown. **3.** (right) John Wood's design of 1732 for the East Front of the chapel.
(Both reproduced by courtesy of Bath & North East Somerset Council: Victoria Art Gallery, Bath)

Pitman made several attempts to purchase land as a site for a new building, until in June 1874 he seized the opportunity of buying part of Kingston Buildings when the Earl of Manvers placed his extensive property on the market. He reported later that

4. Ordnance Survey map of 1886 (Somerset sheets XIV.5.14/15) showing Kingston Buildings and Church Street. (*Reproduced by courtesy of Bath Record Office*)

at the auction, which was held over two days, Thursday and Friday 28 and 29 May 1874, and which realised a total of about £44,000, 'lots 100 and 101 consisted of two houses, nos. 6 and 7 Kingston Buildings, near the Abbey Church'. His new acquisition, 'a block of buildings, five storeys high, faces the north, and has seven windows at uniform distances, on each floor ... No. 6 being a corner house, facing Church Street on the west, has also windows on that side, and no. 7 is lighted both front and back ... The houses are only one room in breadth from front to back ... originally built as one house whose spacious hall and staircase now belong to no. 6'. Pitman continues 'this house [no. 6] is thirty feet by sixteen feet four inches, and no. 7 is 25 feet by 20'[5] (fig.4). At the time of the auction sale both houses were occupied 'as private residences' with a Mrs. A. Lambert and a Henry O'Brien, artist, being in no. 6, and a tailor, Wm. Crowley, in no. 7.[6] But Pitman 'arranged with the present tenants to take possession' at the end of June 1874.[7]

Pitman hoped to complete the necessary alterations to the building in three months, and to spend another three months placing 'a boiler, engine and printing machine on the basement, and the different departments of the business in the several rooms above, with the necessary fixtures and furniture'. The cost would, he hoped, be borne by the subscriptions to a fund which had been opened in 1859 for the express purpose of providing a new Institute, and which was slowly approaching £1,200. As is usual with building contracts, he erred somewhat on the optimistic side concerning both the time needed to complete it, and the expense involved. The stone of the Roman Doric portico from St. Mary's Chapel was to be re-used to raise the ceiling of the top storey to a full working height, and probably to help reconstruct the roof then 'old and out of repair'. This proposed development is confirmed by an elegant tinted sketch of the north elevation of 6/7 Kingston Buildings (in Bath Record Office) which shows the plan for the present four-storey façade. A decorative corner entrance was conceived but never incorporated, no doubt because so much money had to be spent on the more utilitarian improvements. The drawing is subscribed with the name of Thos. W. Gibbs, who was a solicitor in Bath, and it is dated 6 July 1874. In the bottom right-hand corner, a faint entry in Pitman's own immaculate shorthand script, reads 'Frederick John Williams, architect, Bristol'. There is no record in the accounts of any direct payment to Frederick Williams, who may have been a surveyor, not an architect, but Pitman sometimes paid professional fees in cash. A fee of 15 guineas for Wilson, Wilcox and Wilson, however, is entered on 4 August 1874. We can reasonably assume that this was payment for design work on the top storey of the Fourth Institute.

It seems likely that the columns of the portico from St. Mary's Chapel were not adapted for use on Kingston Buildings. Pevsner notes the suggestion that they were taken to Heathfield, a house on Lansdown.[8] This is possibly true of the two square Doric outer pillars, parts of which could be those now supporting the lintel at the entrance gate. Some surviving columns of the Ionic order, of which one complete example can be seen near the Cleveland Bridge, have excited speculation and received a mention on the Bath Preservation Trust plaque at the site of the former

5. Pillars at the entrance to Heathfield, Lansdown.

chapel. However it is likely that these were not from the portico but were interior columns, described by Ison as being of the Roman Ionic order. The distinction can be seen in figures 5 and 6.

If the portico pillars went elsewhere, so perhaps also did the ten triglyphs which once featured along the frieze above the pillars of the chapel. On the other hand, most of the carved panels, or metopes, between the triglyphs can possibly be identified. Seven rosettes which now appear between the windows of the top storey on the north face of the Fourth Institute must surely have come from the original frieze. An eighth panel, shown on the left of fig.7, is different, having a laurel wreath carved on it. The three spaces between the windows on the west face now have blank recessed panels, but in pictures of the Institute which are contemporary with Pitman's occupation of it (see for example fig.8) two more rosettes and one other laurel wreath are to be found. This total of nine rosettes coincides

6. Pillar in a garden near Cleveland Bridge.

7. (below) Decorative panels on the north face of nos. 6 & 7 Kingston Buildings.

neatly with the number of metope panels which Pitman acquired from the St Mary's portico, and which are shown on Lansdown's watercolour (fig.2). The wreath panels are not depicted there but they or something similar can be seen on Wood's drawing (fig.3), which suggests that this design may have been executed elsewhere in the portico, later to be purchased and re-used by Isaac Pitman.

The advantage of Pitman's work in raising the height of the attic storey can be judged from the appearance of Kingston Buildings (now known as Abbey Chambers), both in the past (fig.8) and in the present day. The roof-line of Pitman's building over-tops that of the neighbours, whose present sky-line must be similar to that of nos. 6 and 7 before this was remodelled.

8. The Fourth Phonetic Institute, Kingston Buildings, Abbey Churchyard, c.1877. (*Alfred Baker, 1913, facing p.196*)

Messrs. Bladwell undertook a good deal, if not all, of the building work for Pitman. Their bills were particularly heavy at the turn of 1874-5, amounting as they did to over £500, which was paid in three instalments. A sum of £100 was paid on 12 December 1874 when the work was completed, the workmen having left the building on 7 December ('eight weeks after the expiration of the contract term' while the masons were employed on the outside of the house), and a further £200 was paid on each of 27 February and 27 April 1875.

Bladwell's bills were not all for the reconstruction of the roof, and just as much work, if not more, was going on five floors down in the basement. At the time of his move to the new premises, Pitman was anxious to increase both the size and the distribution of the weekly *Phonetic Journal*, the house publication which carried news and exercises in both phonography (shorthand) and phonotypy (phonetic spelling), and which now provides us with most of our information about the work undertaken in his new premises.[10] In order to achieve this expansion in production he needed to purchase and instal one of the recently developed steam-operated presses. He therefore took steps to purchase a steam engine, a boiler to go with it, and a press to replace his existing manual one. The origins of the engine and boiler remain obscure, although Pitman's surviving account and bank books show that on 22 October 1874 an individual or firm of the name of Hornsey was paid the sum of £60.12.6d 'for engine and boiler etc.', and Reed tells us that it was a two horse-power vertical engine.[11] Pitman also spent £100 on a second-hand 'platen' press to go with his engine and boiler. From scattered references to the press, or 'machine' as it was usually known, we learn that it weighed five tons, was a 'double platen' press, and needed a 'walled pit' to house it. A further minor item 'for the machine' was the purchase, probably in December 1874, of 'straps' from Ashman of Bristol.[12] A report, which was reprinted three years later in the *Phonetic Journal*, describes the press more specifically as a 'double platen, double crown, press, by Messrs. J. Brown & Co., Kirkcaldy, Scotland'.[13]

Pitman's choice of printing machine was apparently a well-advised one, even if he found that his staff had a lot to learn about the new, much more complicated machinery. The double-feeder bed and platen press was particularly sought after as a machine for reproducing copy of a meticulous clarity, such as Pitman's shorthand certainly was. Developed initially around 1830 as a superior alternative to the powered rotary press, some of the earliest models remained in use with specialist printers at least until the 1930s. Pitman was lucky enough to pick one up second-hand just at the moment when 'other recently-invented presses [had] now partially superseded them',[14] so that the price of £100 which he paid compares very well with those of from £400 to £1400 which were being asked by Napier for similar machines only a short time before.[15]

The installation of engine, boiler and press was almost certainly the combined work of Samuel Griffin, engineers and millwrights in the Lower Bristol Road, Bath, and Joseph Bladwell, Pitman's regular builders, of 5 Railway Place. Both firms received part payments at the end of 1874: Bladwell receiving £100, as we have seen, as a 'first payment' for his building work, while Griffin received £15, later to be topped up by a further £25 on 1 February 1875, as a 'balance of account for general work'.

However, all was not well with the engine. After the first two issues of his expanded, 16-page Journal at the beginning of January 1875, Pitman headed his next, shrunken 8-page, issue 'A DISAPPOINTMENT' and explained that:

when the time arrived for printing [*Phonetic Journal*] No. 1 we found that our large printing machine ... could not be worked with our comparatively inexperienced hands fast enough to do the required 10,000 copies in time, and we were compelled to send the two 'formes' of type to Frome, to be machined by Messrs. Butler and Tanner. We hoped that another week's experience would suffice, but it only showed that our supply of water was inadequate for the daily wants of the engine, and No. 2 was, of necessity, also printed at Frome, at a very great additional outlay.[16]

Both the inadequacy of the supply of water and the ineptitude of the operators were being exaggerated by faults of which Pitman was not then aware. Meanwhile he arranged to have a more 'continuous supply of water from the fire-main of the city', and while his new and augmented staff learned to grapple with the recalcitrant machinery he accepted 'the kind offer of Mr. Lewis, of the *Bath Express & County Herald*, to work a single forme of type each week on one of his machines'. This could indeed have been a kind offer, as there is no trace of a payment for the work of printing the next three 8-page issues (nos. 3, 4 and 5). On the other hand, each of these bore a declaration that they were 'Printed by Isaac Pitman (Inventor of Phonography) at the Phonetic Institute, Kingston Buildings, Bath'. Perhaps this was a compromise statement in that Pitman did print his own 8-page Journal, but on Lewis's machine.

With issue no. 6 Pitman was able to resume his bumper 16-page numbers, which were published from 6 February 1875 to 27 March, a run of eight weeks' issues. But his problems were far from over and they were evidently making production of the paper on his own premises a nightmare. Writing in the issue of 3 April, he lamented that:

impediments have arisen from having to use a boiler that leaks. A small leakage was discovered soon after its erection. It was speedily enlarged by use, and the fire that is kept up to generate steam to drive the machine is rendered ineffective by the leakage of the boiler to such an extent that we can work but one or two hours, but then have to stop to get up steam. The boiler cannot be repaired without being taken down; we have therefore had a new boiler set ...

But it was not only the boiler which had to be replaced. By the beginning of May 1875 Pitman confessed frankly to his 'difficulty of getting our machine [i.e. the printing press] to work at all, through our having been deceived in the purchase of an engine and boiler that eventually proved not worth the cost of erection ...' He gave no further details of his travails with the engine, but we learn from his notice published in the issue of 3 April that, in addition to replacing the boiler he eventually had 'a new engine made' which was a horizontal four horse-power engine. 'We are promised', he continued, 'that the new engine shall be at work in a fortnight from this date, 22 March.'[17]

Pitman's new engine was made for him by Samuel Griffin. There is no specific reference to a payment for an engine, but Pitman as we have seen met several bills from Griffin at about this time, and the report from the *Printer's Register* in 1877, already quoted, states that the engine then *in situ* was 'a small horizontal engine with high-pressure speed-governor, made by Mr S. Griffin, of Bath'. The report went on to explain that 'the exhaust steam [is] utilized for warming the building and drying the sheets as they leave the machine'. Although we have no further details of the engine itself, it is probable that one similar was supplied to Bowler's in about 1876 when the production of mineral waters began at Corn Street, where it may have been used to drive the pumps. A small engine like that which is now in the Bath Industrial Heritage Centre (known as the Victoria Engine) would easily have operated such a press as Pitman had bought: little power is required because the moving parts are well counterbalanced.[18]

Whilst the hardware was creating mechanical difficulties for its inexperienced operators, Pitman had, in his enthusiasm for the advancement of his project, entirely overlooked the environmental effects of installing his new technology in the confines of an inner city tenement. He later reflected ruefully that 'the noise caused by the printing machine is so great as to constitute a "nuisance" to the occupier of No.8 Kingston Buildings: it is heard in every room of his house'.[19] Pitman did not name the neighbours, but they can be identified from the contemporary *Post Office Directories* as T.J. Tuttell, surgeon chiropodist, and Mrs E.S. Tuttell, surgical chiropodist.[20] Mr Tuttell seems to have tolerated the continued use of Pitman's equipment once it was in full working order and a 16-page Journal was produced from 6 February to 27 March, evidently printed by Pitman. But an undertaking was given to move the machinery away from the neighbour's wall. Arrangements had been made to replace the boiler and to order a new engine, and advantage was taken of these changes to move both of them away from the 'neighbour to the east'. But the press needed substantial structural changes for its re-installation, and on 22 March Pitman wrote that, 'in removing the printing machine to another part of the premises' he had to 'make a new walled pit for it, and turn one of the underground arches in front of the Institute into a habitable room for the workmen and the machine'.[21]

The expression 'one of the underground arches' requires some explanation. Many, if not most, of the properties in the centre of Bath are provided with vaulted cellars which extend in front of the house at basement level, often reaching out to a common underground party wall with the houses on the opposite side of the road. In the case of Kingston Buildings there are no houses on the other side of the road, but the Abbey itself. The 'underground arches in front of the Institute' therefore reached out almost to the footings of the Abbey wall, and provided a spacious, but isolated area which would normally have been used for storage – of coal for example. In Pitman's case he used this conveniently remote part of his new premises to house his most anti-social piece of machinery – his printing machine. In 1995 this space was rented from the owners of Kingston Buildings and incorporated in the Abbey vaults. In anticipation of this move an archaeological excavation was undertaken in 1993 and a walled pit was discovered. This was at first thought to have been a steam engine base,[22] but it now seems however that just such a provision would have been made for a large press like Pitman's. A widely conducted search for the structural details of this particular machine has so far drawn a blank, but it has attracted much helpful advice, especially the information that a press with a similar specification, D. Napier and Son's Patent Double Platen Printing Machine, has dimensions and seating requirements similar to those uncovered in the Abbey Vaults, and as described by Pitman[23] (figs.9 & 10).

9. Napier's Patent Double Platen Printing Machine. (*Moran, 1973*)

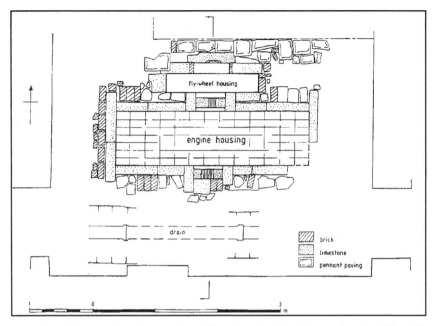

10. Plan of the machine base in the Abbey Vaults. (*BIAS Journal, 26 (1993), p.32*)

In contrast to this heavyweight printing machine, Griffin's new little steam engine need not have called for more than a wooden baseblock, measuring perhaps 5ft by 1ft 3ins, possibly with a small recess for the flywheel (fig.11). This engine was apparently removed at least twice within the basement of Kingston Buildings without any recorded problems. Presumably it was located near the boiler, which was so situated that the flue from its fire fed into the chimney stacks adjacent to the 'neighbours to the south' – whose reaction to this unwelcome supplementary heating Pitman was soon to experience.

For practical reasons the engine and any belt drive would be kept well away from the press and the paper in order to prevent soiling the work, as grease or other lubricants were liable to be spattered around moving parts. It seems likely that an underfloor shaft would have led from the engine to the cellars where the printing machine was established. It is true that Pitman had little experience of engines and engine-driven presses, so would not have known enough to insist on this, but Griffin was certainly more knowledgeable and could well have advised on the eventual layout of the equipment. Clearly Griffin had won the confidence of Pitman, since he had been asked by him to build his new engine, and to install and maintain it.

11. Griffin's steam engine, now in the Bath Industrial Heritage Centre. (*Photograph reproduced by courtesy of Stuart Burroughs*)

Pitman's hopes of 22 March 1875 that the work then in hand to adapt his cellar space would be completed a fortnight later were again disappointed, and on 3 April he had to tell his readers 'we regret to be compelled again to issue for two or three weeks an 8-page Journal, which we must get printed off the premises, while removing our printing machine, and getting a new boiler and engine, shafting etc. to work'.[24] This was finally achieved, and on 24 April he announced with relief that 'we have this week the pleasure of printing this Journal again on our own premises, but in consequence of the interruption caused by the presence of engineers, masons and carpenters for three weeks we are not in a position to print a 16-page Journal in time for this week, but shall do so next week.' This he did, for just one issue, for if one consequence of the relocation or replacement of his equipment was the successful production of one 16-page *Phonetic Journal*, another was an immediate, and peremptory verbal assault from his 'neighbour to the south'.

The attack took the form of a personal harangue from the medical gentleman who used the ground floor of the premises, swiftly followed by a letter from his lawyers Maule, Robertson and Maule of Northumberland Buildings, who demanded immediate compensation or cessation of the nuisance caused, principally, by the noise of the steam engine. Pitman was at first outraged, but then told his readers that:

> within three days after ... the lawyer's letter ... means had been devised to so reduce the amount of noise, and the heat from our boiler fire, the smoke of which passed into a stack of chimneys common to the two houses that we hope soon to be safe from an action at law... Masons and engineers [Bladwell and Griffin] are now engaged in carrying out the plan, which will take about a month from the date of this Journal. Our first neighbour, to the east, bore the infliction of the noise of the engine with even an excess of patience for three months in the hope that on the erection of our second engine, and the removal of the machine [i.e. the printing press] to a greater distance, there would be no further trouble. Our second neighbour, to the south (this being a corner house) was as unmercifully prompt ... as the other was kind and forbearing ... [When] the engine was removed to the other side of the room, and an additional wall built, the sound of the engine could not be heard, but the sound of the [printing] machine was now heard, which before was overpowered by the greater and nearer noise of the engine.[25]

It is unfortunately not clear from this account at what juncture 'the engine was moved to the other side of the room', but perhaps this took place during Pitman's enforced cessation of work between the issues of 30 April and 22 May. It is also unclear what plan 'the masons and engineers' were 'engaged in carrying out' as the issue of 22 May was prepared. Was this, for example, when the separate vent pipe, which we see appearing above the roof next to the chimney stack in pictures of the Institute, was run up through the building from the steam engine in the basement? (see fig.8)

Pitman never reveals the identity of the 'medical gentleman' to the south. In the pictures of the period the premises are labelled 'Dispensary ...', although no such appellation appears in the Directories until 1884 when 4 Lower Church Street [not 5, as stated by Pitman] is called the Dispensary for Skin Diseases. In 1888 the occupier is listed as 'H. Culliford Hopkins esq., surgeon and physician', so perhaps he was the offended party; he was the only resident in either street to aspire to the title of 'esq.'. In 1875, however, only the lodgers' names were listed, for as Pitman tells us

'The house in question is let out in unfurnished apartments, except the ground floor, which the lessee, a doctor, keeps for receiving patients between 12 and 1 o'clock at noon'. In an attempt to placate him, wrote Pitman, 'we promised to stop the engine during this hour each day'. The only result was 'another lawyer's letter ... [which] was returned to the writer'.[26]

It was another seven weeks before, on 10 July 1875, a 16-page Journal was resumed. This was presumably printed on the premises, but we cannot be quite sure because the surviving copies of the Journal lack the outer covers, until we come to the issue dated 4 September 1875. And then, at the foot of the back cover, we have, triumphantly:

> Printed by Steam Power by Isaac Pitman (Inventor of Phonography) at the Phonetic Institute, Kingston Buildings, Bath ...

Mr & Mrs Tuttell, surgeon chiropodists, continued to attend to their ladies and gentlemen next door, to the east; by 1878 Mr Tuttell had acquired, or assumed, the title of Professor. The Dispensary for Skin Diseases continued to occupy the premises to the south. Both parties were still in occupation when in March 1889 Isaac Pitman moved out of Kingston Buildings to his last, purpose-built Fifth Institute on the Lower Bristol Road. Its opening was celebrated by a 'substantial' tea; the celebrants were lucky, as Pitman had not always been so tolerant of stimulating liquors. His firm survives there as the Bath Press.[27]

Postscript

Since May 1995 the ground floor of Kingston Buildings has been occupied by Bath City Tourist Office. This circumstance could offer an opportunity to exploit the coincidence that the building was home to a movement guided by a man whose reputation has been more widespread than that of any other Bath resident. The extent of his influence can be judged from two reports over 100 years apart. In the first, his biographer Alfred Baker recalled that in Isaac Pitman's last public address in September 1893 he remarked:

> In every part of the world where our noble tongue is spoken, phonetic shorthand is written. It has been adapted to the writing of fourteen foreign languages, and eleven foreign systems have been published ... the Debates in the Japanese Houses of Parliament are reported in Phonography.

In 1997 the Editor of the *Bath Chronicle* wrote:

> In spite of all the developments in modern technology, accomplish-ment in shorthand remains an absolute priority for today's aspiring journalist ... while other forms of speed writing and shorthand come and go, the Pitman method enjoys the greatest longevity ... once conquered, it remains a qualification for life.[29]

These pages have tried to reflect the strength of Pitman's commitment to the promotion of a cause which he was convinced was supremely worthwhile, and to show how this indefatigable pioneer fought and won the battle of the Fourth 'Fonetik Institut'.

Notes

1   See two major biographies of Isaac Pitman: *Biography of Isaac Pitman* by Thomas A. Reed (Bath, 1890) and *The Life of Sir Isaac Pitman* by Alfred Baker (Bath, 1913).
2   Reed, p.84.
3   Reed, pp.84-85.
4   *The Phonetic Journal* (*PJ*), 26 April 1873. The journal was published weekly from January 1873 until 1905 when it became *Pitman's Journal* and then (in 1925) *Pitman's Journal of Commercial Education*, and from 1930 evolved into *Office Training* and the teacher's companion volume.
5   *PJ*, 13 June 1874, p.185.
6   *Post Office Directory*, 1874.
7   *PJ*, 13 June 1874, p.186.
8   Nikolaus Pevsner, *North Somerset and Bristol* (1958), p.122n.
9   Walter Ison, *Georgian Buildings of Bath*, (1948: reprint, Bath, 1991), p.72.
10 *PJ*, 1874, *passim*.
11 Pitman's Bank Book, in the Pitman Collection,University of Bath Library; Reed, p.128.
12 Pitman's Account Book, Pitman Collection, University of Bath Library, 6 January 1875, cost £6.3s.0d.
13 *PJ*, 3 November 1877, p.520, reprinted from the *Printer's Register* for August of that year.
14 John Bryson, *Industries of Kirkaldy and District* (1972).
15 James Moran, *Printing Presses* (1973), p.120, drawn to my notice by Bernard Seward, printer at Bristol Industrial Museum and Matthew J. Hume of Summerlee Heritage Trust.
16 *PJ*, 16 January 1875, p.25: Butler's account for printing numbers 1 and 2, together with the paper, cost Pitman £44.3s.3d., which he paid promptly on 15 January 1875.
17 *PJ*, 8 May 1875, p.195; Reed, p.128.

18   Information from Stuart Burroughs and Alan Stock, Bath Industrial Heritage Centre.
19   *PJ*, 3 April 1875, p.146.
20   It seems likely that Pitman was a good customer of T. J. Tuttell, as he made him a payment of £50 in January 1885, perhaps for the previous year's treatment. Pitman's Account Book, p.113.
21   *PJ*, 3 April 1875, p.146.
22   Robert Bell, 'A horizontal steam engine in the centre of Bath', *BIAS Journal* (1993), Vol.26, pp.30-32
23   See note 15, p.120.
24   *PJ*, 22 March 1875.
25   Describing the location of Pitman's works, the correspondent of the *Printer's Register* for August 1877 said 'It stands at the corner of Church Street and Kingston Buildings, the names of which are written up in phonetic characters', see fig.18.
26   *PJ*, 22 May 1875. A reader's letter, in a sympathetic allusion to the lawyers' names, refers to Pitman having been 'mauled' by his neighbour.
27   The premises of the Fourth Institute in Kingston Buildings were taken up as the offices of the then recently created Bath Stone Firms Ltd. See Norman Bezzant, *Out of the Rock* (1980), p.166.
28   Baker, p.291.
29   *Bath Chronicle*, editorial column for 22 January 1997.

Acknowledgements

The main source of data for this paper has been the Pitman Collection at the University of Bath, in the care of Tony Holbrook, Social Sciences Librarian. Because many of the notes are in Pitman's own immaculate but minuscule shorthand, assistance in reading them has been crucial. The initial excavation of the machinery base which led to this study was by Robert Bell of Bath Archaeological Trust, who has encouraged this further examination of the written records. This study has benefited from facilities available at the University of Bath through the Centre for the History of Technology (Director, Professor R. A. Buchanan).

In addition to those mentioned in the notes, the assistance of the following in matters of detail is gratefully acknowledged: Ralph Emanuel (lecturer in the history of architecture at Bath University), Graham Gerrard (Bath City Engineering Services), Andy King (Bristol Industrial Museum), Colin Johnston (Bath Record Office), Susan Sloman (Victoria Art Gallery, Bath), and Peter Martin (Head Verger, Bath Abbey).

Errors in interpretation are, however, the author's own responsibility.

CHARLES RICHTER AND BATH CABINET MAKERS:

THE EARLY YEARS

Sally Festing

'We are informed that Messrs Norris & Co have discharged all the cabinet makers in their employment who came out on strike last week and that they intend to carry on their business as on non-society principles.'[1] In history, there are no real beginnings, yet Bath Cabinet Makers (BCM) owes its very existence to the strike at the Albion Cabinet Works in December, 1891. By 1901 the new firm was employing a hundred men, sixty years later the staff had grown to 600.[2] Unlike its thirty-six fellow cabinet makers[3], BCM was to trade for sixty-seven years before being taken over by Yatton Furniture. The name and the goodwill, moreover, survived for more than a century.

The growing population of Bath in the nineteenth century included a thriving service industry. Because of its rapid expansion and a rich eighteenth-century architectural heritage, the city had long been a centre for making furniture.[4] Cabinet making is the skilled making of furniture fitted with drawers or shelves in wood. It is not necessarily concerned only with

1. Charles Augustus Richter (1867-1946). (*Family photograph, c.1900*)

cabinets, but strictly speaking does not include the construction of chairs, which is done by specialists, or of framed-panel furniture, jointed at the corners and slipped into grooves above and below, which is the province of joiners. The joiner might supply the cabinet maker with sawn and planed planks, but inevitably there was an overlap, and a sizeable cabinet-making concern employed chairmakers, joiners and carvers along with the authentic cabinet makers, equipped to design, shape and assemble, dowel, carve, finish and, since the reign of King Louis XIV, to use veneers. Cabinet making in all its manifestations was where Charles Richter (1876-1945), artist, designer, businessman, socialist and determined idealist, chose to employ his considerable energies for more than fifty years.

JC Rogers's *Modern English Furniture* (1930)[5] celebrated the work of forty-two designers among whom Richter takes his place with notables like Edward and Sidney Barnsley, Edwin and Robert Lutyens, Gordon Russell and Robert Lorimer. To furniture dealers and furniture historians of his period, BCM's founder and luminary has a distinguished name, but he remains strangely unsung in the annals of Bath. It is my feeling that the very spread of his talents has marginalised his recognition. Even those who know his furniture might not realise that he modelled his firm on the Arts and Crafts Society to which he was later elected a member.[6] Basically, this meant a continuous effort to improve the standard of design, notoriously low towards the end of the Victorian period despite the example of a few notables like Norman Shaw and William Morris. Morris's Arts and Crafts business had been set up in 1861, yet art furniture was appreciated by a very small minority. But what chiefly distinguished Richter from the other proponents of Arts and Crafts, were his views on production. Morris thought that the machine itself was responsible for bad design, and since hand work was necessarily time-consuming, his furniture was too expensive for the very people he wanted to supply. Richter, in contrast, deplored asking men to perform monotonous and arduous tasks that could well be accomplished by machine. He spoke as a natural progressive and an erstwhile worker. The pace of life being no longer conducive to medieval workshop methods, it was the duty of the trade to produce designs adapted specifically for machines. This was the premise of the man whose vision, tenacity, artistic ability and commercial aptitude was the bedrock of BCM. Under him the firm won an international reputation.

Charles Augustus Richter was born on 27 August 1867, the third son and child of Sarah and Johannes Friedrich Wilhelm Richter. Although it is not recorded in the biography of Charles's younger brother, Herbert,[7] their father was a Prussian groom, trained in the royal stables at Potsdam, who had sailed to England when he was eighteen to accompany a race horse bought from his employer King Frederick William IV of Prussia, by a client in England. The groom settled in Sussex and married an English girl. Romance and circumstance are knit in a tale of Dickensian poignance. Though Sarah Davis was working as a laundry maid when Richter met her, her background was more illustrious than her predicament suggests. Sarah's mother had been a pupil at a private art school in Chelsea run by William Davis. Her wealthy parents, the Duffields, had predictably disapproved of the match with the art teacher and the couple eloped. Thereafter, the Duffields broke off all relations with their daughter. Both Sarah's parents died in her early youth from ill health, penury, and the struggle to raise a string of children. Despite this, Charles Richter's mother was a flame of energy and tenacity.

Charles was brought up on the Woodendean estate – now 'Woodingdean' in the parish of Ovingdean – where his father worked for a wealthy race-horse owning eccentric, Mrs Strangways, who had estates both there and in Bath. The relations between Mrs Strangways and her groom were, for the time, surprising. Between the two, out of understanding and affection for the animal kingdom, there grew a close relationship that kept them together for the rest of his working life.[8] Five Richter children reached maturity, a daughter and four sons, of whom three were exceptionally intelligent and two were artistic. Samuel Smiles's *Self-Help* being the family rule, discipline was firm but not severe. Sarah instilled in her children a high standard of ethics, the ability to fend for themselves, and perhaps most important, a passion to create. Thanks especially to her, several had distinguished careers. Frederick became a teacher at Bath Technical College, Herbert (H Davis) was an architectural and flower painter, President of the Pastel Society and of sufficient repute to earn himself a *Times* obituary,[9] and Charles's contribution speaks for itself; besides his career with BCM, he became President of the National Federation of Furniture Trades, lectured widely, and served on Lord Gorell's Royal Commission on Art in Industry, in connection with which he gave evidence in the House of Commons. What is more, he rivalled Herbert in painting.

The only check to an early life that Charles Richter was to remember as idyllic, was an irrepressible desire to ask questions, a tendency towards which not all school masters took a tolerant attitude. Charles left school at eleven and a half, by which time his two elder brothers were already apprentice joiners, a trade from which they could work their way, if they chose, into other fields. Instead of following suit, Charles opted for the Brighton office of *Southern Weekly News*.

In the last two years of the 1870s, the rainfall was phenomenal. Poor crops on top of the abolition of the Corn Laws aggravated the decline of arable farming, and the English market overflowed with American grain. By 1880, some hundred thousand fewer farm labourers were tilling the earth than just ten years before. It is not known whether the national situation influenced Mrs Strangways, but she left the countryside and moved to her Bath estate. Here Richter was joined by Sarah and the three younger children.[10] In Bath they resided in the Lodge to Lansdown Place (enlarged in 1900 to become the present house, Cresthill), at what must be one of the highest points in the city, close to its boundary and handy for the racecourse. For thirteen year-old Charles, longing to do something more creative than shorthand and bookkeeping, Bath opened the path to progress.

After an abortive spell with a firm of engravers called Wilkinsons – 'All they did was drink beer' – he advertised his skills in a local newspaper and in either 1881 or 1882,[11] he was taken on by the Norris brothers at the 'spic and span' Albion Cabinet Works on the Upper Bristol Road.[12] About the same time, he undertook an intensive programme of self education.[13] Thomas Carlyle was a seminal influence. From Carlyle's gospel of work, Richter reinforced his mother's teaching. He read and imbibed literature, philosophy, history and politics. And with his new awakening, he acquired a determination to capture experiences. On bits of paper, in notebooks, exercise books, old envelopes, anything to hand, he charted his intellectual and emotional progress. Much as he had loved the Sussex countryside, his waking consciousness was moved at a profound level by the pale tiered city in its amphitheatre of hills. He was never to leave his second home.

Alongside the larger cabinet-making firms, small family businesses continued to flourish, indeed specialist work was often sub-contracted to them. Simeon Norris had started in 1870 and Charles A Porter, designer and manager, was brought in some ten years later (at the same time as Richter joined the firm), when Frank and Albert, Simeon's sons, had taken the helm. Porter's employment was a prestigious move. So often had he won the national competition for furniture design run by the Benn Brothers publishing firm in conjunction with their publication, *The Cabinet Maker*, that he was asked to stand down to give other competitors a chance. It was observed that, 'One of the secrets of success was ... Porter's aptitude in giving practical guidance to the men ... Frequently in the carving department, Mr Porter could be seen taking over the job in hand and putting it into the form he required ... Their first class cabinet work, both in design and workmanship, soon found its way to all the leading shops throughout the country.'[14] By mid nineteenth century the factory system of manufacture was being developed and power-driven machines were being installed. The Albion Cabinet Works was, according to Keevil, 'considerably in advance of other firms in the city, with perhaps the exception of Wadmans'. [15] It was nevertheless, essentially a hand carving enterprise.

The 1860s had seen a Queen Anne revival, and latterly, a return to favour of eighteenth-century styles, especially Chippendale. After 1870, the British public wanted heavier furniture, mahogany, rosewood, ebonised cabinets, sideboards and overmantels, carved and inlaid, particularly in ivory. No single style was produced in the Albion workshops, but a variety of fashionably popular derivatives ranging from modern Adam to Italian Gothic. Most of it was 'shaped' or curved, as was the main body of the late Victorian trade, love of richness and sinuous outline being chief selling points.

Though Richter was apprenticed to Porter in business management, it was soon evident that in a general way the Norrises had an outstandingly able recruit. While busy installing the first costing system, Richter was also benefiting from Porter's expertise in design. From 1883, his notebooks are peppered with sketches of furniture, architecture, and anything else he fancied as raw material from which to extrapolate[16] (fig.2). His touch was always light, nineteenth-century 'Chippendale' rather than the 'Early English' or 'Modern English Gothic' promoted by Charles Eastlake and developed by William Morris's firm. Nor was he influenced by the spindly Japanese furniture that aesthetes extolled.

On Wednesday 10 September 1884, as a contemporary jotting informs us,[17] Richter performed an errand for Mr Porter, carrying volume 2 of the *Universal Instructor* to the bookbinder, Cedric Chivers, to readjust the binding so as to include eighteen errant pages. His shopping list was for 'oil colours, Painting, 3 Tools, and Screws', half aesthetic (oil colours, painting), and half practical (tools and screws) symbolizing the balance of his activities. On 13 December, 1884 he was paid 1s 5d for a drawing of a cabinet, and the following January he received 16s 9d for a drawing of a casquet. On 11 September 1885, he was paid 7s for a drawing of a satinwood cabinet. A few days later he received the same amount for a drawing of a mahogany cabinet.[18] The earliest piece of his furniture of which we have a record is a cabinet of 1900,[19] which means there are only his notebooks to fill in the sixteen intervening years.

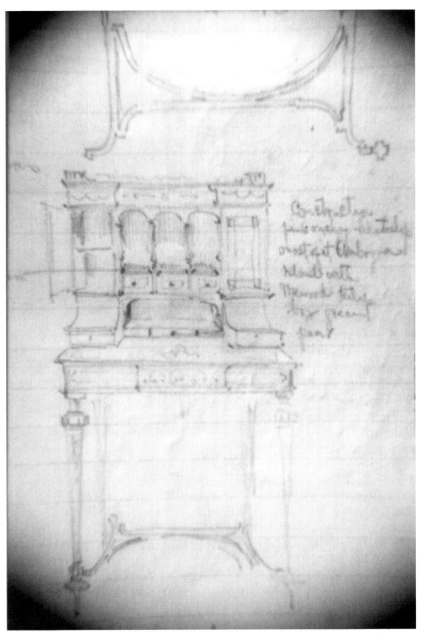

2. Design for a cabinet from C A Richter's notebook of 1883. (*Family archive*)

Another of Porter's apprentices at Norris's was Frank Keevil, father of H T Keevil, the author of *The Cabinet Making Trade of Bath 1740-1964*. Keevil was seven years older than Richter and had the advantage of receiving from *his* father a training in ecclesiastical furnishing, architecture and furniture trades. After his term with Norris, he went into partnership with his brother in Bristol. Then, in 1891 or 1892, the same time as Richter started his first venture, Keevil set up his own business on the Lower Bristol Road. On Monday, 20 October 1890, Richter and Keevil discussed Emerson and Carlyle at the Twerton Club. A week later, and on various other occasions, they met and talked again.[20] It seemed at first likely that a serious occasional literary correspondence with 'Frank' was addressed to Richter's fellow apprentice, but as Keevil is always noted by his surname it is more probable that his correspondent was Frank Norris, under whose guidance he was rapidly being promoted. The letters were profoundly important to Richter who records dates on which he received and sent his somewhat earnest missives. Unfortunately, they add nothing to our knowledge of the writers' common trade.

Towards the end of the 1880s, rather to the Norris's amusement, their young employee entered one of *The Cabinet Maker's* competitions. The magazine's circulation was over 50,000 a year[21] and entries were received from all over the country. Both Norris brothers sent off drawings and one of them was commended – Richter however received a first prize. In 1891, Charles's younger brother, the seventeen-year-old Herbert Richter, then also employed at Albion under Charles Porter, was to win another first; £10 for a drawing of a Dining Room in Italian Renaissance style and a prominent double-page spread.[22] 'Although the prizes have not been effective in producing anything very original in character' the judge commented, 'they have brought to light some drawings which we venture to think will be of interest to the trade'. The Norrises were to feel for 'these damn Richters', increasing respect. In 1887, at the age of twenty, Charles Richter represented the Albion Cabinet Works at the Paris Exposition where his drawings were on display. By 1891 he was helping with the management of the business despite the fact that he was working only half time. The remainder was devoted to study. That year he took, passed and won a prize for London University Extension examinations in a variety of subjects.

During the first half of the 1880s, Trade Union policy had been pacific. The big unions had won most of what they set out to win and there were a few miners' representatives in Parliament. The sense of accomplishment was false, as Tom Mann and John Burns recognized when they set about organizing the sweated trades where unionism was weak. Pitched battles occurred in the Metropolis and unrest spread in the cities. By 1891 there was still plenty of scope for improvement. Charles Booth's analysis of London's poor showed that some thirty per cent of Londoners habitually fell below the poverty line.

A family firm such as the Norris's was in a difficult position since the management showed a certain avuncular concern for its workers. Notwithstanding, men with families to house and feed worked long hours in unskilled, poorly paid jobs, and practices long accepted were resistant to change. When a spindle moulding machine was installed, the cabinet makers were 'greatly alarmed' that it would usurp their duties,although in practice, as Keevil attests,[23] the machine created rather than eliminated work. What the men's reaction actually signified was chronic insecurity. By the last decade of the nineteenth century, timber was being shaped in steam presses and new glues were used which eradicated traditional joinery. Veneer-cutting machines were on the market, of which the rotary-slicer in particular encouraged a minor revolution. New machines minimised waste and thin veneers could form three-layer plywood construction. To the precariously balanced manual workforce, change was a threat.

Warning had come in mid-1891 that all was not well at the Albion Cabinet Works. On 25 July and for the next two days, Richter's diary records, 'Cabinet-makers agitations, locked out, work prevented'. Through his reading of Robert Owen and Carlyle in particular, Richter had become a socialist. On Tuesday 1 December, when 'the cabinet-makers struck work at twelve o'clock', he was reading, appropriately, about the Co-operative Movement. On the Wednesday, the carvers likewise struck work. Frank Norris refused to see a deputation and before the week's end, in an unsympathetic gesture, removed all tools from the works. On Saturday, reading Carlyle's *Past & Present*, Richter was moved to expostulate, 'Ah me! Ah me!'.[24] His sympathies were with the workers, and once again, it was Carlyle who prompted his conscience – 'Hold fast to the duty that lies nearest'. A quandary was brought to a head: attending university had been an alluring possibility but Richter now made a fateful decision. He must do what he could to help the men.

Twelve of Charles Richter's notebooks cover the 1890s, with a daily record of the hours worked, the cash made, books read, engagements undertaken (birthdays, concerts, lectures), and of his problems and sensibilities. Other documents which show his concerns at this time include the Oxford Extension Lecture Syllabus for 1891, endless scribbled memos for cabinet making, instructions from clients, courses that Charles and his younger brother taught at Bath Art and Technical School (one of them on Period design), the minute book for BCM's first year and the Minutes of the Education Committee of the Works. In one maroon paper-covered, lined and yellowing exercise book, first penned at the *Garrick Head Hotel* on the penultimate day of 1891, lay the embryo of the later international company, launched as The Bath & West of England Co-operative Cabinet Makers Ltd under the motto 'Labour is Worship'. By 16 January 1892, Richter had been elected General Manager at a salary of £3.5.0. per week. The shareholders of the Society were represented by five committee members of whom Richter had known the Bath-born Cedric Chivers at least since he joined Norris's.[25] The others were T B Silcock, Edwin Hill, John Henshaw and Basil Dyer. Bath had a 'model parliament' and all were on the council. Each put in £50 and Richter contributed £100. His mother, father, sister and brother Fred joined in, and friends were persuaded to buy shares which were also advertised in the local press. The workers were represented by Messrs Oliver Hewlett, Hawkins, Milton and Coaffee, each of whom contributed £10 before work began in rented accommodation opposite Twerton Railway Station.

The other members of the Committee played no active part in the firm, but Richter was activator, promoter, bookkeeper, buyer and salesman. He it was who drew up a prospectus and solicited orders. He had been at Norris's for some years, and to his gratification he was now successful wherever he went. Eight months into the life of the firm, he was able to reveal: 'Your committee has great pleasure in reporting the continued growth of the Society and the extension of its business month by month, notwithstanding that the general state of the cabinet trade has been one of almost unprecedented depression'. There was never a dearth of orders, and good wages were being paid to the three carvers, eleven cabinet makers, three polishers, one machinist, five lads, and occasional upholsterers, chair-makers, marquetry-cutters.[26] The only reservation at this stage was the firm's unwieldy title. The Committee voted to dispense with the term 'Co-operative'. Whether this was Richter's wish is not known, but customers were not included in the profit-sharing so the firm was under no obligation to use the word, and the 'high principle' by which the Society [that is, Richter] stood, was reckoned by some to run the risk of alienating buyers. At all events, the name was contracted to 'The Bath Cabinet Makers Ltd'.

By September 1892, the future of the firm looked auspicious, and Richter was keen to expand:

> Your committee wish to impress upon the shareholders the necessity of the society adopting and acquiring all the advantages, methods, appliances & machines which other manufacturers possess so that the Society may increase its trade & employ a much greater number of its members. Reducing laborious manual toil will enable us to produce finer & higher class work at moderate but remunerative prices. As the wet season advances, the want of machinery will be still more seriously felt.[27]

It is known from private accounts that the Manager was frustrated by what he felt was the other shareholders' lack of vision: 'They knew they were on to something good and they wanted to keep it small'.[28] Richter's instinct proved correct. After eighteen months, profits at BCM began to decline. He was working day and night – at a machine, supervising packing and labelling, even helping to load crates onto the vans – but he could not entice the men to follow suit. It was a discouraging time. Richter doubted his influence and half of him longed to abandon the whole business and return to his books. In reality, there had never been sufficient capital, a situation aggravated by failure to expand when it was appropriate.

There is only Harold Keevil's version of events to attest the fact that Richter walked out of BCM, probably in late 1893 or early 1894. For a short period, the three Richter brothers set up on their own in Parsonage Lane with an office at Nassau House, Orange Grove; Fred, the eldest, who now called himself a cabinet maker rather than a joiner, Charles, and Herbert, whose late-developing talents had taken him to South Kensington's newly founded Technological Institute and to the Bath School of Art.

A music cabinet displayed in Bath's Holburne Museum in the autumn of 1985 probably dates from this period.[29] The design is said to have been done by Herbert, the joinery and veneering by Frederick, and the carving by Charles, but it is likely that the division of labour was not entirely clear cut. French Rococo in design, and exquisite in craftsmanship, the small bow-fronted mahogany and satinwood piece was conjured expressly to display the range of the brothers' skills (fig.3). Cabriole legs make the corner posts to a mahogany cupboard with a solid single door, protected from warping by a 4 inches wide, deeply carved, inset ebony cross. The corners are decorated with parquetry in various woods including tulip. Above the cupboard, there is a single drawer bearing a rectangular, similarly

3. Music cabinet of 1892 by Frederick, Charles and Herbert Richter. (*Family archive*)

carved, central ebony plaque. The whole is surmounted by a domed vitrine of four glass panes set into a satinwood cage. The display compartment is hinged at the back, and lifted by a single carved handle at the front. It supports a plain rectangular platform on which a vase might stand. The legs, the sides of the cupboard and the ribs of the vitrine are heavily carved with fern-like and acanthus leaf decoration.

Despite the skills displayed in this individual piece, the real potential still lay with Bath Cabinet Makers. For shareholders, especially the Richter family, its failure meant more than disappointment, it involved serious financial loss. To protect his honour and save those who had helped him, Charles felt that he should try to make a fresh start, and when the Society called him back[30] he re-launched it as a limited liability company, taking over the assets of the co-operative society at the end of 1894. This time, he was Managing Director, and his younger brother, Herbert, head of the Design Department. All their combined energies went into the business. It succeeded and the success was long-lasting, though the company had its struggles through, for example, the copying and pirating of designs. Richter expected a lot, both from himself and of others, and his methods were not always orthodox. On one occasion, when the men had been kept working late at night to get an order dispatched, the vanmen, who were waiting to load up the goods, refused to stay any longer. After other methods of persuasion had failed, Richter gave some pretext to get them into the lift, quickly closed the doors, pulled the lift half way up, and left them stranded until the goods were ready. Fortunately they took it in good part. Richter 'struck a hard bargain' as one of his long-time employees remarked. At the same time, he engendered a good deal of loyalty amonst his men. It is said that when Tom Mann, the Trades Union leader, addressed his members at Bath, one of BCM's workers named Hewlett hurled a jug of water at him for casting aspersions on 'the Management'. Like its predecessor the new firm paid good wages. Every employee, on becoming a shareholder of the Society, was eligible for a share of profits, and as before, an Education Committee was set up to broaden the quality of the workers' lives. The *Minute Book* tells of weekly lectures on subjects like 'Co-operative Vistas' (C A Richter), 'The Land Question' (Mr Gilbert), and 'The Miners of '43' (Mr Cannings), and a library for public reading including Darwin's *Origin of Species* and Carlyle's *Heroes and Hero Worship*. Before the year was out the Committee was renting additional rooms, one for draughts and chess, another for the use of a cricket club.[31]

In 1895 Richter collaborated with local architects Messrs Silcock & Reay on the design of a factory in Bellotts Road, a grand stylish affair, flying its company name in giant letters from a low-hipped roof (fig.4). From a machine shop that was one of the largest and best equipped in the West of England, flowed luxury furniture, often elaborately carved. In 1899, BCM undertook the complete interior decoration, woodwork, fittings and furniture of Hotel Cecil in the Strand (subsequently demolished for a Shell-Mex building). A hectic period followed as one after the other, stores and hotels clamoured for a new look to embody the spirit of the turning century. Many were large-scale commissions and all had to be done at once. While Charles organized production, Herbert designed, and co-ordinated operations. His drawings were being reproduced in *The Building News*, *The British Architect*, *Academy Architecture* and other journals.[32]

In 1900 the firm's reputation was consolidated with five medals at the Paris World Exhibition, a gold, two silver and two bronze. From this time forth their headed paper proudly displayed the fact. BCM's work, the *Art Journal* considered, had 'the distinction of being on novel lines, without

4. Bath Cabinet Makers Factory in Bellotts Road, Twerton. (*Family archive*)

overstepping the bounds of good taste in any instance', and the company's display 'did more than its share towards saving the situation in the British section.'[33] The gold medal went to a Mr Coy, the bronze to George M Elwood and A J Crocker, the silver to each of the Richter brothers. A writing desk from this exhibition,[34] illustrated in the Holburne Museum Catalogue, is a weird, top-heavy looking object with art nouveau decoration. By contrast, CA Richter's award-winning mahogany display cabinet, also shown at the Holburne Museum,[35] is light in appearance, (though apparently not weight) with narrow crossbars in glass doors mounted at the top and bottom with Burne Jones-type art nouveau designs in aluminium, an expensive metal at that time. Its chief interest to us is in anticipating the designer's increasingly stylish forms of the new century. After the exhibition the piece was sold at Christie's and taken to the USA.

In more ways than one, 1900 was a memorable year for C A Richter who had married in January the daughter of an Aberdeen hotelier, Frances Mann. For another thirty-four years he ran BCM, through good times and bad, with extraordinary industriousness, daunting energy and great personal mobility. Some of these qualities are revealed in extracts from his papers.[36]

Selected Extracts from Letters and Memoranda, C A Richter's Notebook, June-July 1911

Mr Pidgeon: call a board meeting for Monday July 31. Notices to be sent the middle next week ... Get cigars from Caters ...

Mr S Trier: Are you following up Mr O's enquiry for hotel furnishing & for chairs for the Imperial Hotel, Regent St. or can I do anything in the matter. I asked you if we had heard anything about the Buffet we made for him ... Ask Mr Lansdown if already written to M Trier [Dr M Trier].[37]

Mr Joseph Trier in Darmstadt:
Mr H returned to Zurich on Saturday. His entire order will probably total £1400 but he is going to write me definite instructions after conferring with M. Keller. I will send you particulars. The order includes a considerable amount of plaster decoration upon which there is only a narrow [profit] margin, but no doubt we can arrange this to our mutual satisfaction. I also have important enquiries from him for which I am preparing special drawings.

M. L Huve,
Marbier
62 Rue St Sabin, Paris.
We will be much obliged if you will send us catalogues of reproductions of 18th century English Marble mantelpieces. We do a very large mantelpiece trade & could doubtless make good use of your productions.

Mr Bergnor:
We have discussed the proposed arrangements for your agency at a board meeting today and the same were approved ... I will write you fully in the course of a day or two. I cannot do so now as I am called from town on important business ... Meanwhile, if you can send the plans of the hotel at Venier [or, possibly, Venice] I shall be pleased to prepare designs for the furnishing.

Herr Prienin, Berlin.
There is a balance of 9/- owing to us on a former account. We shall be pleased if you will remit this amount & so save further correspondence.

Remind Mr Richter [Bert] to send set of drawings & photos to M Joseph Trier.

Mr Pidgeon: Please do your best to obtain a more competent typist. If you cannot get a man, engage a girl. We could perhaps do with two.

Dear Mr Robertson
I was in M last week & was surprised to see displayed in the window at Goodalls, a bedroom suite of my design (with very slight modifications) made & supplied by you. I cannot think that you would have deliberately copied my design, & I am sure you will oblige me by letting me know in confidence how this design came into your possession. We have suffered so much of late from the copy of our designs that I am determined in the interests of our customers no less than in that of my firm, to take all possible steps to prevent it ... We are registering all our more recent running designs but are conscious that this affords but slight protection as the alteration of a few details evades the law ...

Mr Wentworth: A German customer living in London is to call at the L.S.R. [London Show Room at 18, Berners Street] to buy lacquered cabinet. Quote plus 20%.

BCM furniture was on constant display in London stores like Maples and Harrods, and trade became ever more far flung, with sales in North America and on the Continent. To complement the external network, every department within the firm was intricately dovetailed by the links and responsibilities of men like Mr Coaffee, Timbershop and Machineshop Foreman, under whose supervision wood was selected, sorted, pointed, planed, grooved, mortised, tenoned, moulded, veneered, sandpapered and generally prepared for the cabinet fitters; and Mr Williams, Foreman of the Cabinetmakers, who saw the mantels glued and screwed together. The business of Mr Marsh, the General Foreman, was to colour, polish, and dispatch, whilst Mr May, a spindle moulder in the company's employment, entered on a time sheet every day the work on which he had been engaged.[38]

The firm had grown, but it was unwieldy and Richter was increasingly away from home. In the latter part of 1912 he knew, quite suddenly, that he would have to instigate a series of reforms. The least pleasant of his duties was to dismiss a number of loyal workers, some of whom had been with him since the inauguration of BCM.

September 1912
I did not finish till after 11.pm. I had made some important decisions, so necessary, though regretfully performed. – I cannot describe the sadness which invaded me & which I could not shake off at having to beat a retreat from the proposed course & parting with those I so much valued and respected. Men who had served me to the best of their ability. So willingly. – How heavy my heart none can tell.[39]

Richter was an old-fashioned master – a dwindling species. Unlike the new management, who knew all about a balance-sheet but little about how the product was made, he understood every process from start to finish and kept the organization tightly under his control. For him, there was no other way, yet the price he paid was a strain upon his energies. With keen interest, he had watched the progress of his younger brother. Though he still provided drawings for the firm, the reputedly cautious Herbert had left it in 1909 to try his luck as a painter. Four years later he was holding his first one-man exhibition. With a view to following suit, Charles travelled to London to attend classes at the London School of Art and at Heatherleys. Unfortunately, his plans for early retirement were interrupted by the First World War.

A Prussian background and a German name were not the most comfortable attributes for a prominent businessman. To guarantee his own and his family's survival, Richter sought safety in Government commissions. The factories were converted to manufacture aircraft parts and wooden boxes for munitions, and afterwards restored to panelling, joinery and high-class furniture. Some of the unskilled labour taken on during the war was retained on contract work, making gramophone and wireless cabinets. A further concern, the Bath Guild of Handicraft and Design Ltd,[40] was launched under the able administration of Herbert's wife, Gertrude Barber, and Charles's sister, Florence Schottler,[41] to make tapestries, cushions, and the fabrics required for interior decoration in the large restaurant, hotel and shipfitting contracts then being taken on.

Even before the war, BCM had been shipping furniture to America, India and Germany. When it was over, Richter travelled to Italy to negotiate an order from the Italian Government for luxury liners. The panelling and decorations were all constructed in Bath, then transported to Trieste, where they were installed by a body of workmen sent over from BCM. Orders were subsequently obtained for work on other liners, including the giant Cunarders, the *Queen Mary* and the *Queen Elizabeth*. Interiors were also provided for London's County Hall and the new Bristol University buildings.

Once again, Richter was able to spare time and thought to his work as a designer. He could probably be called eclectic, since he designed inspired period furniture. Indeed, he was on one occasion amused to discover that a cabinet he had made for a Louis XVI setting so accurately caught the spirit of the age that it was acquired as authentic by a South Kensington Museum. But his first interest was increasingly in moving from Victorian extravagance, through Art Nouveau and Art Deco, to the graceful lines and good proportions of modern design (fig.5). No mere draughtsman, Charles chose his material at the time of conception – besides weather oak, he had a penchant for exotic woods like French walnut, figured mahogany, paroba and laurel. At the other end of the range, he draughted a good deal of simple, moderately priced furniture, some of which he mass-produced in tubular steel. He also designed cut glass and china ware, which was specially made for him by Wedgwood. Further recognition was obtained at the Wembley Exhibition of 1924 and the Paris Exhibition of 1925, whilst year after year, he aired his views in the trade journals, at lectures for the Royal Society of Arts, through organizing exhibitions of industrial art, and at meetings of the Furnishing Trades Federation of which he became President. An undated photograph shows him wearing the decorative chain and medal of his office.

5. Sideboard designed by C A Richter, probably in the 1930s. (Family archive)

All was not well, however, as 1922 brought the boom to an end, with the years that presaged the big industrial slump. With large-scale unemployment, business everywhere came to a standstill, and the last thing anyone wanted was luxury furniture. Profits were seen gradually to be drying up, leading to profound dissatisfaction and unrest among company shareholders, but under Richter's leadership the company survived, continuing in family ownership after his retirement in 1934.

Perhaps it was ironical that an erstwhile pacifist should have aided the war effort, and a socialist made a private fortune. About 1920 Richter had bought a distinctive Georgian house, once the home of the Duke of Cleveland – Bathwick Hill House, at the top of Bathwick Hill, where he and the family lived for many years surrounded by furniture and furnishings of his own design. Despite his personal achievements he continued to demonstrate his egalitarian principles with dramatisations at BCM. He was acquainted with George Bernard Shaw who travelled down to Bath when they put on *Caesar and Cleopatra* – a performance, incidentally, for which Richter was responsible for the stage settings.

Charles Richter was intensely alive until he died, on 28 May 1946. Typically, his twelve-year retirement was spent in painting, gardening and study. He never achieved Herbert's success as a painter, perhaps due in part to the younger brother's ease among his clients. Herbert was close to the actress, Maud Allan, and had a very wide circle of friends. From Neitzsche Charles learnt that 'Nothing is true; everything is possible.' In order to read his favourite philosopher in the original, Richter taught himself German, which, strangely, he had not learnt as a child. He is buried in Lansdown Cemetery, together with his wife, father, mother, and two cabinet-making brothers. Charles and Frances's gravestone lies a few paces west of the large cedar tree. It is a simple, horizontal, blue fossil limestone with typical Art Nouveau lettering in lead around the perimeter. The gravestone of the other four Richters lies in the old, overgrown part of the cemetery, between the road and Beckford's Tower.

Appendix: The Richter Family

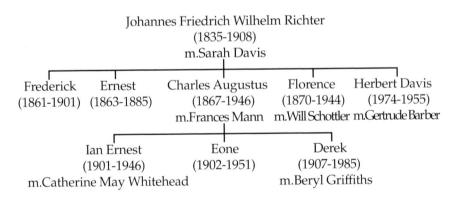

Johannes Friedrich Wilhelm Richter
(1835-1908)
m.Sarah Davis

Frederick	Ernest	Charles Augustus	Florence	Herbert Davis
(1861-1901)	(1863-1885)	(1867-1946)	(1870-1944)	(1974-1955)
		m.Frances Mann	m.Will Schottler	m.Gertrude Barber

Ian Ernest	Eone	Derek
(1901-1946)	(1902-1951)	(1907-1985)
m.Catherine May Whitehead		m.Beryl Griffiths

Acknowledgements

I would like to thank Philippa Bishop and Geoffrey Beard for reading the article, Desmond Brown for his guidance in Lansdown Cemetery and my cousin, Nicholas Richter, for helping to describe the music cabinet stolen from my father.

Notes

1   *Bath Chronicle*, 10 December 1891, p.8.
2   *Bath Critic*, Vol.3, 'A Story of Craftsmanship', p.254.
3   Numbers fluctuated. According to *Post Office Directories*, there were 36 in 1892, the firm's first active year. Twelve years before, there were 48, and six years later there were 60.
4   See *Furniture Made in Bath* (Holburne Museum Exhibition Catalogue, 1985).
5   J C Rogers, *Modern English Furniture* (Country Life Publications, 1930). A classic in its time.
6   Information about Charles Richter and Bath Cabinet Makers comes largely from private and business papers in the possession of the author, including notes taken down by her father Derek Richter from the family, chiefly his father, C A Richter.
7   H Granville Fell, *The Art of H. Davis Richter* (Benfleet, 1935).
8   Mrs Strangways was recorded in the 1871 census as 'widow', and later as unmarried.
9   *The Times*, 24 August 1955.
10 *Post Office Directories* show J F W Richter in Bath by 1878-9. It seems probable that his wife and children did not follow him for a year or so.
11 Harold T Keevil's *The Cabinet Making Trade of Bath 1740-1964* (Bath, 1964) says 1887. This account of furniture-making in Bath, though valuable for the inside material about the industry, contains many inaccuracies about BCM. Whether these permeate the whole text is uncertain, but the possibility is alarming since much research has relied upon this text. It is likely that a certain competitiveness existed between the families.
12 *Bath Chronicle*, 10 January 1889, p.5.
13 Every book Richter bought is listed in Cash Accounts of this period, and the titles of what he read daily.
14 Keevil, p.15.
15 *Ibid*.
16 Notebook, 1880s-1.
17 Notebook, 1880s-1.
18 Notebook, 1880s-6.
19 *Furniture Made in Bath*, Exhibit 12.
20 Notebook, 1890s-7, pp.49, 53, 59.
21 *Cabinet Maker*, July 1891 and others.
22 *Cabinet Maker*, July 1891.
23 Keevil, p.14.
24 Notebook, 1890s-5, pp.35, 69, 71.
25 Minute Book of Bath & West of England Co-operative Cabinet Makers Ltd., pp. 1,4. Eleven years younger than C A Richter, Chivers had started a bookbinding business, first in Union St and then in 1886 at 39 Gay St in 1886. In 1890 he joined the city council as a Liberal member for Kingsmead ward and served on it except for a short break until 1914. In 1922 and 1924 he was to be elected Mayor.
26 *Ibid*., pp.40-41.
27 *Ibid*., p.42.

28   See note 5.

29   *Furniture Made in Bath*. Exhibit 11 is dated c.1892, which is probably a couple of years too early. The cabinet is described as 'Mahogany, with domed glass top and cabriole legs. height overall 50 in/127 cm; width 22 in/55.9 cm. [Some time after 1946, when my grandfather died, this extraordinary little piece (delicate but somewhat 'over the top') came into my life. In my memory, the vitrine always contained, on a base of pale green velvet, the ivory chess set that my grandfather and then my father played. It remained in the family until 1995 when it was stolen from my father's home. The sadness is that whoever now possesses this unique piece of furniture has no idea of the affection with which it was conceived and wrought by three young brothers. In a way it carries its own legend; Bert's refined aesthetic, Fred's precision-conscious execution, and Charles's imaginative spark. S.F.]

30   Keevil, p.17.

31   Minute Book of Education Committee, pp.9,11.

32   Fell, pp.13-14.

33   Fell, p.12, from a special edition of the *Art Journal* published for the Paris World Exhibition, 1900.

34   *Furniture Made in Bath*, Exhibit 13, and described on p.22.

35   *Ibid.*, Exhibit 12, and illustration in Christie's Catalogue, *British Decorative Arts from 1880 to the Present Day*, January 1986, where it is described as a 'mahogany display cabinet ... with overhanging dentilled cornice and moulded frieze above two hexagonal columns inlaid with brass stringing, the faceted bowed cabinet with two glazed cupboard doors mounted with pierced metal bands 198.2cm. high, 163.7cm. wide, 57.5cm. deep'. It was sold for £2,500.

36   Notebook, 1911-2.

37   Four of the Trier family worked for or helped BCM in various capacities, a father in Darmstadt and his three sons. Owing to Richter's Prussian origins, he made a point of employing immigrants who might otherwise have found it difficult to obtain work.

38   Notebook, 1912-2.

39   Notebook, 1912-1.

40   At first the Bath Guild of Handicraft and Design was established on the Lower Bristol Road. In the late 1920s, its upholstery department was based at The Pavilion on North Parade and the firm also acquired the premises of The Bath Artcraft Company at 6-7 Avon Buildings; the Bellotts Road premises is described in the 1929 *Post Office Directory* as a wholesale and timber yard. (*Furniture Made in Bath*, p.25)

41   Even Richter's father-in-law, Charles Mann, was brought into the company, not, as Keevil suggests (p22), as a 'sleeping partner' in Baker and Mann. Mann went bankrupt in 1901, shortly before Richter married his daughter, so providing a job for him was a kindness, even if Mann did not receive very much. In March 1910, when Mann started work, Richter wrote 'I intended paying you 25/- per week since you started at Bakers ... I fervently hope to give more time to help you and send you out travelling.'

THE FLOODS OF BATH

R. Angus Buchanan

On the evening of Wednesday 10th July 1968, West Country members of the Institution of Civil Engineers held a Reception in Bristol to celebrate the 150th anniversary of the foundation of the Institution in 1818. The guests assembled in the City Art Gallery, through the glazed roof of which the proceedings were punctuated by vivid flashes of lightning and tremendous cracks of thunder. A summer storm, which had already been rumbling for several hours, terminated a long period of drought with a phenomenal downpour of rain. Some of the speakers at the Reception were tempted to boast of the way in which engineering had successfully tamed the forces of Nature. In the event, this was an extraordinary declaration of *hubris*, because the storm wreaked exceptional havoc across the West Country. Underground aquifers erupted on the Mendips; rivers rose alarmingly; roads and embankments were washed away; and many bridges, including the County Bridge across the Avon at Keynsham and the bridge at Pensford across the Chew, were destroyed. In Bath, streams in all the tributary valleys flooded quickly and the Avon rose ominously. The way back to the city was blocked late that night by a torrent at the Saltford end of the newly-constructed Keynsham by-pass, and a double-decker bus was abandoned in flood waters at Pennyquick. The level of the Avon itself rose steadily until, by the afternoon of the next day, the river had flooded Southgate Street, as it had done so many times before.[1]

This, after all, was only the latest of a long series of floods which had regularly disrupted life and transport in the City of Bath, and had caused enormous damage to property over the years, even though there had been remarkably few fatalities. The sight of water lapping the parapets of the Old Bridge; of the inundation of large areas of Dolemeads, Avon Street, Green Park and Twerton; and of swans sailing up Southgate Street had become all-too-familiar features of Bath experience, and views which the citizens had come to take largely for granted in the eighteenth and nineteenth centuries. Even then, however, steps had been taken to alleviate the recurrent scourge of serious flooding, although most of the schemes which were considered were either inadequate or too expensive to be put into practice. With the twentieth century, the demand for effective action became more articulate, and after a particularly serious inundation in 1960 the determination and resources were at last found. The scheme which resulted from this disaster was being put into practice when the summer flood of 1968 struck, but it proved to be the last occasion on which the River Avon was allowed to get seriously out of control in the centre of the city. It would be unwise to claim that such an event can never happen again, but within the limits of imaginable contingencies the engineering arrangements now in place should make a recurrence of serious flooding very unlikely.

The problem of flooding is one which affects all settlements adjacent to irregular and unreliable rivers. The Bristol Avon is as variable in its behaviour as any British river, subject to the range of the national weather which, although generally temperate, is notoriously unpredictable in detail. Downstream in Bristol its behaviour is complicated by the unusually high range of the tidal reaches as far as Netham Weir (and occasionally as high as Hanham Weir), and by its confluence with the River Frome in the centre of the city. In Bath, however, the water level is normally about 40ft above the highest level of the tide in Bristol, although the backing-up effect of a high tidal surge coinciding with a flood in the catchment area remains a remote possibility. The special features of Bath floods have been the result of a large increase in the volume of river water channelled by the topography of the Avon valley into a series of 'bottlenecks'. These have restrained the flow of the river and caused it to flood out over the narrow strips of low ground between the bluff on which the original settlement of Bath was built and the bulk of Beechen Cliff to the south. The growth of the city has involved increased pressure to build on this flood plain, and all the developments in Walcot, Bathwick, Dolemeads and downstream to Twerton and Weston have been hostages to the fortune of floods from the moment they were built. The first such development was from the traditional South Gate of the city to the Old Bridge – the Southgate Street which figures on maps from the sixteenth century.[2] But it was the popularity of the city as a spa town in the eighteenth century, and the flourishing industrial expansion along the river between the Old Bridge and Twerton in the nineteenth century, which caused the main encroachments on these vulnerable areas. They were all built-up except for the pieces which became the Recreation and Cricket Grounds, always prime victims of any flooding. At the same time, the building and paving of the city up both hillsides away from the river increased the volume of run-off water into the Avon and thus accentuated the danger of flooding in the low-lying areas (fig.1).

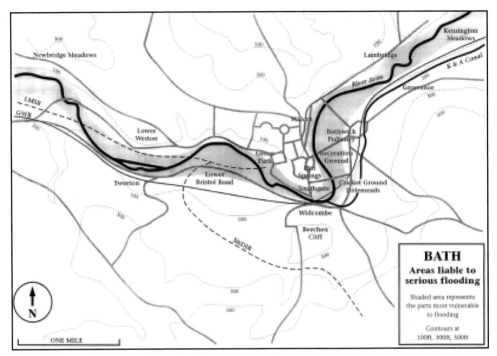

1. Bath: Areas liable to serious flooding.

While it is safe to infer that the valley of the River Avon has always been prone to flooding, this has only become a serious problem to the people of Bath with the growth of the city. The mineral springs which formed the nodal point of the original settlement emerged in a marshy declivity in the middle of a more or less level terrace which rose some 50ft above the normal level of the river. This would therefore rarely have been affected directly by flooding in the valley, although the backing-up effect of spring water unable to make its usual escape into the river would have added considerably to the marshiness in the vicinity of the springs. These effects were not sufficient to deter the Romans from establishing their great baths and temple complex on the site, and the complete settlement, as indicated by the line of the wall round the city, stood firmly on the terrace above the flood plain of the river. For the greater part of three centuries Roman engineering and drainage coped adequately with any tendencies to succumb to flooding.[3]

Towards the end of the Roman occupation, however, flooding became an increasing problem. Professor Cunliffe observes that, tackled at first by expensive re-floorings, the problem eventually:

became more serious as the water table rose and eventually the Baths had to be abandoned. Thus the drainage system soon fell into disrepair and the mineral water, unable to drain away, ponded up, allowing silt and mud to clog both the temple and the Baths.[4]

The buildings gradually collapsed, largely under the pressure of their own weight as their foundations shifted, and partly as a result of robbing and deliberate destruction. The resulting pile of monumental rubble was slowly engulfed by the silt around the springs, and lost to sight for several centuries.[5]

Meanwhile, a new town grew in the medieval centuries on the same site as that settled by the Romans, with its own Abbey Church, walls and market. Placed above the river flood plain, the periodic floods would have been only a slight inconvenience to movements into and out from the city. But as the settlement expanded southwards towards the five-arch masonry bridge erected over the River Avon in the thirteenth century, so the danger of annual inundation of buildings in its vicinity became a regular feature of Bath life.[6] The Old Bridge, or St.Lawrence's Bridge as it became known on account of the small oratory to the saint incorporated into its northern parapet, itself contributed to the danger by acting as a bottleneck to pond back any flood water. Despite several rebuildings, this masonry structure remained an impediment to the smooth flow of flood water until it was finally replaced by the single-span Churchill Bridge in the 1960s.[7]

Commentators on the Bath scene before the nineteenth century appear either to have taken periodic flooding for granted or not to have thought the subject worthy of mention, so that there is little documentary evidence of the problem. The Rev.Richard Warner, in his monumental work of antiquarian scholarship, *The History of Bath*, first published in 1801, discusses the use of the river as a highway for trade and as a source of power for mills but has nothing to say about it as a cause of floods.[8] Neither did John Wood in his valuable but idiosyncratic study, *A Description of Bath*, published originally in 1742-3.[9] We know from other sources that the 'Tempest' of 1703 caused extensive flooding and disrupted life over much of south west England; and that in 1774 another flood seriously damaged the 'new' bridge built by Ralph Allen for the Bath Turnpike Trust in the mid-1730s, so that it had to be rebuilt as the present single-span Newbridge.[10]

Only in 1838, with the appearance of *Annals of Bath from the year 1800*, by Captain Rowland Mainwaring, RN, do we find an attempt to record carefully the effects of floods in Bath. Mainwaring saw his study as a sequel to Warner, but by arranging his material in the form of a year-by-year chronology he was writing a different sort of book. It was under his heading for the year 1809 that he took note of the first serious flood in his period:

> It falls to our lot next to relate the distressing ravages of a flood,
> hitherto unprecedented in the records of the city. From the particular
> situation of Bath, surrounded on all sides by steep acclivities, and
> subject, of course, to frequent overflowings of the river, many had
> been witnessed at various times, but never with such devastating
> effects as at the present. At Monks Mill, near the Orange Grove, a
> high flood was marked in 1725, and a second in 1774, neither of which
> were so high, by two feet and a half, as that which we now record.[11]

This passage suggests that Mainwaring was aware of both the long-standing
nature of the problem and the novel features showing in 1809 that it was
becoming worse. He cites only the year for the incident, but the Bath Chronicle
for 26 January 1809 reported:

> The appearance of the immediate suburbs and the lower streets of
> this city during the noon of today has been equally novel and
> distressing. The sudden thaw of a heavy accumulation of snow,
> accompanied by a violent rain, produced a flood of greater depth
> and extent than has occurred here for the last forty years.[12]

The details given – the loss of seven lives in Bedford Street, off the London
Road, where three houses were washed away, and the disruption of the mail
coach – 'The Volunteer coach, in an attempt to force its passage through the
waters, unfortunately lost two horses' – are also narrated by Mainwaring,
who goes on to describe how the inhabitants of the Quay, Southgate Street,
Milk Street and Avon Street 'were obliged to retreat to their upper apartments',
and how in the Dolemead area:

> the most agonizing spectacle was that of a cradle floating down the stream,
> from which an infant now and then endeavoured to raise its head ...

The child was rescued at the Old Bridge.

Mainwaring also thought it worth mentioning, as an aspect of the singularity
of the 1809 flood, that 'the magistrates and clergy' of Bath promptly raised a
fund for the relief of distress which amounted to the considerable sum of
£3,495. In an interesting comment on the spirit of the times he explains that
the recipients were divided into two classes, one to whom grants of £5 or

less were made, totalling £1,008; and the other consisting of shopkeepers and suchlike who had lost property and stock, who received a total of £1,799. The remainder was dispensed on provisions, £355; rewards, £74; and advertisements, £16; leaving a balance for contingencies of £240.[13] It became a regular feature of these events to raise an appeal for flood relief, but the generosity of the response on this occasion was an indication of its novel seriousness, and inaugurated the modern period of Bath floods.

Several other floods were recorded by Mainwaring in the period covered by his chronology, especially in 1821, 1823, and 1828. For 1821 he reported:

> At the termination of the year, public attention was particularly called to the unfortunate inhabitants of those miserable abodes recently built on that low, swampy spot of ground, called the Dolemeads ... [where torrential rain in the last two weeks of December] ... caused the river to overflow its banks full twelve feet above the customary level; and the Dolemeads presented one immense sheet of water.[14]

But there were no fatalities as in 1809, and the relief fund amounted to a mere £881.[15] Dolemeads was again the main area to suffer in 1823, when heavy rain at the beginning of November brought renewed flooding to the lower end of the town:

> the view presented from the Abbey Tower was of the most desolate description. Several of the houses appeared with little more than their roofs above water; and the Avon rushed onward in its impetuous course, as if to overwhelm everything within its reach.[16]

On this occasion a load of timber was washed downstream and blocked part of the Old Bridge, contributing significantly to deepening the flood. For the first time, serious remedial measures were contemplated. Mainwaring observed:

> These frequent overflowings, and their lamentably devastating effects, at length called for the serious attention of the Municipal Authorities.

In the next year, 1824, a 'Flood Relief Committee' was established, and the great civil engineer Thomas Telford, at that time the leader of his profession, was invited to report on the situation. Telford responded with characteristic thoroughness, recognizing that the problem, although serious, was soluble by the provision of some fairly simple engineering works – removing obstructions to the flow of water, replacing the Old Bridge by a single arch bridge (preferably in iron), and making some realignments in the course of the river. His estimated cost was £47,848 but when the Committee saw no hope of raising this sum Telford's report was shelved indefinitely.[17] The flood reported by Mainwaring in 1828 differed from its predecessors, which had all been winter floods brought on by heavy rain and/or melting snow, by coming in the summer months. This type of flash flood, following a violent summer storm, could cause serious damage in Bath, as we have already noted in that of 10th July 1968, so although less frequent than the winter floods they have to be reckoned with:

> On the night of 8th July, an alarming and destructive inundation occurred, occasioned by a tremendous fall of rain, so sudden and powerful that it appeared as if a huge water-spout had burst over the city, accompanied by thunder and extremely vivid lightning, and which continued, without intermission, for many hours.[18]

The storm caused the Widcombe Mill dam to burst, flooding the lower part of the village suddenly, including the *White Hart* public house, and several people were drowned.[19]

The next serious flood was a winter one, reported in 1841. Under the headline 'The overflowing of the Avon', the *Bath Chronicle* described the familiar situation:

> The rapid thaw which commenced on the night of Friday last caused a more extensive flood along the banks of our river than has been known since November 1823 ... The effects of the flood were, as usual, the most severely felt in the Dolemeads.[20]

After that, there appears to have been something of an intermission to 1866. There were certainly wet years with gales and snow in evidence, but none in which inconvenience to the citizens of Bath seems to have made an impression. The fact that the flood in January 1866 was also the first to be recorded on the southern abutment of the Widcombe Footbridge, and that this was probably the first year of the existence of the abutment, suggests that our records for the previous two decades may be deficient. However, the pattern of a couple of serious floods in every decade resumes at this point, and continues for a century thereafter. In 1875, there were two floods, one in the summer (July) and the other in the winter (November). The flood of October 1882 received full attention in the local press, with an emphasis on the remarkable number of horses, pigs, sheep and other animals lost. This is a reminder of the large population of animals normally resident in the town in the nineteenth century, not only in the transport service but also kept in back yards to supplement the diet. A widow living in a cottage near North Parade refused to be rescued from the flood in 1866 because she had moved her four pigs upstairs into her bedroom and intended to look after them there.[21]

Newspaper comment on Bath floods increased in the nineteenth century with the emergence of popular local journalism, and flourished further in the twentieth century, aided by the advent of newspaper photography. It has to be admitted that the photographs were frequently dull and repetitive black and white images, but their drama lay in what they showed – the torrent lapping the parapets of the Old Bridge, or swans swimming up Southgate Street. The episodes do not bear detailed re-telling, as so many of the events recalled are depressingly similar. However, a glance at figure 2 will serve to indicate the incidence of serious flooding in Bath over the last two centuries, with as much of the available statistical information as is relevant to this pattern. It will be sufficient for our purposes to pick out a few of the highlights and more dramatic incidents. Fortunately, there were few fatalities involved in the Bath floods, so that newspaper comment tended to concentrate on the more bizarre and amusing incidents, and the narrative often assumed something of what a later generation would call the 'Dunkirk spirit', of adversity stoically and even heroically borne.

2. The incidence of floods in Bath (opposite).
• Heavy lines denote years in which serious flooding has occurred in Bath in the last two centuries.
• The month in which the flood occurred is indicated where known, showing that the majority of inundations were in the winter months (September to April) but that a significant minority may be regarded as summer flash floods (May to August). Specific dates generally refer to newspaper comments.
• The height of flooding is given where known, expressed in feet and inches as at the time of the incident. These figures are derived from several sources and are not completely consistent. They generally refer to the height above normal at Pulteney Weir. The most comprehensive set of figures is contained in a note in the Large Red Cutting Book on Bath Floods in Bath Central Library (B551.57BAT).
• Sources: the chart has been compiled from references in Bath newspapers, especially the *Bath Chronicle* which is available on microfilm in Bath Central Library (BC); R. Mainwaring, *Annals of Bath* (M); F. Greenhalgh, *Bath Flood Prevention Scheme* (G); and other Bath Library records (Lib). Also useful in filling in background information has been: Barry Horton, *West Country Weather Book* (1995) (H); and the physical evidence provided by flood marks on the south abutment of the Widcombe Footbridge (W) (fig.3).

Year		
1809	26 Jan 12'6"	(BC) (M)
1821	27 Dec 12'0"	(H/BC) (M)
1823	6 Nov 13'3"	(H/BC) (M)
1828	8 July	(H/BC) (M)
1841	21 Jan	(BC)
1866	18 Jan 8'3"	(W/BC)
1867	28 Mar 8'0"	(W/BC)
1873	Mar 3'6"	(Lib)
1875	22 July 4'6"	(W/BC)
1875	18 Nov 7'3"	(W/BC)
1877	29 Nov 6'6"	(W/BC) (Lib)
1882	26 Oct 12'6"	(W/BC)
1888	15 Nov 7'3"	(W/BC)
1889	28 Mar 9'6"	(BC)
1891	6'6"	(W/G) (Lib)
1894	15 Nov 12'0"	(W/BC)
1897		(W)
1899	31 Dec 14'0"	(W) (Lib)

Year		
1900	Dec	(BC)
1903	18 June c.4'	(W) (BC)
1914	28 Dec 2'6"	(BC)
1918	26 Jan	(BC)
1925	3 Jan	(W/BC)
1929	30 Nov	(BC)
1932	1 May 14'6"	(BC)
1935	26 June	(BC)
1947	22 Mar 9'10"	(BC)
1960	29 Oct	(BC)
1968	10 July	(BC)
1972	10 Feb	(BC)

176

3. Widcombe Footbridge south abutment. (*R.A. Buchanan*)

On some occasions the newspapers published supplements to bring together their coverage of the bigger floods. This happened in 1894, and again in 1932 and 1968. The pamphlet reprinted from the *Bath Herald* in 1894 amounted to a sixteen-page dossier on the events of the 'Great Floods'.[22] The publishers claimed that 100,000 copies of the original newspaper reports had been sold. There was widespread agreement that the 1894 flood was one of the biggest. A contemporary comment claimed that:

> The present flood is the fourth great inundation of the city during the present century, the other three being 1809, 1823 and 1882. Of course there have been numerous other occasions ... when the river has risen to a great height, flooding the lower parts of the city, and causing great anxiety and distress ...[23]

On the same day in November 1894, the headlines in the *Bath Herald* told the story in outline: 'The Great Flood', 'Highest on Record', 'Exciting Rescues', 'Hundreds of People Homeless', 'Measures for Relief', 'The City in Darkness', and 'Collapse of Bathford Bridge'. The flood continued for three days following heavy rain at the beginning of November, and it had two distinct peaks, on 13th and 15th November. Gas-lighting was cut off to much of the city when a barge hit the gas main across the river at the gas works, so that the distribution system was flooded.[24] The newspaper claimed that the flood: 'reached the highest point ever recorded, exceeding even those early in the century which had hitherto held the record', and this judgment is supported by the levels inscribed on the Widcombe Bridge abutment, where that for 1894 is well above the next highest.[25]

Further flooding occurred in 1897, 1899 and 1903, according to the Widcombe Bridge floodmarks, but they received little newspaper attention, apart from the disruption of the Cricket Festival caused by the summer flood of 1903:

> The Recreation Ground presented a unique appearance, with the tents which had been erected in connection with the ill-fated Bath Cricket Festival, standing in about three feet of water, and the ground almost submerged.

The paper also recorded a flood, not marked on the bridge, in the first issue of 1901, but as this started on 24th December it should be regarded as an event of 1900.[26]

4. The River Avon in flood behind Claverton Street, before redevelopment, c.1960. (*Photograph by Rev.W.H.Parsons, reproduced by courtesy of K.Evans*)

There were then more wet winters, with 1914, 1918, 1925, and 1929 all producing inundations. Newspaper comment in January 1918 can be regarded as fairly typical. Under the heading 'The Avon in Flood', it reported:

> Though comparatively little damage was done, considerable discomfort and inconvenience were occasioned in Bath and district by the Avon rising so rapidly on Saturday afternoon and evening to the height of 10ft 6ins above its normal level. Happily on Sunday the water receded almost as quickly as it had risen and the high wind which blew in the latter part of the day had a welcome drying effect.[27]

Amongst the details reported, the road under the GWR bridge at Bathford was flooded, preventing trams from getting through; the meadows at Bathampton, Batheaston and Lambridge were flooded, as were the open spaces of the Recreation Ground and Cricket Club; the Grosvenor Suspension Bridge was cut off for some hours and its toll house isolated; parts of Dolemeads, the Lower Bristol Road and Oldfield Park were under water, preventing the trams getting through to Twerton; and the Rev.Richard

5. Southgate Street under flood water, looking towards the Old Bridge and Beechen Cliff, c.1960. (*Photograph by Rev.W.H.Parsons, reproduced by courtesy of K.Evans*)

W.Windsor of St.Paul's Vicarage appealed for help in support of his poor parishioners in Little Corn Street, The Quay and Lower Avon Street.[28]

In January 1925 a newspaper declared: 'Bath Floods – Worst Inundation for 24 Years – Hundreds imprisoned in their bedrooms'. The river was reported to be 12ft above normal, and the Dolemeads and Lower Bristol Road to be worst affected, while 'Southgate street was impassable this morning to all save dairy errand boys and water-loving dogs'. Under the heading 'Long Night of Terror' another newspaper reported: 'For the first time for years the Roman Baths have been flooded ... what is to become of the famous goldfish?'[29] The Mayor, Alderman Cedric Chivers, donated £100 'as the nucleus of a distress fund'.[30] This intervention by the Mayor represented a familiar pattern of aiding distressed victims of Bath floods. We have already noted Mainwaring's reports of such assistance in the early nineteenth century, and the Guildhall Archives contain a box of documents dealing with such formal appeals between 1875 and 1901. In each case, subscription books were opened in leading banks and institutions, and the sums raised varied from £2,328 in 1882 to a mere £199 in 1900. Allocations were then usually made through local clergymen and other public figures, a high proportion going to the residents of Dolemeads,

6. The River Avon in flood, looking downstream from the Old Bridge, c.1960. (*Photograph by Rev.W.H.Parsons, reproduced by courtesy of K.Evans*)

and being used to purchase coal to help the drying-out process.[31]

There was a violent thunderstorm on May Day 1932 which caused a sudden serious flood in Bath, and led the local newspaper to produce a six-page supplement of text and photographs to cover the event. The Avon was reported to be 14ft 6ins above normal in the 'Lightning Deluge' which rose and fell quickly, producing the usual list of inconveniences, and one unusual disruption:

> 'River, stay 'way from my door', played the Bath Municipal Orchestra at the Pavilion popular concert on Monday night, but the Avon paid no heed to the plea. Nearer and nearer crept the yellow-brown waters, until they had transformed the hall into a moated palace and then invaded the floor ... There was a struggle to rescue the chairs – and the takings, which fell in an attache case into the depths until rescued by a window-pole.[32]

Another of these summer floods occurred only three years later, in June 1935, when the 'Worst Thunderstorm in Living Memory' struck the south-west of the country and caused severe dislocation to traffic in Bath.[33]

7. The Lower Bristol Road under flood water, c.1960. Note the men with the boat. (*Photograph by Rev.W.H.Parsons, reproduced by courtesy of K.Evans*)

There were more wet and cold years in the 1940s and 1950s, but the only serious flood was in 1947, with lesser disturbances in 1950 and 1959. Another inundation in 1960 tipped the scales of public opinion in favour of a determination to do something to deal with the problem. It was argued that the cost of an improvement scheme would be no more than the damage occurring to property in any one flood in Bath, and this led to a resolution to put in train the improvements in the river-flow which, by their completion in the mid-1970s, brought an end to the regular flooding of low-lying parts of the city. There have been plenty of wet winters since, such as that of 1979, which in the old days would have led to extensive flooding, but the waters have been safely confined to the river and its immediate environment. The improvement scheme has thus, to date, been a considerable success, and it is worth understanding how it works.

The scheme, as we have seen, was not the first to be considered. Telford had made his report in 1824 and had recommended the sort of improvements in the flow of river water which were essentially those incorporated in the modern plan. But at the time the local authority could not find the resources to adopt the plan, and it was abandoned. In 1877 a scheme based on the improvement of the existing weirs was promoted by

8. The Parade Gardens under flood water, c.1960. (*Photograph by Rev.W.H.Parsons, reproduced by courtesy of K.Evans*)

Alfred Mitchell, but not even such minimal adjustments were attempted. In 1882, the engineering consultants Messrs Coode, Son and Matthews were invited to make a report, but their recommendations for deepening the river bed and modifying the weirs, costed at £106,545, were disregarded like the previous reports.[34] In 1894, Mr.G.Remington proposed diverting flood water in the River Avon through a tunnel from Limpley Stoke to Twerton, at an estimated cost of £69,300, and this also produced no response.[35] A leading article in *Keene's Bath Journal* at the time of the flood in November that year reflected:

> The flood and nothing but the flood is still the theme of all ... If reports would bring their own cure Bath by now would be the best conditioned city to be found. We have seen how many reports have been invited upon the question of the floods yet no remedy has been attempted... it will indeed be a good day for Bath when a finish is put to the deliberations over flood prevention.[36]

Three years later a letter in the press showed how fully the principles of flood prevention in Bath had been grasped:

9. The River Avon in flood at Pulteney Bridge, c.1960. (*Photograph by Rev.W.H. Parsons, reproduced by courtesy of K.Evans*)

> Dredging, I fearlessly assert, will be one of the most important parts of any scheme of Flood Mitigation which may hereafter be adopted, and taken in connection with the control of the weirs, the removal of restrictions, including the greatest of all obstructions, the Old Bridge ... the graduation or equalization of width of the river below the city, the smoothing of the inequalities of the river banks which retard the outflow, and the construction of relief culverts are in fact all measures which ultimately must be adopted.[37]

But it was many years before realistic action was taken.

The situation began to look more promising with the Land Drainage Act of 1930, under which the River Avon (Bristol) Catchment Board was established in the following year. The first engineer to the Board was Mr. Horace Mercer, who prepared the 'Netham-Bathampton Flood Alleviation Scheme' in 1936, following the main lines of the Coode scheme of 1882 but costed at £260,000. Despite delays caused by the Second World War and its aftermath, and the cost mounting to an estimated £700,000, a start was made with improvements at Netham. As far as Bath was concerned, however, no material improvement had been made by 1960.

Mercer was succeeded as engineer to the Board in 1953 by Mr. Frank Greenhalgh, and it was he who was at last able to guide the Bath Flood Prevention Scheme through to a satisfactory conclusion.[38] Greenhalgh had modified Mercer's scheme and re-estimated the cost at £760,000. The Board had accepted this in principle, and approached the newly established Hydraulics Research Station at Wallingford in November 1953 to commission a model of the River Avon. The Director at Wallingford, Sir Claude Inglis, was sympathetic but unable to undertake the task quickly, so the Board turned to Sir Alfred Pugsley, Professor of Civil Engineering at the University of Bristol, to make a model study, and this was immediately put in hand. River modelling is based on the theory of dynamic similarity, whereby the behaviour of fluids under various configurations can be reproduced accurately on different scales. The theory was first elaborated by Professor Osborne Reynolds of Manchester, and was first applied successfully on a model of the Mersey estuary in 1893. It has become a very valuable technique for determining the best way of proceeding in order to achieve a required effect with river works, and the Pugsley team soon produced a carefully detailed plan of what needed to be done to cope with floods in the Bristol Avon.

Funding the scheme remained a problem. The Board, which had become the Wessex Water Authority, had been unwilling to finance Mercer's scheme in full, and the detailed proposals now put forward by Professor Pugsley were estimated to cost £1.4million. But the catastrophic floods of December 1960 caused damage amounting to £1.14million so that the scheme came to appear as an economy measure, and the long-suffering population of the lower-lying parts of Bath had become weary of official inaction. As Greenhalgh himself observed, 'the 1960 floods and the public feeling which they aroused changed all that, and quickly!'[39] He spelt out the options for improvement as either (i) providing an up-stream reservoir to contain impending flood water, or (ii) constructing a by-pass to carry flood water past Bath, or (iii) raising the river banks throughout the city, or (iv) deepening the existing course of the river and removing obstructions to the easy flow of water. Having dismissed the first three as impracticable for the Bath situation, Greenhalgh came down firmly in favour of the fourth option and drew up his plans accordingly. Agreement was at last reached to go ahead with this scheme, although it was necessary first to complete works at Melksham, Chippenham and Eastville which had already been approved by the Board. But in the winter of 1963-64, work began in Bath.

The first phase involved a new retaining wall at Broad Quay, and the fear that the 1960 floods had weakened the Old Bridge led to a plan for its relief and then to its complete replacement by the new Churchill Bridge and footbridge. Both were single-span concrete structures, thus removing the serious retardation of water-flow caused by the narrow five arches of the previous bridge. The services – gas and electricity mains – were carried in conduits in the new footbridge. These works were completed by May 1965. Meanwhile, channel works between Saltford and Twerton and protection works at Newbridge had been dealt with, and work had begun on the trickier tasks of replacing the old weirs and re-lining the river walls through the city with steel sheeting. The two weirs at Twerton were replaced by a modern balance-gate sluice. At Pulteney weir a new balance-gate was built on the site of the old Bathwick Mill, and a new three-step horseshoe weir was constructed to allow for the smooth passage of a greater bulk of water than the old single-step weir could accommodate. Pulteney Bridge itself was underpinned, its original timber piles being concreted. The success of the design of weir, bridge and sluice-gate was recognized with a Civic Trust Award in 1973.[40]

The final phases consisted of dredging the river through the city, and completing the various services, and these were finished in March 1974. There have been minor problems since, especially difficulties with the balance-gate sluices, but overall the scheme has been an outstanding success. The problem of flooding has been solved in Bath by improving the existing channel rather than by introducing radically new engineering works, and this arrangement has been demonstrated to be both economical and effective. But, as Frank Greenhalgh warned readers of his report, the scheme was designed to cope with any flood since 1809 and its success depends upon 'continuous maintenance of the river channel and control apparatus'.[41] It is important that the citizens of Bath should remember these limits to the effectiveness of the scheme.

Thanks to the success of the Flood Prevention Scheme, the River Avon through Bath has been able for the last twenty-five years to contain the flow of even the heaviest rainfall within its steel-shod and deepened channel. The story of the floods of Bath has thus become a matter of history, and it is to be hoped that it will remain such. But in the past complacency and inaction have led to repeated disasters, and in the future it is possible that changes in natural conditions and human management of the catchment area may re-create a situation in which floods could recur. The lesson of history, here as elsewhere, is to remain vigilant.

Notes

1　This introduction is based on personal recollection, but for details of the flood of July 1968, see J.D.Hanwell and M.D.Newsom, *The Great Storms and Floods of July 1968 on the Mendips*, Wessex Cave Club Occasional Series 1 No.2 (Wessex Cave Club, Oakhill Press, 1970); and Terry Staples, *The Great Flood of 1968* (Bristol, 1988).

2　Pictorial representation of the southward extension of buildings from the South Gate in Bath is apparent on early maps, such as John Speed's map of 1610 and that of 1694 by Joseph Gilmore: see Stephen Bird, 'The Earliest Map of Bath', *Bath History*, Vol.I (Gloucester, 1986), pp.128-149.

3　Barry Cunliffe, *Roman Bath*, No.24 in Reports of the Research Committee of the Society of Antiquaries of London (1969). Professor Cunliffe has maintained a close interest in the archaeology of Roman Bath and has updated his views in *The Book of Roman Bath* (1995).

4　Cunliffe, 1969, pp.5-6.

5　*Ibid.*; see also Cunliffe, 1995: 'it seems that throughout the third and fourth centuries the sea level had been rising and with it the general water table of the inland areas, causing a series of floods of gradually increasing severity', p.115.

6　For the thirteenth-century origin of the bridge see E.Green, 'Bath Old Bridge and the Oratory thereon', *Proceedings of Bath Natural History and Antiquarian Field Club*, Vol.7 (1893), pp.25-34.

7　R.A.Buchanan, 'The Bridges of Bath', *Bath History*, Vol.III (Gloucester, 1990), pp.1-21.

8　Rev. Richard Warner, *The History of Bath* (Bath, 1801). In the Index, printed separately, there is no entry for 'Floods', and the few entries on 'Avon, River' relate to it as a highway or a source of power. The single entry on 'Dolemeads', a frequent victim of flooding, is a botanical reference.

9　John Wood, *A Description of Bath* (3rd ed., Bath, 1765; reprinted Bath, 1969), devotes no space to any discussion of flooding.

10　See R.A.Buchanan, *op.cit.* A correction and apology is in order here, because that account fails to recognize the rebuilding in 1774 which drastically changed the appearance of Newbridge. As observed by Brenda J.Buchanan in 'The Avon Navigation and the Inland Port of Bath', *Bath History* Vol.VI (Bath, 1996), p.78 and note 33, it was the earlier bridge of the 1730s which was criticized by Wood and painted by Anthony Devis circa 1770.

11　Capt. Rowland Mainwaring, RN, *Annals of Bath from the Year 1800 ...* (Bath, 1838), p.83.

12　*Bath Chronicle*, 26 Jan 1809; see also the almost identical report, in the *Edinburgh Annual Register*, 26 Jan 1809, inserted in *Bath Floods*, a large red cutting book in Bath Central Library, B551.57 BAT.

13　Mainwaring, *op.cit.*, pp.85-7. The discrepancy of £3 in the total figure is accounted for by the omission of shillings and pence from the addition.

14　*Ibid.*, pp.228-9.

15　*Ibid.*, p.483. This is Appendix No.9, listing 30 occasions between 1805 and 1834 when the citizens of Bath had raised subscriptions for charitable purposes. The flooding of the Avon was the cause in 1809 and 1821: the other occasions included the 'Battle of Waterloo' (£3,773 for widows, orphans and wounded in 1815) and 'Distress of the Weavers in the Northern Districts'(£3,978 in 1826). Six other occasions were the result of 'Severe Weather' which could have included some flooding (1811, 1813, 1814, 1816, 1820, and 1830).

16   *Ibid.*, pp.249-50; see also *Bath Chronicle*, 6 Nov 1823.

17   *Ibid.*, pp.253-7; see also my reference to the Telford Report in R.A.Buchanan, *op.cit.*, p.5, n.6.

18   *Ibid.*, pp.297-8.

19   The Widcombe Mill was presumably that on the site of the present garage below Widcombe Manor: the mill ponds are now ornamental lakes in the grounds of the manor. See also *Bath Chronicle*, 17 Jul 1828, where it is recorded that: 'At the top of Holloway a considerable body of earth fell into the road'.

20   *Bath Chronicle*, 21 Jan 1841.

21   *Bath Chronicle*, 18 Jan 1866 and 26 Oct 1882.

22   *Record of the Great Floods in Bath*, reprinted from the *Bath Herald*,1894, consisting of 16 pages incorporating half a dozen photographs.

23   *Bath Herald*, 15 Nov 1894.

24   *Op.cit.*, note 22 above, pp.14-15: 'To such a great height had the flood risen that neither the Electric Light Company or the Gas Company thought it within the range of possibility that they would be enabled to continue their supply'. In the event, the electricity supply was maintained, but 'the gas supply was cut short entirely'. Recalling the incident many years later, this was attributed to a barge hitting the pipe across the river at the gas works, allowing the mains to become flooded – see *Bath Chronicle*, 3 Jan 1925.

25   The flood marks on the south abutment are clearly visible from the river-side footpath: some are worn or partially obliterated, but that for 1894 stands clearly above the others.

26   *Bath Chronicle*, 18 Jun 1903: 'Flood in Bath'; also 3 Jan 1901.

27   *Bath and Wilts Chronicle*, 21 Jan 1918: 'The Avon in Flood'. In 1894 it had been reported that 'it is a superstitious belief of old Avon watermen and "bargees" that a quick falling flood will soon be followed by another, but a slow dropping means that this is to be the last of the series': *Bath Herald*, 15 Nov 1894, p.8.

28   *Bath and Wilts Chronicle*, 21 Jan 1918: cutting in small white bound book in Bath Central Library, B551-57 BAT.

29   *Bath Herald*, 3 Jan 1925.

30   The donation of Mayor Chivers is recorded in *Bath Chronicle*, 3 Jan 1925.

31   Bath Record Office (BRO): 'Funds, Subscriptions, Presentations, Etc' Box 9, Bundle 102 – 'Flood Relief'. Each flood is covered by a collection of about ten subscription books and accounts of varying degrees of completion. About £200 was raised in 1881; £2,328 in 1882; £279 in 1885; £302 in 1889; and £634 in 1901.

32   *Bath Herald*, 3 May 1932: 'Bath's Very High Tide'.

33   *Bath and Wilts Chronicle & Herald*, 26 Jun 1935 (complete copy filed in Bath Central Library, B551.554 BAT / A 606582).

34   Frank Greenhalgh, *Bath Flood Prevention Scheme* (Wessex Water Authority, 1974), Bath Central Library at B627.4, Chap.1 'Historical Background'.
35   Geo. Remington, *Mitigation of Floods – Bath*, 17 Nov 1896. Proposal for a culvert 4 miles 7 furlongs from Limpley Stoke to Twerton, with report and maps: in BRO.
36   *Keene's Bath Journal*, 24 Nov 1894: 'The Floods of Bath'.
37   The printed letter, from Jas. Baster of Beechen Cliff, is in the 'Funds, Subscriptions, Presentations, etc', Box 9, Bundle 102, packet 9: in BRO.
38   This summary of the Flood Prevention Scheme is based on Greenhalgh, *op.cit.* It is a well illustrated book in landscape format, 44pp.
39   *Ibid.*, p.12.
40   Bath Flood Defence Scheme, National Rivers Authority, pamphlet, n.d.
41   Greenhalgh, *op.cit.*, p.43.

ACKNOWLEDGMENTS

The author would like to thank the Librarian and staff of Bath Central Library; the Bath City Archivist Mr. Colin Johnston; and others who have assisted in his enquiries. He is grateful to Mr. Ken Evans for making readily available the dramatic photographs of some of the last Bath floods taken by the late Rev. W.H.Parsons of Widcombe Baptist Church, and to Hilary Strickland for her assistance with the map and diagram. And he would also like to thank the Editor for encouraging him to persevere in the study of this subject, and for her valiant editorial efforts on it.

INDEX TO *BATH HISTORY* VOLUMES I-VII BYAUTHOR

INDEX TO *BATH HISTORY* VOLUMES I-VII BY TITLE